Presidents from
Nixon through Carter,
1969–1981

PRESIDENTS FROM NIXON THROUGH CARTER, 1969–1981

Debating the Issues in Pro and Con Primary Documents

AIMEE D. SHOUSE

The President's Position: Debating the Issues
Mark Byrnes, Series Editor

GREENWOOD PRESS
Westport, Connecticut • London

Library of Congress Cataloging-in-Publication Data

Presidents from Nixon through Carter, 1969–1981 : debating the issues in pro and con primary documents / [compiled by] Aimee D. Shouse.
    p. cm.— (The president's position : debating the issues)
    Includes bibliographical references and index.
    ISBN 0–313–31529–9 (alk. paper)
    1. Presidents—United States—History—20th century—Sources. 2. United States—Politics and government—1969–1974—Sources. 3. United States—Politics and government—1974–1977—Sources. 4. United States—Politics and government—1977–1981—Sources. 5. Nixon, Richard M. (Richard Milhous), 1913—Political and social views. 6. Ford, Gerald R., 1913—Political and social views. 7. Carter, Jimmy, 1924—Political and social views. I. Shouse, Aimee D. II. President's position.
    E176.1.P9217   2002
    973.92'092'2—dc21   2002016098

British Library Cataloguing in Publication Data is available.

Library of Congress Catalog Card Number: 2002016098
ISBN: 0–313–31529–9

First published in 2002

Greenwood Press, 88 Post Road West, Westport, CT 06881
An imprint of Greenwood Publishing Group, Inc.
www.greenwood.com

Printed in the United States of America

The paper used in this book complies with the Permanent Paper Standard issued by the National Information Standards Organization (Z39.48–1984).

10 9 8 7 6 5 4 3 2 1

CONTENTS

SERIES FOREWORD

When he was running for president in 1932, Franklin D. Roosevelt declared that America needed "bold, persistent experimentation" in its public policy. "It is common sense to take a method and try it," FDR said. "If it fails, admit it frankly and try another. But above all, try something." At President Roosevelt's instigation, the nation did indeed take a number of steps to combat the Great Depression. In the process, the president emerged as the clear leader of American public policy. Most scholars see FDR's administration as the birth of the "modern presidency," in which the president dominates both domestic and foreign policy.

Even before FDR, however, presidents played a vital role in the making of public policy. Policy changes advocated by the presidents—often great changes—have always influenced the course of events, and have always sparked debate from the presidents' opponents. The outcomes of this process have had tremendous effects on the lives of Americans. The President's Position: Debating the Issues examines the stands the presidents have taken on the major political, social, and economic issues of their times as well as the stands taken by their opponents. The series combines description and analysis of those issues with excerpts from primary documents that illustrate the position of the presidents and their opponents. The result is an informative, accessible, and comprehensive look at the crucial connection between presidents and policy. These volumes will assist students doing historical research, preparing for debates, or fulfilling critical thinking assignments. The general reader interested in American history and politics will also find the series interesting and helpful.

Several important themes about the president's role in policy making emerge from the series. First, and perhaps most important, is how greatly the president's involvement in policy has expanded over the years. This has happened because the range of areas in which the national government acts has grown dramatically and because modern presidents—unlike most of their predecessors—see taking the lead in policy making as part of their job. Second, certain issues have confronted most presidents over history; tax and tariff policy, for example, was important for both George Washington and Bill Clinton, and for most of the presidents in between. Third, the emergence of the United States as a world power around the beginning of the twentieth century made foreign policy issues more numerous and more pressing. Finally, in the American system, presidents cannot form policy through decrees; they must persuade members of Congress, other politicians, and the general public to follow their lead. This key fact makes the policy debates between presidents and their opponents vitally important.

This series comprises nine volumes, organized chronologically, each of which covers the presidents who governed during that particular time period. Volume one looks at the presidents from George Washington through James Monroe; volume two, John Quincy Adams through James K. Polk; volume three, Zachary Taylor through Ulysses S. Grant; volume four, Rutherford B. Hayes through William McKinley; volume five, Theodore Roosevelt through Calvin Coolidge; volume six, Herbert Hoover through Harry Truman; volume seven, Dwight D. Eisenhower through Lyndon Johnson; volume eight, Richard Nixon through Jimmy Carter; and volume nine, Ronald Reagan through Bill Clinton. Each president from Washington through Clinton is covered, although the number of issues discussed under each president varies according to how long they served in office and how actively they pursued policy goals. Volumes six through nine—which cover the modern presidency—examine three presidencies each, while the earlier volumes include between five and seven presidencies each.

Every volume begins with a general introduction to the period it covers, providing an overview of the presidents who served and the issues they confronted. The section on each president opens with a detailed overview of the president's position on the relevant issues he confronted and the initiatives he took, and closes with a list of recommended readings. Up to fifteen issues are covered per presidency. The discussion of each issue features an introduction, the positions taken by the president and his opponents, how the issue was resolved, and the long-term effects of the issue. This is followed by excerpts from two primary documents, one representing the president's position and the other representing his opponents' position. Also included in each volume is a timeline of significant events of the era and a bibliography of sources for students and others interested in further research.

As the most prominent individual in American politics, the president receives enormous attention from the media and the public. The statements, actions, travels, and even the personal lives of presidents are constantly scrutinized. Yet it is the presidents' work on public policy that most directly affects American citizens—a fact that is sometimes overlooked. This series is presented, in part, as a reminder of the importance of the president's position.

Mark Byrnes

TIMELINE

1968
November 5   Richard Nixon elected president

1969
March 17   Secret bombings of Cambodia authorized by President Nixon
July 20   First manned spacecraft lands on the moon; Neil Armstrong the first astronaut to walk on the moon
July 25   Nixon Doctrine announced
November 3   Nixon's Vietnamization speech

1970
March 7   Nixon outlines plans for U.S. space budget
April 30   U.S. troops invade Cambodia
April 22   First Earth Day
April 29   Nixon calls for creation of the Environmental Protection Agency
May 4   Kent State University shootings
May 14   Jackson State University shootings
June 24   Congress repeals the Gulf of Tonkin Resolution

1971
March 29   Wage and price controls implemented
April 20   Supreme Court upholds the constitutionality of busing in *Swann v. Charlotte-Mecklenburg Board of Education*
June 13   *New York Times* begins publication of the Pentagon Papers

1972
March 17   President Nixon advocates a moratorium on busing to accomplish school integration
February 17   President Nixon departs for China

May 22–30	President Nixon visits Moscow; SALT I signed
June 17	Watergate break-in
October 20	Revenue sharing proposed
November 7	President Nixon defeats George McGovern

1973

January	Watergate burglars go to trial
January 27	Paris Peace Accords signed
July 26	Senate Watergate Committee subpoenas White House tapes
October 6	Egypt and Syria attack Israel on Jewish holiday of Yom Kippur
October 15	Vice President Spiro Agnew resigns; Nixon appoints Gerald Ford to position of vice president
October 19	OPEC oil boycott begins as a result of U.S. support of Israel during Yom Kippur War
October 20	President Nixon orders Special Prosecutor Cox to be fired
November 7	Congress overrides President Nixon's veto of War Powers Act

1974

March	OPEC boycott lifted
August 8	President Nixon resigns
August 9	Gerald Ford becomes president
August 12	President Ford announces his "Whip Inflation Now" campaign
September 8	Ford pardons former President Nixon
September 16	Ford announces his clemency plan for Vietnam War resisters

1975

April 10	Ford requests additional military and humanitarian aid for South Vietnam
April 29	Ford announces that all remaining Americans and many Vietnamese were evacuated from Saigon, as Ho Chi Mihn took control of the city
May 12	*Mayaguez* incident
August 1	Helsinki Accords signed
November 27	Ford supports loan program to prevent New York City from going bankrupt

1976

| February 18 | Ford supports limiting the use of electronic surveillance of American citizens |
| November 2 | Presidential election between Gerald Ford and Jimmy Carter; Carter wins election |

1977

January 20	Carter announces full pardon for Vietnam War resisters
March 28	Human rights linked to U.S. foreign policy
September 7	Panama Canal Treaty signed

1978

| September | Camp David Peace Accords signed |
| October 24 | Carter's anti-inflationary measures announced |

October 24	Airline deregulation legislation signed into law
November 9	Carter's energy legislation passed

1979

January	Shah of Iran flees in face of Islamic Revolution
June 18	SALT II treaty signed
October 17	Department of Education formed
November 4	Iranian demonstration takes 52 American hostages in Tehran
December 24	Soviets invade Afghanistan

1980

January 4	Grain embargo announced
January 20	Olympic boycott announced
January 21	Carter Doctrine toward Middle East outlined
April 28	Attempt to free Iranian hostages
November 4	Presidential election, California Governor Ronald Reagan (R) defeats President Jimmy Carter
December 11	Superfund environmental legislation passed

1981

January 20	Iranian hostages released

INTRODUCTION

The years from 1969 through 1980 witnessed incredible change, both within the United States and around the world. At home, societal changes in both the values and opinions of the public brought about significant political changes. In addition, the U.S. government also responded to events outside the boundaries of the United States, as the country's relations with other nations changed markedly in response to events largely out of the control of the U.S. government. Yet this general characterization of the period from 1969 through 1980 could be used to describe almost any era in the history of the United States. It is the specifics of this period, the types of societal changes, and the specific dynamics of international relations, that distinguish it from any other time in history.

The presidencies of Richard M. Nixon, Gerald R. Ford, and Jimmy Carter reflect the different personalities and policy goals of the individuals occupying the office of president. However, there are some common themes across the three presidencies that helped characterize the 1970s. First, the economy played a fundamental role in the policy decisions of all three presidents, as each struggled to ease the burden of a lengthy recession that had been coupled with a high rate of inflation across the country. A recession is a period during which the economy is slowing down, producing less, and employing fewer people. Inflation, however, refers to an economic condition in which prices increase over time for the same goods. In short, the same amount of money will purchase less in an inflationary period.

Prior to the 1970s, the country had generally experienced either a recession or high inflation, but not both at the same time. Government solutions to each problem were generally well understood. To put it simply, a recession was addressed by getting more money into the economy, either by lowering taxes or by lowering the interest rates for borrowing money. Conversely, a high rate of inflation was countered by contracting the money supply, by raising the rates of interest to borrow money, for instance. In the 1970s, however, both conditions occurred simultaneously, a condition referred to as *stagflation*. Policies designed to counter one problem could easily exacerbate the other situation. However, all three presidents tended to focus on the problem of inflation, with each advocating a different approach to address the problem. The approaches ranged from the dramatic, as in the case of Nixon's mandatory wage and price freeze, to the comical, as with Ford's peppy call to "Whip Inflation Now," to the pessimistic, as with Carter's tone of gloom and doom in a speech on inflation to the American public. Although there were some economic ups and downs across the 1970s, no consistent upturn in the economy took place until the 1980s, after Ronald Reagan had assumed the presidency.

Besides the more traditional approaches taken to alleviate the stress of inflation, each president took some unique steps to boost the economy. Nixon and Ford, both Republicans, tended to favor greater economic discretion being given to the states, with the national government playing a lesser role than it had played during the immediately preceding administrations of John F. Kennedy and Lyndon Johnson. Nixon, for instance, chose to turn some of the federal tax revenue over to the states. His policy of revenue sharing would allow state governments more autonomy in determining how the state could best use its resources, rather than having the national government compel certain actions to be taken by the states. With this approach, greater government spending could take place at the state level, a level of government that is closer to the people than the national government. President Ford was faced with a unique economic crisis when New York City announced in 1975 that it would probably go bankrupt without the assistance of the federal government. Although he was not easily convinced, Ford eventually chose to use the resources of the federal government to help alleviate New York's economic woes.

Although Democrats have traditionally favored using the national government to accomplish a higher proportion of their policy goals, Jimmy Carter did not always make a dramatic break with his predecessors when it came to policies used to influence the economy. For instance, Carter favored a diminished role for the national government in certain industries, such as the airline and trucking industries, thinking that the move would enhance competition within each industry. Such competition, he believed, would help lower prices and create greater demand for their services. Similarly, in his energy legislation, Carter favored the deregulation of prices for domestic oil.

Domestically, the Nixon, Ford, and Carter presidencies were marked by considerable social upheaval, including political protests and activism involving issues as disparate as civil rights, environmentalism, and America's involvement in Southeast Asia. The civil rights movement was already in high gear by the time Richard Nixon took office in 1969. African Americans had achieved great legislative victories in the fight against discrimination with the Civil Rights Act of 1964 and the Voting Rights Act of 1968. By the time Richard Nixon took office, the concerns of the movement had largely shifted away from broad grants of protection against discrimination to more focused issues, such as busing to achieve school integration and the implementation of the civil rights laws. Numerous cases in the federal courts also testified to the constitutional protection afforded individuals from discriminatory acts. However, while changing the law to reflect the nation's heightened concern for equality was not a particularly easy process, it was simpler to change the law than it was to change a social system that had systematically favored whites over any other race for centuries. One response to continued discrimination was to bring lawsuits against those who were discriminating, as in the case of *Swann v. Charlotte-Mecklenburg Board of Education* (1971), in which busing was mandated by the Supreme Court as a remedy for segregated schools. The question of racial discrimination came before the High Court again in 1978, when the case *Regents of the University of California v. Bakke* addressed the issue of affirmative action and "reverse discrimination." Although most of the major civil rights legislation banning racial discrimination was passed in the 1960s, it was in the 1970s that these laws were put into practice, which is sometimes as difficult and contentious a process as actually changing the laws.

Black Americans were not the only group seeking equality. Women were also active during this period, specifically pursuing opportunities in employment and education equal to those afforded men. Although the Civil Rights Act of 1964 had specified that it was illegal to discriminate based on sex, the law was not enforced as rigorously for victims of sex discrimination as it was for victims of racial discrimination. In the early 1970s, women's rights organizations, such as the National Organization for Women (NOW), took direct action against employment discrimination, picketing newspapers, for instance, for discriminatory hiring practices and for placing gender-specific "help wanted" advertisements. They also fought to add an amendment to the Constitution that would expressly prohibit discrimination based solely on one's sex. The amendment stated that "Equality of rights under the law shall not be denied or abridged by the United States or by any state on account of sex." Congress passed the Equal Rights Amendment, known as the ERA, in

1972, but for the amendment to be added to the Constitution, it had to be ratified by thirty-eight states. This ratification process spanned all three presidencies during this period, ultimately falling short by three states and failing to be ratified in 1979. While all three presidents expressed support for the ERA, they were not particularly outspoken advocates of the amendment. First Ladies Betty Ford and Rosalyn Carter, however, actively campaigned on its behalf.

During the 1970s, environmentalists were also becoming actively involved in the political process and were able to achieve some great successes. The public was realizing that economic progress in the United States had contributed to the degradation of the natural environment and, as such, environmental interest groups began putting pressure on the federal government to make policies reflecting these concerns. As a consequence of the enhanced political role of environmentalists, groups that were opposed to greater environmental regulation were also motivated to put greater pressure on the policy-making process, creating a much more contentious political environment regarding environmental policy. Groups such as the Sierra Club and the Audubon Society lobbied on behalf of greater environmental protection while companies and industries that would bear the brunt of increased environmental regulation tended to oppose these policies. Despite the heightened conflict between competing interests, a wide range of environmental legislation was passed during the 1970s, including the creation of the Environmental Protection Agency in 1970, the Clean Air Act of 1970, the Federal Water Pollution Control Amendments in 1972, the Endangered Species Act of 1973, the National Forest Management Act of 1976, and the Superfund legislation in 1980.

Although many of the more significant environmental policies were passed during the presidencies of Richard Nixon and Gerald Ford, President Carter had a particular interest in this area of public policy. It was during his presidency that issues of energy efficiency and conservation came to the fore. The stage for new energy policies was undoubtedly set by the artificially created shortages of oil that was being imported from the Middle East, but Jimmy Carter capitalized on the increased awareness of American dependence on foreign oil and successfully shepherded many energy policies through Congress during his administration. The maximum speed limit across the country was set at fifty-five miles per hour, and there was greater attention paid to the energy efficiency of consumer products, such as automobiles and household appliances.

Another trend seen domestically during the 1970s, a trend related to both civil rights and environmentalism, was the increase in activist politics, especially in the early years of the decade. Although voting and writing letters to one's representatives are conventional and common forms of political participation, some people do not believe that these are the most effective means of making one's voice heard in the political arena. This is especially true among groups whose members do not feel that they are well represented in the mainstream political system. During the 1970s, and in some cases up to the present, the concern with under-representation applied most often to minority groups, women, and younger Americans. For instance, until the ratification of the Twenty-sixth Amendment to the Constitution in 1971, persons under twenty-one years old could not vote. This is often offered as a reason why so many college campuses erupted in protest demonstrations in the late 1960s and early 1970s, primarily in protest against the American military presence in Vietnam. In short, a young man eighteen years of age could have been drafted, but he couldn't vote. While the momentum of college protests didn't last long into the 1970s, Richard Nixon was forced to address the issue, establishing a commission to study the violence and protests on college campuses. In short, Nixon was not particularly sympathetic to-ward protest tactics, believing that such tactics tended to degenerate into violence, as happened in May 1970 at Kent State and Jackson State University. He felt that his actions reflected the views of the "silent majority" of Americans who were not as vocal or demonstrative in their appeals for government action.

College protests against the Vietnam War expressed a growing op-position to U.S. foreign policy toward Southeast Asia, in particular, and communism, in general. During the years from 1969 through 1980, the U.S. concern with communism influenced much of the nation's foreign policy. While the period definitely witnessed a thaw in the tense rela-tionship between the United States and the Soviet Union that had char-acterized the 1950s and 1960s, the Cold War was still very much in place during all three presidencies of this era. Richard Nixon did much, how-ever, to open doors between the United States and the communist coun-tries of the Soviet Union and China. For instance, the inroads made by Nixon with his visit to China in 1972 were solidified when President Carter formally recognized the People's Republic of China in 1979. How-ever, suspicions still ran high among the three countries across this pe-riod.

Much of the American foreign and defense policy during the first half of the 1970s focused on preventing the spread of communism and min-imizing the possibility that an alliance would form between the Soviet Union and China. The fear of the spread of communism was particularly pronounced during the Vietnam War. U.S. policy makers were convinced that communism would spread across Southeast Asia if Vietnam were to fall to the communists in a so-called "domino effect." The assumption was that Vietnam and any other country succumbing to communism would then become virtual extensions of China. The "win at all costs" strategy pursued by the United States in Vietnam failed, however, and the communist North Vietnamese took control of the country in 1975.

Another feature that marked the mood and policies of the 1970s was the proliferation of nuclear weapons around the world. Both the Soviet Union and China possessed nuclear capabilities by the 1970s, along with France and Great Britain. However, while the concern with China was focused more on its potential to spread communism across Asia, the concern with the Soviet Union was based largely on its stockpile of nuclear weapons. Like the United States, the Soviets had put large amounts of resources into nuclear technology and escalation. Part of this escalation in arms was based on the assumption that only an approximate parity between the United States and the Soviet Union would prevent a nuclear war. This concept of nuclear deterrence had been used to justify expansion of the American nuclear arsenal since the Soviet Union had tested its first atomic bomb in 1949, and it was still very much in place during the 1970s. However, by the time Richard Nixon took office, both countries had begun working on new strategies to minimize the risk of nuclear war. Two treaties were signed in the 1970s to limit the number of nuclear weapons possessed by each country. The first Strategic Arms Limitation Treaties (SALT) were negotiated and signed in 1972 by Richard Nixon, and although it was never ratified by the Senate, SALT II was signed by Jimmy Carter in 1979.

One further foreign policy trend during this time period was a shift by 1975 in U.S. attention away from Southeast Asia and to the Middle East, the world's new political "hot spot." After the last Americans were evacuated from Vietnam in 1975, the United States had little to do with the countries of that region. For instance, it was during these post-Vietnam years that Cambodia fell to the communist Khmer Rouge and millions of Cambodians were killed at the order of leader Pol Pot. The response by the United States was minimal. By the time Jimmy Carter took over the presidency, the region of prime concern had become the Middle East.

The rise of Islamic fundamentalists in many countries such as Afghanistan and Iran was a troubling phenomenon for the United States for several reasons. First, many of the Middle Eastern governments most vulnerable to being overthrown had been put in place largely with the assistance of the United States and other Western countries. Were these governments to fall to militant Islamic groups, the United States would lose its influence with many countries in the region. Second, most of the Islamic groups vying for power were greatly opposed to the U.S. presence in the region. This resentment was spurred in large part by continued U.S. support of Israel, support that was perceived by Islamic groups to come at the expense of the Palestinian Muslims who had been displaced by Israel at the creation of the state in 1948. Third, because the

United States relied so heavily on oil imported from the Middle East, our government felt it was in the best interest of the country to maintain ties with the governments of the region.

Jimmy Carter in particular articulated the American interest in the region, basing his Carter Doctrine on the premise that the United States would intervene were its interests in the region threatened by an outside country. His stance on the Middle East was shaped by the reality of the Soviet invasion of Afghanistan in 1979. In retrospect, however, the greatest threat to American interests came from within the region, not from without. In November 1979, fifty-two Americans were taken hostage by Iranian protestors who had stormed the American embassy in Tehran. They were not released for fourteen months, not until after Ronald Reagan had taken the oath of office in January 1981. The hostage crisis contributed to American suspicions regarding Middle Eastern countries, and had far-reaching consequences, as relations between the United States and Iran were strained into the twenty-first century.

Foreign and defense policies during these three presidencies were often dominated by extremes. For instance, President Nixon expressed his desire to withdraw troops from Vietnam, yet also enlarged the sphere of the war by bombing and invading Cambodia. President Ford was accused of using a heavy-handed approach in dealing with Cambodia after the Cambodians boarded the American commercial ship *Mayaguez* and held its crew hostage. The American loss in Vietnam certainly played a role in Ford's response, yet more troops were killed in the rescue operation than there were crew members to rescue. On the other extreme, Jimmy Carter responded to the Soviet military invasion of Afghanistan by refusing to sell grain to the Soviets and boycotting the Moscow Olympics of 1980. These were simply not effective means of addressing such an aggressive act of war. The more moderate policies of the period generally came with U.S. agreements with other countries that were negotiated over periods of years, such as the Helsinki Accords and the two SALT agreements.

The one event that most defined the 1970s was Watergate. What began as a burglary attempt at the Democratic National Headquarters in the Watergate office complex ended in the only resignation by an American president. What the burglary represented was a president who was willing to abuse the power of his office in an attempt to manipulate the outcome of the presidential election of 1972. It became evident over the course of the investigation that Nixon wanted the office more than he valued the American democratic system of government. Certainly, other presidents have skirted the edge of the law at times, and possibly even crossed it. But few have so clearly violated the very principles of democracy. For instance, during the Watergate investigations, it was discovered that Richard Nixon had used federal agencies to investigate and harass his critics, had established an illegal fund to accept campaign contributions from corporations and large donors, and had lied about his knowledge of the Watergate break-in. Despite all his achievements in the area of foreign policy, it is Watergate that marks the Nixon presidency.

The consequences of Watergate extended far beyond Nixon's resignation. At the simplest level, the term "Watergate" is now used to represent any potential violation of the law by the president. In addition, the American public has become considerably more cynical of government since Watergate and less trusting of the information provided by all elected officials, not just presidents. The media, too, has a changed relationship with presidents since Watergate. Journalists are much more willing to dig for information about presidents and presidential candidates, regardless of the information's relevance to the person's qualifications for or performance in office. While other policies and events that occurred during these three presidencies have colored the years that followed, Watergate, more than any other, cast a pall on the office of the presidency that has been hard to remove.

This volume includes some of the most significant policy proposals from the presidencies of Richard Nixon, Gerald Ford, and Jimmy Carter. For each of these three presidents, an introduction outlines the major events and issues of the presidency and the president's general approach to policy making. Following the introduction to each president, some of the more important issues addressed by the president are considered in chronological order. In Chapter 1, fourteen of Richard Nixon's policies are considered. Eight of Gerald Ford's policy stances are covered in Chapter 2, while Chapter 3 examines fourteen of the key policies of Jimmy Carter's presidency.

For each of the thirty-six issues considered, an introduction will provide the reader with background information regarding the issue, as well as give some insight into the political context at the time the policy was considered. This introduction is then followed by two original policy statements. The first is a statement by the president about the issue. These presidential statements are taken from various sources, including presidential addresses to the nation, press conferences, campaign speeches, State of the Union addresses, and town meetings. The second original statement represents a position countering the president's view. The sources of these statements are quite varied, including statements from members of Congress, the comments of interest group representatives in congressional committee hearings, editorials from newspapers and periodicals, and a Supreme Court decision. Each chapter concludes with a list of recommended readings about the policies of that president.

relations with these two countries during his presidency. Despite these successes, Nixon was plagued with the failures of the Vietnam War, often finding himself at odds with a Congress that was attempting to reign in the presidency's powers to make war.

However, the president's difficulties were not limited to the areas of defense and foreign affairs. There was plenty of discontent at home in the United States, as well. President Nixon's administration witnessed numerous events related to the civil rights movement for African Americans, such as controversy over busing to achieve integration in the public schools, as well as the women's rights movement, whose leaders were also demanding equal rights, including an Equal Rights Amendment to the Constitution. The American economy was also beginning its descent into a prolonged recession during the early part of Nixon's administration. He took numerous steps to alleviate these problems, including the unprecedented imposition of wage and price controls across the country, the distribution of federal revenue to the states, and a refusal to spend money already appropriated by the Congress. Despite these trouble spots, the national pride and excitement of the United States putting the first person on the moon also occurred during Nixon's administration, and he was supportive of continuing American efforts in space.

The most destructive aspect of the Nixon administration involved his decisions related to the Watergate affair, in which it became evident that the president had known about, and subsequently covered up, the break-in of the Democratic National Committee headquarters in the Watergate office complex. The president's involvement went much further than his knowledge of the burglary attempt, however. During the investigation, it became evident that the president had also used his position to accomplish other political goals as well, including using the FBI to investigate his political "enemies," defying federal subpoenas for information, and firing federal investigator Archibald Cox when he came too close to discovering Nixon's true involvement in the affair. It was this deception and abuse of power that ultimately led to Nixon's resignation.

In this section on President Nixon, fourteen different issues will be considered. The first two issues relate to Richard Nixon's early foreign and defense policies. In November 1969, Nixon's policy of "Vietnamization" was announced to the public in a nationally televised address. In the speech, he outlined his plans to change the nature of American support for the South Vietnamese. Instead of relying on American troops to help fight the communist North Vietnamese, he would instead begin removing American troops and start putting additional resources into assisting the South Vietnamese in fighting their own war. The lack of details in Nixon's speech concerned many opponents of the war, however. Senator Frank Church (D-Idaho), well known for his opposition to the war, expressed his doubts that the president's plan would fulfill the hopes of Americans seeking the country's complete withdrawal from Vietnam.

In early 1970, Nixon outlined his philosophy of détente, which was a shift America's previous relationship with the Soviet Union and China. The second issue presents Nixon's speeches to both the Congress and the United Nations, in which he explains that the United States and the Soviet Union must, in essence, agree to disagree, building on the mutual interests of each country, rather than focusing on their ideological differences. While few would disagree that a warming of relations between the United States and the Soviet Union was a positive step, most critics of détente focused on the president's actual policies, not his stated philosophy. Fred Warner Neal, professor at the Clarement Graduate School, testified before a House Foreign Affairs subcommittee that Nixon's actions looked more like a continuation of the Cold War than any type of new direction in foreign policy.

Two issues arose in March and April 1970 that demonstrate well the ups and downs of Nixon's early presidency: the space program and the invasion of Cambodia. In March the president outlined his commitment to the U.S. space program. For most Americans, interest in space peaked in 1969 by the first manned mission to the moon. The success of the mission came after watching the Soviet Union beat the United States to numerous milestones in space exploration, and as such, was especially welcomed by most Americans. However, when it was time to actually appropriate more money to NASA's space program, the question of whether the money could be put to better use was raised. Representative Edward I. Koch (D-N.Y.) pointedly asked this question in a dissenting opinion to a report prepared in the House of Representatives for the NASA appropriations bill. In contrast to the nation's support of the space program was the violent reaction to the news that the president had ordered the invasion of Cambodia in Southeast Asia. In an address to the nation, Nixon explained the move as a necessary step to protect Cambodia from communist forces. However, these assurances rang hollow on most college campuses, as protest after protest was organized to express outrage at the decision. Eleven East Coast university newspapers ran an editorial calling for protests of the actions. The Columbia University *Spectator* was one of the papers involved in the editorial, which is reprinted in issue four.

The fifth and sixth issues detail some of Nixon's domestic initiatives. In July 1970, the president submitted to Congress a plan to reorganize the executive branch in order to create a new agency to oversee environmental policy. The Environmental Protection Agency was formed in a political environment that was increasingly concerned with the environmental degradation caused by human progress. The nation's first Earth Day was held only three months before the reorganization plan was sent to Congress. Representative John Dingell (D-Mich.), who did not believe the plan submitted by the president was the most effective way to address the nation's environmental problems, expressed concern over Nixon's policy. A year later, the president's attention had turned to the U.S. economy, which was experiencing two problems that rarely occur simultaneously: inflation and recession. The president attempted to curb the inflation by mandating a freeze on all wages and prices across the country. Consumer advocate Ralph Nader countered in a hearing of the congressional Joint Economic Committee that the wage and price freeze put an undue burden on the workers of the country and that there was no comparable freeze on corporate earnings during the freeze.

The election year of 1972 saw a flurry of activity, with the next five issues brought to the fore in that year. In each case, the president's policy stance was designed to appeal to the majority of the country and build a positive image for himself as he headed into the November election. In February 1972, Nixon took an unprecedented trip to communist China. The trip generated tremendous media coverage, with American journalists covering every aspect of the whirlwind trip. Yet, it was the carnival-like atmosphere of the trip that caused Edwin O. Reischauer, professor at Harvard University and former ambassador to Japan, to criticize Nixon's approach to building relations with the Chinese, especially when viewed through the eyes of other Asian allies. In March, following his return from China, Nixon tackled the issue of busing to achieve racial integration in the public schools. Most Americans opposed the policy of busing and Nixon expressed his shared opposition in an address to the nation. His approach was to impose a moratorium on any additional busing, a policy that was heartily criticized by Clarence Mitchell, director of the Washington Bureau of the National Association for the Advancement of Colored People. He voiced the view that the moratorium was "anti-black," and simply a means to placate white Americans.

The next issue was the signing of the Strategic Arms Limitation Treaty, or SALT, in May 1972. After years of negotiations, President Nixon visited Moscow and signed a treaty that would limit the use of antiballistic missiles by both the United States and the Soviet Union. He also signed an interim agreement on the use of other types of nuclear weapons. In a joint communiqué to members of both chambers of Congress, he explained the strengths of SALT and why the treaty should be confirmed by the Senate. In a statement before the Senate, however, Senator Ernest F. Hollings (D-S.C.) opposed the interim agreement, which he believed put the United States at a strategic disadvantage by permitting the continued use of certain weapons by the Soviet Union.

President Nixon again tackled the issue of the economy in July 1972, pitting his administration squarely against Congress when he refused to spend funds appropriated by the Congress. The president set the stage for these actions in a message to Congress in which he accused the legislature of making irresponsible spending decisions and explained that he would take all steps necessary to curb these wasteful habits. When the president simply refused to spend the funds appropriated by Congress for waste treatment facilities, Senator Frank Church (D-Idaho), in an article in *The Nation* magazine, accused Nixon of violating the constitutional separation of powers. The president's last efforts to address the economy before the November elections was a bill passed in October to share national tax dollars with the states. At the bill-signing ceremony, Nixon explained the benefits this revenue sharing would have on the economy. In comments made before the House of Representatives, Representative John W. Byrnes (R-Wisc.) expressed his opposition to the policy, believing that it would promote a continued reliance on federal funds by the states.

The last three issues demonstrate the strain on the president during the latter half of 1973, after the Watergate cover-up started unraveling and trust in the president had waned. In August 1973, it was discovered during testimony at the Watergate trial that the Oval Office was equipped with recording devices. Thinking that access to the tapes would uncover once and for all the president's role, if any, in the illegal activities of his staff, the tapes were subpoenaed in the Watergate investigation being conducted by Special Prosecutor Archibald Cox. At first, Nixon flatly refused to submit the tapes, and in a televised address to the nation explained that the confidentiality between the president and those who advised him was a trust that could not be violated. In 1974, the Supreme Court, in the case of *United States v. Nixon*, ruled otherwise, explaining that the president was not exempt from the law and that the needs of the courts prevailed in a criminal investigation. Nixon's response to the thoroughness of Special Prosecutor Archibald Cox's investigation was to fire him. The thirteenth issue highlights Nixon's rationale for firing Cox, in both a letter to Acting Attorney General Robert Bork and Nixon's comments at a news conference after Cox had been fired. Because the act appeared to be motivated purely by Nixon's political concerns for holding onto the office of president, he encountered a great deal of criticism for the decision. Chesterfield Smith, president of the American Bar Association, explained the view from the legal community in the *ABA Journal*. In short, he explained that special prosecutors could never effectively investigate possible illegal activity by the president as long as the prosecutor was answerable to that president. He instead called for special prosecutors to be independent of the president.

Last, the veto of the War Powers Resolution is considered. When Congress passed the War Powers Act to reclaim a role for itself regarding war activities and to consequently constrain the independence of the president in this regard, the president claimed that the act violated the constitutional powers of the president as commander-in-chief. As such, Nixon vetoed the bill, explaining in his veto message his reasons for doing so. Congress promptly overrode the veto. Representative Michael J. Harrington (D-Mass.), in a statement before the House of Representatives, explained that the violation of the separation of powers had taken place when the president had omitted the Congress from decisions related to the war. Overriding the veto, rather than violating the president's authority, would permit Congress to reclaim its rightful role regarding war powers.

VIETNAMIZATION

When Richard Nixon was elected in November 1968, the United States was already fully embroiled in the Vietnam War. Although U.S. intervention into the communist revolution in Vietnam had started during the administration of John F. Kennedy, it was President Kennedy's successor, Lyndon B. Johnson, who had increased the U.S. presence in the war to such a point that, in 1968, 536,000 American troops were serving in Vietnam. As U.S. involvement in Vietnam escalated during Johnson's presidency, so did the level of public protest and dissatisfaction with the war. Student protests, in particular, became more commonplace during Johnson's administration, culminating in violent demonstrations at the 1968 Democratic National Convention in Chicago.

Of course, not everyone was protesting during the late 1960s; there were many who resented the antiwar attitude that seemed to emanate from college campuses during this time. Richard Nixon, in his bid for the White House, attempted to appeal to this latter group, a group he called, the "silent majority." Generally, these were people who favored ending the war, but perceived protests and other similar tactics as anti-American, unpatriotic, and unsupportive of democracy. Thus, while Nixon was not responsible for the initial U.S. involvement in the war, he knew he would ultimately be held responsible for ending it.

After the election of 1968, the president had hopes that the United States could slowly withdraw U.S. forces yet continue to contribute to the efforts of the South Vietnamese against the communists of North Vietnam by providing them with military equipment and supplies. Nixon had to balance many competing goals with regard to the country's policy on Vietnam. On the one hand, he didn't want to give the impression that the United States had abandoned its allies, only to have them taken over by a communist regime, and it was paramount that any withdrawal not appear to be a military loss by the United States. On the other hand, the country was ready to wash its hands of this undeclared war and see U.S. involvement ended. Too many young people had died and too much controversy had been stirred up at home over a war that was taking place half a world away.

Nixon recommended that the United States slowly withdraw its troops, yet provide massive military assistance to the South Vietnamese, suggesting that this would allow them to more effectively fight their own war. The United States would attempt to resolve the conflict with the North Vietnamese peacefully by encouraging negotiations with its communist leaders, but the bulk of the fighting would fall to the South Vietnamese. The president referred to his policy as the "Vietnamization" of the war, indicating that we would be turning responsibility back to the South Vietnamese, but offering assistance to help prevent the country from falling to the communists. It was hoped that this policy would placate the opponents of the war, yet would also allow the United States to "save face" in withdrawing from a conflict that had lasted significantly longer than anyone had imagined.

The president introduced his policy of Vietnamization in November of 1969. Within a month, the Senate Committee on Foreign Relations was considering the administration's policy, taking statements from Melvin R. Laird, secretary of defense, and William P. Rogers, secretary of state, on the president's policy objectives. One of the most significant criticisms of Nixon's policy was its timing; the president would not indicate how long he thought the process of Vietnamization would take. Congressional "doves," or opponents of the war in Vietnam, wanted more specific information about the president's timeline on troop withdrawal. Senator Frank Church, Democrat from Idaho, pressed this point in comments made during the Senate Committee hearing. He was not hopeful that Vietnamization would work, fearing that the policy would drag U.S. involvement out for several more years. Interestingly, there was some merit to these fears, as the United States did not fully withdraw from Vietnam until April of 1975, over five years after Nixon's policy statement was made. While the number of troops in Vietnam decreased during Nixon's administration, the final evacuation of troops, a frantic process as the North Vietnamese took over the city of Saigon, did not occur until after Gerald Ford had assumed the presidency.

NIXON'S ADDRESS TO THE NATION ON THE WAR IN VIETNAM

Address from the Oval Office, November 3, 1969

Good evening, my fellow Americans:

Tonight I want to talk to you on a subject of deep concern to all Amer-

icans and to many people in all parts of the world—the war in
Vietnam. . . .

Now, let me begin by describing the situation I found when I was
inaugurated on January 20.

—The war had been going on for four years.

—31,000 Americans had been killed in action.

—The training program for the South Vietnamese was behind schedule.

—540,000 Americans were in Vietnam with no plans to reduce the
number.

—No progress had been made at the negotiations in Paris and the
United States had not put forth a comprehensive peace proposal.

—The war was causing deep division at home and criticism from
many of our friends as well as our enemies abroad.

In view of these circumstances there were some who urged that I end
the war at once by ordering the immediate withdrawal of all American
forces.

From a political standpoint this would have been a popular and easy
course to follow. After all, we became involved in the war while my
predecessor was in office. I could blame the defeat which would be the
result of my action on him and come out as the peacemaker. Some put
it to me quite bluntly: This was the only way to avoid allowing Johnson's
war to become Nixon's war.

But I had a greater obligation than to think only of the years of my
administration and of the next election. I had to think of the effect of my
decision on the next generation and on the future of peace and freedom
in America and in the world.

Let us all understand that the question before us is not whether some
Americans are for peace and some Americans are against peace. The
question at issue is not whether Johnson's war becomes Nixon's war.

The great question is: How can we win America's peace? . . .

Now, many believe that President Johnson's decision to send American combat forces to South Vietnam was wrong. Any many others—I
among them—have been strongly critical of the way the war has been
conducted.

But the question facing us today is: Now that we are in the war, what
is the best way to end it?

In January I could only conclude that the precipitate withdrawal of
American forces from Vietnam would be a disaster not only for South
Vietnam but for the United States and for the cause of peace.

For the South Vietnamese, our precipitate withdrawal would inevitably allow the Communists to repeat the massacres which followed their
takeover in the North 15 years before. . . .

For the United States, the first defeat in our history would result in a collapse of confidence in American leadership, not only in Asia but throughout the world....

For these reasons, I rejected the recommendation that I should end the war by immediately withdrawing all of our forces. I chose instead to change American policy on both the negotiating front and battlefront....

We Americans are a do-it-yourself people. We are an impatient people.

Instead of teaching someone else to do a job, we like to do it ourselves. And this trait has been carried over into our foreign policy.

In Korea and again in Vietnam, the United States furnished most of the money, most of the arms, and most of the men to help the people of those countries defend their freedom against Communist aggression.

Before any American troops were committed to Vietnam, a leader of another Asian country expressed this opinion to me when I was traveling in Asia as a private citizen. He said: "When you are trying to assist another nation defend its freedom, U.S. policy should be to help them fight the war but not to fight the war for them." ...

Well, in accordance with this wise counsel, I laid down in Guam three principles as guidelines for future American policy toward Asia:

—First, the United States will keep all of its treaty commitments.

—Second, we shall provide a shield if a nuclear power threatens the freedom of a nation allied with us or of a nation whose survival we consider vital to our security.

—Third, in cases involving other types of aggression, we shall furnish military and economic assistance when requested in accordance with our treaty commitments. But we shall look to the nation directly threatened to assume the primary responsibility of providing the manpower for its defense....

My fellow Americans, I am sure you can recognize from what I have said that we really only have two choices open to us if we want to end this war:

I can order an immediate, precipitate withdrawal of all Americans from Vietnam without regard to the effects of that action.

Or we can persist in our search for a just peace through a negotiated settlement, if possible, or through continued implementation of our plan for Vietnamization, if necessary, a plan in which we will withdraw all our forces from Vietnam on a schedule in accordance with our program, as the South Vietnamese become strong enough to defend their own freedom.

I have chosen this second course.

It is not the easy way.

It is the right way.

It is a plan which will end the war and serve the cause of peace not just in Vietnam but in the Pacific and in the world....

And so tonight to you, the great silent majority of my fellow Americans, I ask for your support. . . .

As President I hold the responsibility for choosing the best path to that goal and then leading the Nation along it.

I pledge to you tonight that I shall meet this responsibility with all of the strength and wisdom I can command in accordance with your hopes, mindful of your concerns, sustained by your prayers.

Thank you and goodnight.

See "Address to the Nation on the War in Vietnam" (3 Nov. 1969), pp. 901–909. In *Public Papers of the Presidents of the United States: Richard Nixon, 1969* (Washington, D.C.: Government Printing Office, 1969).

TESTIMONY OF SENATOR FRANK CHURCH (D-IDAHO)

Hearing before the Senate Committee on Foreign Relations November 18, 1969

. . . The president has said in his speech that the phaseout will depend upon the ability of the Saigon government gaining strength enough to assume the burden.

Now, the President has said that he will not disclose the timetable, perhaps he cannot, but it would seem to me that the best we can hope for would be to get our combat troops in the field replaced in another year, by the end of this coming year; then, assuming that the South Vietnamese hold up in the field, the removal of the remainder of our forces would be much slower. . . .

Therefore, I think you are operating in a time frame that may very well be 3 or 4 years, even if it works, and based upon all of our past experience with the South Vietnamese forces, there is very little basis, it seems to me, to have much confidence it will work.

I am afraid that the proposal may result in one of two things happening. At best, we may find ourselves with a large force left in Vietnam indefinitely, a kind of interminable war, and the American people will wake up to the fact that it is still costing us $20 billion a year, and we still have a quarter of a million troops there to support this Thieu-Ky regime [presidential administration of Nguyen Van Thieu of the Republic of the South Vietnam]. At worst, as the level of our troops goes down, we may be faced with a collapse on the battlefield, which would then face us with the most difficult of all possible choices at a time when our own forces had been reduced to the level where we are no longer completely capable of enforcing our own will. I foresee these as the inherent dangers in any plan for partial or piecemeal withdrawal, in any formula for keeping us partly in the war rather than taking us completely out of the war in a deliberate, orderly way.

I just do not have much confidence that Vietnamization is going to work out very well. . . .

I have pointed [the risks] out for a reason . . . When the president said we have two alternatives, I must disagree. His first alternative, precipitate withdrawal, is not what any responsible critic is urging the President to do. . . .

Nobody in the Congress is urging the President to preside over a Dunkirk-type evacuation. I do not think the President of the United States would ever accept such a course, and I would not personally urge such a course on him. Moreover, I do not think there is much support for that, even on the campuses, so I think the talk about precipitate withdrawal is really unrelated to the alternatives that anyone in the Government would seriously consider. . . .

I think the actual alternatives are not just the two the President mentioned but three. The third alternative he did not mention is a national commitment to a full and complete disengagement from Vietnam brought about in a way that would permit an orderly transition on the battlefield within a reasonable period of time, whether it is 12 months or 18 months, whatever may be required to withdraw our forces in orderly fashion and to protect them as they are being withdrawn.

I personally think, under the present circumstances, that this third course has become the most intelligent policy for the United States. If we were to inform Saigon that we intended to move out in this manner, then, for the first time, I think we would begin to see these various factions in Vietnam start to work out a settlement. Conversely, as long as the Saigon generals believe that they can continue to depend indefinitely on a very large American military force, I think we will not see the accommodations within Vietnam that are going to be necessary if a viable political settlement is to be achieved. . . .

And I would add that, until we are willing to "bite the bullet" and recognize that our own vital interests are not at stake in such a way as to justify the prolongation of our own participation in this war, we have not laid the groundwork upon which a political settlement is ever likely to be worked out.

See U.S. Senate. Committee on Foreign Relations. *Briefing on Vietnam*. Hearing, 18 Nov. 1969, 91st Cong. 1st sess. (Washington, D.C.: Government Printing Office, 1969), pp. 26–30.

DÉTENTE

Until 1991, a map of Europe reflected geographically the deep ideological differences that existed between Western Europe and the Soviet

Union. This division of Europe into western and eastern blocs after World War II was negotiated in February 1945, when President Franklin D. Roosevelt, British Prime Minister Winston Churchill, and Soviet Premier Joseph Stalin met in the Russian city of Yalta to negotiate the end of World War II in Europe. Although Japan was still actively engaged in the Pacific, Germany was near defeat by early 1945, and the "Big Three," as the three leaders were collectively called, met to discuss the prospects for peace and reconstruction in a Europe devastated by war. Although the United States, Great Britain, and the Soviet Union were united in their opposition of Germany and Japan, the national interests of the two democratic nations differed markedly from the interests of the Soviet Union, which had ambitions to gain control of greater territory. In order to secure Soviet cooperation to end the war in the Pacific, Roosevelt and Churchill made concessions to Stalin, resulting in a divided Germany and Berlin, and additional territories from Poland and Asia were granted to the Soviet Union. These decisions made at Yalta represented the beginning of heightened tensions between the Soviet Union and the West.

The period spanning 1945 through 1991 is often referred to as the Cold War years, reflecting the frosty relationship that developed between the Soviet Union and the United States after World War II and was sustained until the Soviet Union disintegrated in 1991. The tense relationship between the Soviet Union and the West was, at its foundation, based on ideological differences between the two types of governments, yet this tension was magnified greatly by the detonation of the atom bomb on Hiroshima and Nagasaki in August 1945. The United States had won the race to build a nuclear bomb, but the Soviet Union wasn't far behind in developing its own nuclear weapons. Once both countries had developed nuclear weapons, a new race was on to build more and better weapons of mass destruction.

Because the world had changed fundamentally when the first atomic bomb was dropped on Hiroshima, new concepts for maintaining peace were devised that represented this new world. In the late 1950s and 1960s, the concept of "deterrence" was developed, which was based on the idea that neither the United States nor the Soviet Union would choose to make the first nuclear strike against the other if it knew that the other country had the ability to retaliate with the same force. However, the assumption that "mutually assured destruction" would deter a nuclear war prompted both countries to continue building up their nuclear stockpiles.

Although Richard Nixon had been quite vocal early in his political career regarding his contempt for the Soviet Union, by the time he became president, he recognized that the frantic pace of the arms race could not continue indefinitely. Since it was unlikely that the United States would eliminate communism in the Soviet Union, our future relations needed to recognize the fundamental differences between the two countries, yet focus on points of mutual interest. In short, although the value of equal weapons capabilities was still recognized, Nixon knew it was in neither country's interest to maintain the heightened level of conflict as witnessed in the 1960s by incidents such as the attempted placement of Soviet missiles in Cuba. As such, Nixon favored a policy of détente, in which negotiations with the Soviets would replace threats. He expressed these sentiments both to Congress and to the United Nations in 1970. Ultimately, this change in policy would result in an invitation from Soviet Premier Leonid Brezhnev for Nixon to visit the Soviet Union in May 1972, and would pave the way for ultimate agreement on treaties such as the Strategic Arms Limitation Treaty (SALT) in 1972.

Not everyone was supportive of the president's approach toward the Soviet Union, however. The president faced two general criticisms regarding his policies toward the Soviets. First were those who wanted to maintain a hard line against the Soviet Union, and were opposed to any thaw in relations. This criticism was directed more specifically at the SALT treaty between the United States and the Soviets. Second were those who wanted more amicable relations with the Soviet Union but didn't think the president's policies reflected the rhetoric of détente. Thus, many of Nixon's critics weren't opposed to détente, but were instead opposed to the continuation of Cold War tactics under the new, and misleading, title of détente. Professor Fred Warner Neal of Claremont University, in testimony before the Subcommittee on Europe of the House Committee on Foreign Affairs, claimed that Nixon's rhetoric about the creation of a new relationship with the Soviet Union and his actions toward the Soviets simply did not coincide. Instead, he claimed, the Cold War policies of the past seemed very much in place and Nixon's policies toward the Soviet Union did not actually reflect détente. Neal used the outcry over a proposal to reduce the number of NATO troops by Senator Mike Mansfield (D-Mont.), a vocal critic of the Vietnam War, to illustrate his point.

FIRST ANNUAL REPORT TO THE CONGRESS

February 18, 1970

The Soviet Union shares with other countries the overwhelming temptation to continue to base its policies at home and abroad on old and familiar concepts. But perceptions framed in the nineteenth century are hardly relevant to the new era we are now entering.

If we have had to learn the limitations of our own power, the lessons of the last two decades must have left their imprint on the leadership in the Kremlin—in the recognition that Marxist ideology is not the surest guide to the problems of a changing industrial society, the worldwide decline in the appeal of ideology, and most of all in the foreign policy dilemmas repeatedly posed by the spread of Communism to states which refuse to endure permanent submission to Soviet authority—a development illustrated vividly by the Soviet schism with China.

The central problem of Soviet-American relations, then, is whether our two countries can transcend the past and work together to build a lasting peace.

In 1969, we made a good beginning. In this first year of my Administration, we ratified the non-Proliferation Treaty; we made progress in negotiating arms control on the seabed; we took steps to further the prospects of agreement regarding chemical and biological methods of warfare; we engaged in talks on the Middle Eastern settlement; and we began negotiations on the limitation of strategic arms—the most important arms control negotiations this country has ever entered. In concert with our allies, we have also offered to negotiate on specific issues in Europe: history has taught us that if crises arise in Europe, the world at large cannot long expect to remain unaffected. . . . We hope that the coming year will bring evidence that the Soviets have decided to seek a durable peace rather than continue along the roads of the past.

It will not be the sincerity or purpose of the Soviet leadership that will be at issue. The tensions between us are not generated by personal misunderstandings, and neither side does anyone a service by so suggesting. Peace does not come simply with statesmen's smiles. At issue are basic questions of long conflicting purposes in a world where no one's interests are furthered by conflict. Only a straightforward recognition of that reality—and an equally direct effort to deal with it—will bring us to the genuine cooperation which we seek and which the peace of the world requires.

See "First Annual Report to the Congress" (18 Feb. 1970), pp. 179–180. In *Public Papers of the Presidents of the United States: Richard Nixon, 1970* (Washington, D.C.: Government Printing Office, 1970).

THIRD ANNUAL REPORT TO CONGRESS ON FOREIGN POLICY

February 9, 1972

Since the nuclear age began, both the world's fears of Armageddon and its hopes for a stable peace have rested on the relationship between the United States and the Soviet Union. For most of that period, the policies of both countries have been directed more to the fearful possibility than to the larger hope.

But it is not inevitable that our relationship with the Soviets be dominated by an incessant and dangerous contest made all the more ominous by an occasional, but always brief and unproductive, oscillation toward détente. The true interests of neither country require such a relationship. The needs of neither are served by the restrictions it places on the intercourse between two great peoples.

It has been the purpose of this administration to transform the U.S.-Soviet relationship so that a mutual search for a stable peace and security becomes its dominant feature and its driving force. If the ultimate prospect for a stable world peace requires accommodation between China and the United States, both the immediate and the long-term hopes for world stability rest on a more decent and mutually beneficial relationship between ourselves and the Soviet Union.

Such a vision is not quixotic. It has been rendered possible by the end of the bipolar rigidity which characterized the postwar world. It is sustained by the desire of the Soviet people for the benefits which would be theirs if their government could reduce the vast investment of resources in international competition with us. And it is countenanced by the readiness of the American people to search for a new and just approach to lasting peace.

For the three years of this administration, we have, therefore, worked to establish a more positive relationship with the Soviet Union.

Paradoxically, this required that we put aside the temptations of immediate, but shallow, "accomplishments" such as unprepared and unproductive summit meetings. A constructive relationship with the Soviet Union cannot be built merely by mutual assertions of good will. History has amply shown how barren such gestures are of genuine and lasting result.

The issues which divide the United States and the Soviet Union are real and serious. They are at the heart of the security and well-being of both countries. They are not, therefore, susceptible to solution by resort to mere atmospherics. They require, instead, concrete agreements on the specific problems which cause the tension between our two countries.

Such agreements can be obtained only by a careful and painstaking effort by both countries. It requires each to exercise restraint, to recognize and accept the legitimate interests of the other, and to negotiate realistically to accommodate conflicting views. For our part, we are committed to such an approach. We are convinced that it can serve the best interests of the American and Soviet peoples and the peoples of the world.

That is the burden of the message which, in various ways, we have been conveying to the Soviet leaders for the past three years. We hope that what has been accomplished will prove to be the beginning of a transformation of the relationship between ourselves and the Soviet Union.

See "Third Annual Report to the Congress on United States Foreign Policy" (9 Feb. 1972), pp. 204–205. In *Public Papers of the Presidents of the United States: Richard Nixon, 1972* (Washington, D.C.: Government Printing Office, 1972).

STATEMENT OF FRED WARNER NEAL, PROFESSOR, CLAREMONT (CALIFORNIA) GRADUATE SCHOOL

Hearings before the Subcommittee on Europe of the House Committee on Foreign Affairs
June 18, 1971

There have been some American responses to these changed conditions. The tenor of official rhetoric is usually less frenetic; and some subsidiary assumptions have been modified. We have achieved more flexibility. There is less tendency to shoot from the hip. There is more awareness of the difficulty, if not the impossibility, of maintaining global military commitments. There is wider recognition of the desirability, if not the necessity, of reaching some understanding with the Soviet Union and China, and we have, indeed, even concluded certain peripheral agreements with the U.S.S.R.

In spite of all this, it seems to me that the underlying cold war concepts persist in much American thinking about foreign polity, consciously or unconsciously. There could be no clearer illustration of it than the frenzied outcry which arose recently over Senator Mansfield's attempts to reduce our NATO troop strength.

The cold-war concepts continue to pervade our military planning and make us fear the risks of nuclear arms control agreements more than the nuclear arms race. They lead to our opting for the ABM and MIRV systems on the eve of the SALT talks. They are responsible for our objection to a European security conference. They impede our negotiations on Berlin. They condition our thinking about the Middle East and the Mediterranean. They underlie what we do—and don't do—in Southeast Asia.

Indeed, there are few aspects of American foreign policy which in one way or another—either in terms of the beliefs of decision makers or in terms of what they consider, probably correctly, to be the beliefs of a majority of the American people—are not affected in some way by cold-war concepts and assumptions. . . .

It may be useful in this regard to glance briefly at the foreign policy record of the Nixon administration, which has asked to be judged on the basis not of what is said, but what is done. The fact is that thus far much more has been said than done. How much of it reflects considerations of public relations and politics, rather than policy, is, therefore, still an open question. If some of President Nixon's statements seem to indicate a desire to break away from the confines of cold-war concepts, others seem to indicate that these concepts have a continuing hold.

Although the President has said he sought a foreign policy based on "an evaluation of the world as it is, not as it was 25 years ago," he also speaks of "the necessity to stop communist encroachments on the free world."

Although he had referred to being satisfied with a "sufficiency" of nuclear armaments, his Secretary of Defense emphasizes the need for "superior military strength."

Although Mr. Nixon has promised to "end the war—in Vietnam—and our involvement," he also warns that anything short of victory by Saigon "would greatly increase the danger of aggression and also the danger of a larger war in the Pacific and in the world."

With regard to military intervention, we have the Nixon doctrine. The Nixon doctrine, as you, of course, know, is not officially written down anywhere. Emerging from remarks the President made at a press conference in Guam, there is no text and thus no official language. The Nixon doctrine apparently asserts that the United States will not go in for full-fledged military intervention militarily any more unless absolutely necessary.

One may welcome the implication of restraint while remembering that even John Foster Dulles [Secretary of State under President Dwight D. Eisenhower] never advocated intervention when not absolutely necessary. The effort at Vietnamization stems from the ideas implicit in the Nixon doctrine. The Nixon doctrine seems to envisage less abandonment of cold-war concepts than a new kind of cold war, in which other people will do the ground fighting for us while we supply massive air support, money, and material, plus some advisers. Vietnamization appears to be a pilot project. If so, the Nixon doctrine may be to the new-type cold war what the Truman doctrine was to the old one.

The trouble is that if the policy is seen as a way to maintain American influence—in Southeast Asia, for instance—while supporting one side of an internal conflict with everything but ground troops, it is very, very likely to lead to the old kind of cold war in short order. What kind of a cold war there will be if Vietnamization does not work is anybody's guess. . . .

Discovering China via the ping-pong table is encouraging, but so far it is more declaration than policy, and the only discernible results to date have been the stimulation of fears in Moscow. To effect a real reapprochement with China, while also improving relations with the U.S.S.R., would be a great stroke of statesmanship. An attempt to play Peking against Moscow would only be another cold war ploy. This possibility, in my opinion, constitutes a real danger against which we should be on guard, and which we should not permit our desire for a more rational policy toward China to obscure.

In any event, if the record up until now indicates some awareness of the need for new directions, it is still far from being free of evidence of cold war thinking.

See U.S. House. Committee on Foreign Affairs. *The Cold War: Origins and Development.* Hearing, 7, 11, 14, 18 June 1971, 92nd Cong. 1st sess. (Washington, D.C.: Government Printing Office, 1971), pp. 167–69.

SPACE POLICY

Although the U.S. government had been researching and utilizing rockets for military purposes since the 1940s, the country didn't enter the "space age" until January 1958, when *Explorer I*, the country's first satellite, was successfully launched. Yet, while this was an American "first," it was not the world's first manmade satellite. On October 4, 1957, the Soviet Union had surprised the United States with *Sputnik*, the first manmade satellite successfully launched into Earth's orbit. A mere month later, the Soviets launched *Sputnik II*, a second successful effort, which had the distinction of carrying a dog into space. Thus, *Explorer I* represented a frantic and fearful game of "catch-up" for the United States. While the United States had been the first to employ nuclear weapons in 1945, the Soviet Union had followed the United States into the nuclear age in 1949. However, the Soviets' successful development of rocket and missile technology would give them a significant advantage over the United States in deploying such weapons.

In addition to the evident lag in U.S. space technology, the Soviet Premier, Nikita Khrushchev, added insult to injury by openly joking about the failures of the U.S. space program and taunting that *Sputnik* was "lonely" in space. The response by the United States was multifaceted; in July of 1958, Congress passed legislation creating the National Aeronautics and Space Administration (NASA) to streamline programs that had previously been administered by several government agencies. President Eisenhower, along with Congress, also signed the National Defense Education Act, designed to strengthen educational programs in math and science as well as foreign languages. In 1961, after the Soviets beat the United States at putting a man in space by less than a month, President Kennedy raised the stakes by pledging in his State of the Union message that the United States would be the first country to put a person on the moon, and he further urged congressional support for an accelerated space program to create effective communications and weather satellites.

Richard Nixon inherited the program to put a man on the moon when he became president in January of 1969, although the feat had not yet been accomplished. Yet, on July 20, 1969, the first manned lunar landing was accomplished, with Neil Armstrong and Edwin "Buzz" Aldrin as the first humans to walk on the moon. In the midst of the domestic turmoil surrounding Vietnam and civil rights, the successful moon landing offered a welcome boost to national pride.

The space program was an issue that generated excitement and support among the American public. The United States had been bested by the Soviet Union so many times in the space race since 1958 that successfully putting humans on the moon and returning them to Earth had significant symbolic as well as scientific value. Richard Nixon tapped the excitement of the manned moon landing in a speech about the future of the space program. He outlined several broad goals for the program, including more lunar exploration and the increased use of space technology. He also focused on the need to decrease the cost associated with space exploration, briefly mentioning the future development of a reusable space shuttle. In his 1970 budget recommendation to the Congress, the president had provided for a substantial increase in the budget for the space program, in particular the manned space flight program.

When Congress debated the authorization of funds for NASA in late 1969, the amount eventually proposed for continued human space exploration actually exceeded the amount the Nixon administration had requested, even though Nixon's request had been considerably more than had been appropriated during the Johnson administration. While congressional support for the increased authorization was strong, there were members of Congress who believed that increasing funds for the space program was misguided. Representative Edward I. Koch (D-N.Y.), who would later become mayor of New York City, opposed increasing the authorization for the NASA manned space program. While he vehemently opposed the boost in funds proposed in Congress's authorization bill, he also felt that the amount requested by Nixon was excessive. Specifically, Koch thought that there were other, more pressing issues facing the national government, such as the economy, defense, and social programs, and that the excitement over the manned space program should not eclipse these concerns.

NIXON'S STATEMENT ABOUT THE FUTURE OF THE U.S. SPACE PROGRAM

Florida, March 7, 1970

What we do in space from here on in must become a normal and regular part of our national life and must therefore be planned in conjunction with all of the other undertakings which are also important to us. . . .

With these general considerations in mind, I have concluded that our space program should work toward the following specific objectives.

1. We should continue to *explore the moon*. Future Apollo manned lunar landings will be spaced so as to maximize our scientific return from each mission, always providing, of course, for the safety of those who undertake these ventures. Our decisions about manned and unmanned lunar voyages beyond the Apollo program will be based on the results of these missions.

2. We should move ahead with bold *exploration of the planets and the universe*. In the next few years, scientific satellites of many types will be launched into earth orbit to bring us new information about the universe, the solar system, and even our own planet. During the next decade, we will also launch unmanned spacecraft to all the planets of our solar system, including an unmanned vehicle which will be sent to land on Mars and to investigate its surface. In the late 1970s, the "Grand Tour" missions will study the mysterious outer planets of the solar system—Jupiter, Saturn, Uranus, Neptune, and Pluto. The positions of the planets at that time will give us a unique opportunity to launch missions which can visit several of them on a single flight of over 3 billion miles. Preparations for this program will begin in 1972.

There is one major but longer-range goal we should keep in mind as we proceed with our exploration of the planets. As a part of this program we will eventually send men to explore the planet Mars.

3. We should work to *reduce substantially the cost of space operations*. Our present rocket technology will provide a reliable launch capability for some time. But as we build for the longer-range future, we must devise less costly and less complicated ways of transporting payloads into space. Such a capability—designed so that it will be suitable for wide range of scientific, defense, and commercial uses—can help us realize important economies in all aspects of our space program. We are currently examining in greater detail the feasibility of reusable space shuttles as one way of achieving this objective.

4. We should seek to *extend man's capability to live and work in space*. The Experimental Space Station (XSS)—a large orbiting workshop—will be an important part of this effort. We are now building such a station—using systems originally developed for the Apollo program—and plan to begin using it for operational missions in the next few years. We expect that men will be working in space for months at a time during the coming decade.

We have much to learn about what man can and cannot do in space. On the basis of our experience with the XSS, we will decide when and how to develop longer-lived space stations. Flexible long-lived space station modules could provide a multipurpose space platform for the longer-range future and ultimately become a building block for manned inter-planetary travel.

5. We should *hasten and expand the practical applications of space technology*. The development of Earth resources satellites—platforms which can help in such varied tasks as surveying crops, locating mineral deposits, and measuring water resources—will enable us to assess our environment and use our resources more effectively. We should continue to pursue other applications of space-related technology in a wide variety of fields, including meteorology, communications, navigation, air traffic control, education, and national defense. The very act of reaching into space can help man improve the quality of life here on earth.

6. We should *encourage greater international cooperation in space*. In my address to the United Nations last September, I indicated that the United States will take positive, concrete steps "toward internationalizing man's epic venture into space—an adventure that belongs not to one nation but to all mankind." I believe that both the adventures and the applications of space missions should be shared by all peoples. Our progress will be faster and our accomplishments will be greater if nations will join together in this effort, both in contributing the resources and in enjoying the benefits. Unmanned scientific payloads from other nations already make use of our space launch capability on a cost-shared basis; we look forward to the day when these arrangements can be extended to larger applications satellites and astronaut crews. The Administrator of NASA recently met with the space authorities of Western Europe, Canada, Japan, and Australia in an effort to find ways in which we can cooperate more effectively in space.

It is important, I believe, that the space program of the United States meet these six objectives. A program which achieves these goals will be a balanced space program, one which will extend our capabilities and knowledge and one which will put our new learning to work for the immediate benefit of all people.

As we enter a new decade, we are conscious of the fact that man is also entering a new historic era. For the first time, he has reached beyond his plane; for the rest of time, we will think of ourselves as men *from* the planet earth. It is my hope that as we go forward with our space program, we can plan and work in a way which makes us proud *both* of the planet from which we come *and* of our ability to travel beyond it.

See "Statement About the Future of the United States Space Program" (7 March 1970), pp. 250–251. In *Public Papers of the Presidents of the United States: Richard Nixon, 1970* (Washington, D.C.: Government Printing Office, 1970).

OPINION OF REPRESENTATIVE EDWARD I. KOCH (D-N.Y.)

Authorizing Appropriations to NASA
1969

There are several aspects of H.R. 11721, the NASA authorization bill for fiscal year 1970, which I consider objectionable.

Manned Space Flight: The bill authorizes $258 million more for research and development than was requested by the administration, and the bulk of the increase is earmarked for the manned space flight program. Based upon correspondence which I have had with officials of NASA, the purposes of manned space flight are limited to determining the physiological and psychological effects of the space environment upon men, and assessing man's ability to perform in space. It seems clear that the scientific objectives of such flights are secondary, and it appears that in virtually every case these objectives could be achieved more effectively and more economically using automated spacecraft. I am convinced that the greatest values from our vast expenditures in the national space effort have been, and will be, achieved using automated equipment, and I strongly favor an increased effort in the relatively less expensive unmanned program, and a reduced effort in the extremely costly manned space flight program.

In a period of extraordinary and urgent demands upon our national resources brought about by enormous defense expenditures, and pressing economic and social problems many of which are not being met adequately, I regard it as at least unwise, at most outrageous, for Congress to increase the already large-scale expenditures for manned space flight.

It is noteworthy that Congress learned for the first time this year that NASA plans to make 10 manned space flights to the moon after the initial Apollo landing.

In my view, manned exploration of the moon should not be based upon the availability of Saturn-Apollo equipment taking billions of dollars from our needs here on earth, but rather upon genuine scientific objectives and the amount of new information each successive flight can produce. Before committing ourselves to 10 additional manned lunar landings, let us first see what the first ALSEP [Apollo Lunar Surface Experiment Package] and the soil samples brought back by the Apollo astronauts produce. It is possible that the ALSEP and the soil analysis will reveal that there is not enough material of scientific interest on the moon to warrant a total of 10 more manned missions. Must we proceed at a rate of three lunar landings a year (after the initial landing), when there are urgent priorities here on earth?

I support our need and desire to explore space, but there is a matter of priorities which our committee must recognize. Until the hungry in this country, and indeed this planet, are adequately fed, we should take pause before we shoot for the outer planets when those trips could be stretched out and delayed, but not terminated.

In summary, I oppose any increase in the manned space flight budget beyond the amount of the Administration request as entirely unwarranted. On the other hand, I would support a reduction of $29 million in the NASA request, the amount by which the Nixon budget exceeds the Johnson budget for manned space flight for fiscal year 1970.

See U.S. House. Committee on Science and Aeronautics. *Authorizing Appropriations to the National Aeronautics and Space Administration* (H. Rpt. 91–255) (Washington, D.C.: Government Printing Office, 1969).

INVASION OF CAMBODIA

With the announcement of his policy of Vietnamization in November of 1969, President Nixon had raised the hopes of the American people that the end of the Vietnam War was within sight. What the public didn't know at the time was that U.S. forces in Vietnam, at Nixon's direction, had for months been secretly bombing North Vietnamese outposts in Cambodia, a country along the southwestern border of Vietnam. Thus, while the president publicly supported a measured withdrawal from Vietnam, he was actually responsible for escalating U.S. involvement in the war in an unsuccessful attempt to oust the North Vietnamese from Cambodia.

In April 1970, five months after his speech on Vietnamization, Nixon ordered American troops to invade Cambodia to destroy Communist bases and supply routes. He explained in his speech of April 30, 1970 that the incursion into Cambodia was necessary to protect American and South Vietnamese troops from the North Vietnamese who were occupying territory in a country that had declared its neutrality with regard to the Vietnam War. He emphasized that this was not an invasion of Cambodia, but was instead an attack on the North Vietnamese who were stationed in Cambodia.

The response to Nixon's announcement was immediate and, in some cases, violent. An editorial statement was released by the editors of eleven prestigious universities, including Columbia University, which condemned the president for the invasion and the continued American presence in Vietnam. To communicate the opposition to the war that was growing across the country, the editorial called for strikes to be held on all university campuses, endorsed by the entire academic community, including students, faculty, staff, and the administration. Response to the strike was great, with as many as 200 campuses conducting some sort of demonstration against the Cambodian invasion. Two of these incidents, in particular, have come to characterize the trauma and conflict in the United States over the Vietnam War.

On May 4, 1970, less than a week after Nixon's announcement, students at Kent State University in Ohio gathered to demonstrate against Nixon's decision to invade Cambodia. When the demonstration became more menacing, with students threatening to burn down the college's Reserve Officer Training Corps (ROTC) building, National Guard troops were sent in to maintain order. Although many in the crowd of students were merely passing by on their way to class, National Guard troops opened fire on the group, killing four students and injuring nine. A second, similar incident occurred a mere ten days later, at Jackson State University in Jackson, Mississippi. On May 14, 1970, students at this historically African American university were protesting both the Kent State "massacre" and the American invasion of Cambodia. Again, when the demonstrations became more destructive, state police were called to quell the demonstration. These officers eventually surrounded a residence hall on campus and began firing on the group of students that had congregated there. Two students were killed, with twelve others seriously injured from flying glass.

The consequences of the American invasion were certainly felt even more strongly by the Cambodians who were killed or displaced by the American military actions. Anti-American sentiments grew in Cambodia after the 1970 invasion, providing enough backing to the Cambodian communists, called the Khmer Rouge, to support a civil war for control of the Cambodian government. Despite continued U.S. military and financial support, Cambodia fell to the Khmer Rouge in 1975. Although the Khmer Rouge was displaced in the early 1990s by a constitutional monarchy, the period between 1975 and 1979 witnessed the government-sponsored killing of over a million people in the so-called "killing fields" of Cambodia.

FROM NIXON'S ADDRESS TO THE NATION ON THE SITUATION IN SOUTHEAST ASIA

Address from the Oval Office, April 30, 1970

North Vietnam in the last two weeks has stripped away all pretense of respecting the sovereignty or the neutrality of Cambodia. Thousands of their soldiers are invading the country from the sanctuaries; they are encircling the capital of Phnom Penh. . . .

Cambodia, as a result of this, has sent out a call to the United States, to a number of other nations, for assistance. Because if this enemy effort succeeds, Cambodia would become a vast enemy staging area and a springboard for attacks on South Vietnam along 600 miles of frontier— a refuge where enemy troops could return from combat without fear of retaliation.

North Vietnamese men and supplies could then be poured into that country, jeopardizing not only the lives of our own men but the people of South Vietnam as well.

Now confronted with this situation, we have three options.

First, we can do nothing. Well, the ultimate result of that course of action is clear. Unless we indulge in wishful thinking, the lives of Americans remaining in Vietnam after our next withdrawal of 150,000 would be gravely threatened. . . .

Our second choice is to provide massive military assistance to Cambodia itself. Now unfortunately, while we deeply sympathize with the plight of 7 million Cambodians whose country is being invaded, massive amounts of military assistance could not be rapidly and effectively utilized by the small Cambodian Army against the immediate threat. With other nations, we shall do our best to provide the small arms and other equipment which the Cambodian Army of 40,000 needs and can use for its defense. But the aid we will provide will be limited to the purpose of enabling Cambodia to defend its neutrality and not for the purpose of making it an active belligerent on one side or the other.

Our third choice is to go to the heart of the trouble. That means cleaning out major North Vietnamese and Vietcong occupied territories— these sanctuaries which serve as bases for attacks on both Cambodia and American and South Vietnamese forces in South Vietnam. Some of these, incidentally, are as close to Saigon as Baltimore is to Washington. . . .

Now faced with these three options, this is the decision I have made.

In cooperation with the armed forces of South Vietnam, attacks are being launched this week to clean out major enemy sanctuaries on the Cambodian-Vietnam border.

A major responsibility for the ground operations is being assumed by South Vietnamese forces. For example, the attacks in several areas . . . are exclusively South Vietnamese ground operations under South Vietnamese command with the United States providing air and logistical support.

There is one area, however . . . where I have concluded that a combined American and South Vietnamese operation is necessary.

Tonight, American and South Vietnamese units will attack the headquarters for the entire Communist military operation in South Vietnam.

This key control center has been occupied by the North Vietnamese and Vietcong for 5 years in blatant violation of Cambodia's neutrality.

This is not an invasion of Cambodia. The areas in which these attacks will be launched are completely occupied and controlled by North Vietnamese forces. Our purpose is not to occupy the areas. Once enemy forces are driven out of these sanctuaries and once their military supplies are destroyed, we will withdraw.

These actions are in no way directed to the security interests of any nation. Any government that chooses to use these actions as a pretext for harming relations with the United States will be doing so on its own responsibility, and on its own initiative, and we will draw the appropriate conclusions.

Now let me give you the reasons for my decision.

A majority of the American people, a majority of you listening to me, are for the withdrawal of our forces from Vietnam. The action I have taken tonight is indispensable for the continuing success of that withdrawal program.

A majority of the American people want to end this war rather than to have it drag on interminably. The action I have taken tonight will serve that purpose.

A majority of the American people want to keep the casualties of our brave men in Vietnam at an absolute minimum. The action I take tonight is essential if we are to accomplish that goal.

We take this action not for the purpose of expanding the war into Cambodia but for the purpose of ending the war in Vietnam and winning the just peace we all desire. We have made—we will continue to make—every possible effort to end this war through negotiation at the conference table rather than through more fighting on the battlefield.

See "Address to the Nation on the Situation in Southeast Asia" (30 April 1970), pp. 407–408. In *Public Papers of The Presidents of the United States: Richard Nixon, 1970* (Washington, D.C.: Government Printing Office, 1970).

EDITORIAL FROM THE *COLUMBIA UNIVERSITY SPECTATOR*

May 4, 1970

President Nixon's unwarranted and illegitimate decision to send American combat forces into Cambodia and to resume the bombing of North Vietnam demands militant, immediate, and continued opposition from all Americans.

Through his unilateral executive move, the president has placed our country in a state of emergency. He has ignored the Constitutional prerogatives of Congress, and has revealed the sham of his policy of Vietnamization, a policy which, through a tortuous process of inner logic, demands that we escalate the war in order to enable American troops to withdraw. He has demonstrated that American foreign policy still dictates the necessity to sacrifice American lives, to ravish independent countries, and to squander our resources and energies.

The President has tragically misgauged the mood of the country. The anti-war movement, which has marched and protested for years in a vain effort to reverse the United States' role in Southeast Asia, has finally resurfaced in new and larger numbers. With Nixon's lies now finally exposed, the immorality and hypocrisy of our government's actions have been revealed for all to see.

The need for action has never been so great and so urgent.

We therefore call on the entire academic community of this country to engage in a nationwide university strike. We must cease business as usual in order to allow the universities to lead and join in a collective strike to protest America's escalation of the war.

We do not call for a strike by students against the university, but a strike by the entire university—faculty, students, staff, and administrators alike.

The reasons for such a strike are manifold. First, it is a dramatic symbol of our opposition to a corrupt and immoral war. It demonstrates clearly our priorities, for the significance of classes and examinations pales before the greater problems outside the classroom. Moreover, it recognizes the fact that within a society so permeated with inequality, immorality and destruction a classroom education becomes a meaningless and hollow exercise.

But the necessity for a strike extends even far beyond these reasons. The strike is necessary to free the academic community from activities of secondary importance and to open it up to the primary task of building renewed opposition to the war. It is necessary to permit the academic community to first solidify its own opposition, and to then act immediately to extend this opposition beyond the campuses.

We ask the entire academic community to use this opportunity to go to the people, and to bring home to the entire nation the meaning of the President's action. A massive, unprecedented display of dissent is required.

We urge that this strike be directed toward bringing about the following changes:

1. An immediate withdrawal of all American forces from Southeast Asia;

2. Passage of a Senate amendment to the defense appropriations bill to deny all aid for our military and political adventures in Southeast Asia;

3. The mobilization of public support for anti-war candidates in the upcoming primary and general elections;

4. The end of political repression at home, in particular the government's systematic attempt to eliminate the Black Panther Party and other political dissidents;

5. A re-allocation of American resources from military involvement abroad to domestic problems, in particular the problems of our beleaguered cities;

6. And the building of support for a massive demonstration in Washington on May 9 to bring to the nation's capital, in unprecedented numbers, our opposition.

The stage has been set, the issues clearly drawn, the need apparent. It is now time to act.

See "Editorial," *Columbia University Spectator* vol. 114, no. 104, May 4, 1970, pp. 1, 4.

CREATION OF THE ENVIRONMENTAL PROTECTION AGENCY

Before 1970, the condition of the natural environment was not a significant issue for many people in the United States and, as such, was not of much interest politically to elected officials. For most people, the protests of the Vietnam War and the civil rights movement were simply more pressing than issues related to the environment. However, it was becoming increasingly obvious during the 1960s that the quality of the environment was deteriorating. Rachel Carson's book *Silent Spring* was published in 1962, revealing the tragic consequences of using the pesticide DDT for wildlife and the environment. Air and water pollution started gaining more attention as well with events such as a massive oil spill in Santa Barbara, California, in January 1969 and a fire on the Cuyahoga River in Cleveland, Ohio, on June 22, 1969, caused by floating trash and debris in the river. This growing concern for the environment culminated on April 22, 1970 with the first Earth Day celebration.

Earth Day reflected a growing concern for the environment but it also was used as a catalyst to raise consciousness among those people who had not previously considered it a significant issue. Demonstrations and teach-ins were held across the country to alert people to the need for greater environmental protection. These events received considerable media coverage and were successful at putting the needs of the environment on the national agenda. Both President Nixon and members of Congress were swept along with this burgeoning environmental movement in 1970, passing such laws as the comprehensive Clean Air Act, the Environmental Education Act, and the National Environmental Policy Act.

One difficulty in attempting to regulate the quality of the environment was that there was no one unit of the federal government solely charged with environmental issues. Responsibilities for environmental protection were scattered across the federal bureaucracy, in such agencies as the U.S. Forest Service, the National Park Service, the U.S. Fish and Wildlife Service, and the Department of Energy. In July 1970, President Nixon attempted to address this problem by proposing an Environmental Protection Agency (EPA), which would have primary responsibility for implementing environmental policies and coordinating the efforts of other agencies and the environmental efforts of the states. Nixon presented his plan to establish the EPA in a Special Message to Congress on July 9, 1970, along with a plan to establish the National Oceanic and Atmospheric Administration. In it, he outlines his plans for the creation of the EPA and some of the new agency's major responsibilities.

Because it is ultimately the responsibility of the Congress to create and organize units in the federal bureaucracy, each branch of Congress had to consider and vote on the president's reorganization plan; hearings were held on the president's plan in a committee of the House of Representatives in the summer of 1970. In these hearings, Representative John Dingell (D-Mich.) expressed his opposition to the president's plan. His opposition was not based on any rejection of environmental protection, but instead on the manner by which the proposal had been made. First, this opposition was related to the separation of powers between the legislative and executive branches. Dingell thought that the Congress should have played a much bigger role in the reorganization plan, given its constitutional responsibility for the organization of the bureaucracy. Second, Dingell's opposition was based on expectations that this particular reorganization would be confusing and complex and would not result in greater protection of the environment. Ultimately, he believed that plucking responsibilities from a variety of departments and agencies and placing them into a newly created agency would stand in the way of accomplishing the country's environmental goals.

FROM NIXON'S SPECIAL MESSAGE TO THE CONGRESS ABOUT REORGANIZATION PLANS TO ESTABLISH THE ENVIRONMENTAL PROTECTION AGENCY AND THE NATIONAL OCEANIC AND ATMOSPHERIC ADMINISTRATION

July 9, 1970

Our national government today is not structured to make a coordinated attack on the pollutants which debase the air we breathe, the water we drink, and the land that grows our food. Indeed, the present governmental structure for dealing with environmental pollution often defies effective and concerted action.

Despite its complexity, for pollution control purposes the environment must be perceived as a single, interrelated system. Present assignments of departmental responsibilities do not reflect this interrelatedness.

Many agency missions, for example, are designed primarily along media lines—air, water, and land. Yet the sources of air, water, and land pollution are interrelated and often interchangeable. A single source may pollute the air with smoke and chemicals, the land with solid wastes, and a river or lake with chemical and other wastes. Control of the air pollution may produce more solid wastes, which then pollute the land or water. Control of the water-polluting effluent may convert it into solid wastes, which must be disposed of on land.

Similarly, some pollutants—chemicals, radiation, pesticides—appear in all media. Successful control of them at present requires the coordinated efforts of a variety of separate agencies and departments. The results are not always successful.

A far more effective approach to pollution control would:

—Identify pollutants.

—Trace them through the entire ecological chain, observing and recording changes in form as they occur.

—Determine the total exposure of man and his environment.

—Examine interactions among forms of pollution.

—Identify where in the ecological chain interdiction would be most appropriate.

In organizational terms, this requires pulling together into one agency a variety of research, monitoring, standard-setting, and enforcement activities now scattered through several departments and agencies. It also requires that the new agency include sufficient support elements—to give it the needed strength and potential for carrying out its mission. The new agency would also, of course, draw upon the results of research conducted by other agencies. . . .

This reorganization would permit response to environmental problems in a manner beyond the previous capability of our pollution control programs. The EPA would have the capacity to do research on important pollutants irrespective of the media in which they appear, and on the impact of these pollutants on the total environment. Both by itself and together with other agencies, the EPA would monitor the condition of the environment—biological as well as physical. With these data, the EPA would be able to establish quantitative "environmental baselines"— critical if we are to measure adequately the success or failure of our pollution abatement efforts.

As no disjointed array of separate programs can, the EPA would be able—in concert with the States—to set and enforce standards for air and water quality and for individual pollutants. This consolidation of pollution control authorities would help assure that we do not create new environmental problems in the process of controlling existing ones. Industries seeking to minimize the adverse impact of their activities on the environment would be assured of consistent standards covering the full range of their waste disposal problems. As the States develop and expand their own pollution control programs, they would be able to look to one agency to support their efforts with financial and technical assistance and training.

In proposing that the Environmental Protection Agency be set up as a separate new agency, I am making an exception to one of my own principles: that, as a matter of effective and orderly administration, additional new independent agencies normally should not be created. In this case, however, the arguments against placing environmental protection activities under the jurisdiction of one or another of the existing departments and agencies are compelling.

In the first place, almost every part of government is concerned with the environment in some way, and affects it in some way. Yet each department also has its own primary mission—such as resource development, transportation, health, defense, urban growth, or agriculture— which necessarily affects its own view of environmental questions.

In the second place, if the critical standard-setting functions were centralized within any one existing department, it would require that department constantly to make decisions affecting other departments—in which, whether fairly or unfairly, its own objectivity as an impartial arbiter could be called into question.

Because environmental protection cuts across so many jurisdictions, and because arresting environmental deterioration is of great importance to the quality of life in our country and the world, I believe that in this case a strong, independent agency is needed. That agency would, of course, work closely with and draw upon the expertise and assistance of other agencies having experience in the environmental area.

See "Special Message to the Congress About Reorganization Plans to Establish the Environmental Protection Agency and the National Oceanic and Atmospheric Administration" (9 July 1970), pp. 578–579, 581–582. In *Public Papers of the Presidents of the United States: Richard Nixon, 1970* (Washington, D.C.: Government Printing Office, 1970).

COMMENTS OF REPRESENTATIVE JOHN DINGELL (D-MICH.)

Hearing Before the House Committee on Government Operations
July 23, 1970

Reorganization acts probably should be matters that are handled by statute. I really doubt very much whether we are wise in permitting any administration, this administration or any other, to submit to the Congress take-it-or-leave-it proposals which we must swallow whole without chewing, or else reject whatever small good might be present with whatever large evil might be present.

I think these two reorganization plans tend to prove the unwisdom of allowing any executive department or any executive authority completely to reorganize the executive branch of Government with only a veto vote by the Congress of the United States. As these proposals come up to extend the Reorganization Act, I intend to oppose each and every one of them.

I believe my colleagues, as time carries forward, will come to join me in recognizing the unwisdom of allowing the administration power to combine weird mishmashes of good and bad into the kind of monstrosities that we see here before us. . . .

Mr. Chairman, to say that the constitution of EPA . . . will move all agencies having related matters into one particular area is either to demonstrate remarkable ignorance or to deliberately attempt to mislead, because the fact of the matter is that throughout the whole Government structure, such agencies as [National Institute for Health], Federal Trade Commission, and parts of Food and Drug, are going to remain large parts of the responsibility of the EPA. . . .

What we are doing, Mr. Chairman, we are wrenching, by these two plans, two agencies out of departments. We are creating prodigious, fantastic, and totally intolerable levels of confusion and disorganization in these important areas. We are faced, almost certainly, with the absolute surety, Mr. Chairman, that these are only interim steps. I, personally, believe very strongly, apart from the other vices so clearly apparent in the creation of either EPA or NOAA, that one fact alone should militate against these reorganization plans; that is, the prodigious disorganization which will take place is not going to be the final disorganization and misallocation of time, energy, and resources and personnel, but, rather, it is only going to be one step which will lead to a further traumatic experience of exactly the same kind inside the Federal government when we carry forward the next reorganization which is clearly demanded by the kind of orphan structure that we are legislating with the establishment of EPA and NOAA.

It is my hope that you and your committee will recommend disapproval of these two reorganization plans and that, at an early time, you move to see that the House summarily rejects them, as you should, since they are not in the public interest and do not solve the problem. Then we can begin to move in concert with the White House, if the White House wants to, toward a legislative reorganization of the government's affairs by enabling the Congress to participate in that action through the establishment of a Department of Natural Resources and a Department of Environment. In this way, appropriate opportunity will be afforded all persons, and there are large numbers of persons, conservation organizations, members of Congress, Senate, people who have been studying and working on these matters, people in the universities, to participate in the reorganization plans. . . .

With those remarks, Mr. Chairman, I would repeat that this body, the House of Representatives and the Congress, should be consulted in these matters. We should have legislation which would enable operating behind closed doors, so that we can come up with programs which are really going to reflect national need and which will conclude the reorganization of the Government instead of setting up an interminable period of organization which will accomplish nothing.

See U.S. House. Committee on Governmental Operations. *Reorganization Plan No. 3 of 1970: Environmental Protection Agency.* Hearing, 22, 23 July, 4 August 1970. 91st Cong. 2nd sess. (Washington, D.C.: Government Printing Office, 1970), pp. 116, 117–118, 122–123.

WAGE AND PRICE CONTROLS

Although many factors can affect the U.S. economy, the public usually holds the president accountable for the economic state of the country during his term of office. Often, an incoming president is faced with economic conditions not of his own making, but which are rather the result of the previous president's policies or international events beyond his control. Richard Nixon found himself in this situation upon assuming office in 1969. Lyndon Johnson's Great Society social programs, which were intended to address poverty and inequality in America, combined with the costs of the Vietnam War, had contributed to inflation, a situation where the price of goods increase over time and consequently, consumers can buy less for their dollar. Generally, inflation is indicative of a growing economy in which consumers have a higher demand for goods and, in this situation, wages may also increase to maintain consumers' buying power. However, the economy was not growing in 1970 when Richard Nixon assumed office. In fact, the United States was entering a recession in which more people were unemployed and demand for goods was decreasing. This condition, inflation coupled with a slowing economy, is referred to as "stagflation," a particularly difficult economic situation to remedy.

As a Republican president, it was assumed that Nixon would take a conservative approach to the economy, relying less on government policies and more on market forces to address the problems of the economy. In some areas of policy, he complied with this expectation. For instance, it was his premise that the federal government had assumed too much authority during the presidencies of John F. Kennedy and Lyndon B. Johnson. Under his policy of "New Federalism," he recommended that authority over some social welfare policies be divested to the states. Similarly, he supported revenue sharing, which allowed the federal government to provide revenue directly to the states. It appeared that Nixon would take this "hands off" approach to the economy, as well, but by 1971 he decided that more drastic measures were needed to ward off continued economic problems.

In August 1971, President Nixon announced a policy of wage and price controls for a period of ninety days, with a long-term policy to go into effect after the initial controls were lifted. This policy had two facets. First, employee wages were to be frozen at present levels; no raises in wages or salaries could be put into effect during the initial ninety-day freeze. Second, all prices on goods were frozen; with a few exceptions, the price of goods at the commencement of the freeze would stay in effect until the end of the ninety-day period. After the initial period, policies would be put into effect to curb inflationary trends in wages and prices, but there would not be an absolute freeze. It was Nixon's stated hope that these proactive steps would curb inflation.

While the policy was generally met with public and corporate support, there were critics of the program. Ralph Nader, an attorney well-known for his consumer advocacy, was not opposed to the policy in general, but believed that the integrity of such a bold act had been compromised by some of the exclusions to the controls, exclusions that forced poorer citizens to bear a disproportionate burden of the policy. In a statement before the Congressional Joint Economic Committee, which held a hearing on the president's economic policies, Nader also made more dramatic accusations, claiming that there was evidence that the administration had provided an early warning of the price freeze to large corporations before the policy was announced in order for these companies to raise prices before the policy went into effect. As is the case so many times in the creation of public policy, the details of the policy, more than its broad goals, are what drew the most criticism. For Ralph Nader, this was certainly the case.

NIXON'S ADDRESS TO THE NATION OUTLINING A NEW ECONOMIC POLICY

"The Challenge of Peace"
From the Oval Office, August 15, 1971

Good evening:

I have addressed the nation a number of times over the past 2 years on the problems of ending a war. Because of the progress we have made toward achieving that goal, this Sunday evening is an appropriate time for us to turn our attention to the challenges of peace.

America today has the best opportunity in this century to achieve two of its greatest ideals: to bring about a full generation of peace, and to create a new prosperity without war.

This not only requires bold leadership ready to take bold action—it calls forth the greatness in a great people.

Prosperity without war requires action on three fronts: We must create more and better jobs; we must stop the rise in the cost of living; we must protect the dollar from the attacks of international money speculators.

We are going to take that action—not timidly, not half-heartedly, and not in piecemeal fashion. We are going to move forward to the new prosperity without war as befits a great people—all together, and along a broad front. . . .

One of the cruelest legacies of the artificial prosperity produced by war is inflation. Inflation robs every American, every one of you. The 20 million who are retired and living on fixed incomes—they are particularly hard hit. Homemakers find it harder than ever to balance the family budget. And 80 million American wage earners have been on a treadmill. For example, in the 4 war years between 1965 and 1969, your wage increases were completely eaten up by price increases. Your paychecks were higher, but you were no better off.

We have made progress against the rise in the cost of living. From the high point of 6 percent a year in 1969, the rise in consumer prices has been cut to 4 percent in the first half of 1971. But just as is the case in our fight against unemployment, we can and we must do better than that.

The time has come for decisive action—action that will break the vicious circle of spiraling prices and costs.

I am today ordering a freeze on all prices and wages throughout the United States for a period of 90 days. In addition, I call upon corporations to extend the wage-price freeze to all dividends.

I have today appointed a Cost of Living Council within government. I have directed this Council to work with leaders of labor and business to set up the proper mechanism for achieving continued price and wage stability after the 90-day freeze is over.

Let me emphasize two characteristics of this action: First, it is temporary. To put the strong, vigorous American economy into a permanent straitjacket would lock in unfairness; it would stifle the expansion of our free enterprise system. And second, while the wage-price freeze will be backed by Government sanctions, if necessary, it will not be accompanied by the establishment of a huge price control bureaucracy. I am relying on the voluntary cooperation of all Americans—each one of you: workers, employers, consumers—to make this freeze work.

Working together, we will break the back of inflation, and we will do it without the mandatory wage and price controls that crush economic and personal freedom.

See "Address to the Nation Outlining a New Economic Policy: 'The Challenge of Peace' " (15 Aug. 1971), pp. 886, 888. In *Public Papers of the Presidents of the United States: Richard Nixon, 1971* (Washington, D.C.: Government Printing Office, 1971).

NIXON'S ADDRESS TO THE NATION ON THE POST-FREEZE ECONOMIC STABILIZATION PROGRAM

"The Continuing Fight Against Inflation" From the Oval Office, October 7, 1971

Good Evening:

Seven weeks ago I announced a new economic policy to stop the rise in prices, to create new jobs, and to protect the American dollar.

Tonight I want to report to you about how that new policy has been working and to describe how that policy will be continued.

On the international front, I am glad to report substantial progress in our campaign to create a new monetary stability and to bring a new fairness to world trade. This Nation welcomes foreign competition, but we have a right to expect that our trading partners abroad will welcome American competition.

It is a healthy development that the world has come to understand that America believes in free trade as long as it is fair trade. This will mean more sales of American goods abroad and more jobs for American workers at home.

Further on the job front, the House of Representatives just yesterday passed a tax program based on my recommendations that will create an additional half-million jobs in the coming year. I call upon the United States Senate, which has begun hearings on this bill today, to act as promptly as the House so that we can move forward to our goal of full employment in peacetime.

[Treasury] Secretary [Matthew] Connally and I will be meeting tomorrow morning at breakfast with Chairman [Russell B.] Long of Louisiana, of the Senate Finance Committee, to work toward this goal. . . .

Over the past 7 weeks, I have consulted with scores of representatives of labor and business, of farmers and consumers, of the Congress, and State and local government. They have been virtually unanimous in their belief that the battle against inflation must be fought here and now. They are together in their determination to win that battle.

And consequently, I am announcing tonight that when the 90-day freeze is over on November 13, we shall continue our program of wage and price restraint. We began this battle against inflation for the purpose of winning it, and we are going to stay in it till we do win it.

I am appointing a Price Commission to hold down prices. It will be made up of persons outside of government—all public members, not beholden to any special interest group. The Price Commission will develop yardsticks and will be empowered to restrain price and rent increases to the necessary minimum and to prevent windfall profits. Its goal will be to continue to drive down the rate of inflation.

This goal, however, can only be achieved with the active cooperation of workingmen and businessmen, farmers and consumers, Members of the Congress, of our State and local governments. That means all of us.

I am also appointing a Pay Board to stop inflationary wage and salary increases—the kind of increases that do not really benefit the workingman. For example, in the past 6 years workers have received big wage increases, but every wife of a worker who has to do the family shopping will tell you that those increases have practically all been eaten up by rises in the cost of living.

The Pay Board will be made up of representatives of labor, management, and the public. Both the Price Commission and the Pay Board will seek voluntary cooperation from business and labor, but they will be backed by the authority of law to make their decisions stick. Their staffs will be small. Stabilization must be made to work not by an army of bureaucrats, but by an all-volunteer army of patriotic citizens in every walk of life.

See "Address to the Nation on the Post-Freeze Economic Stabilization Program: The Continuing Fight Against Inflation" (7 October 1971), pp. 1023–1024. In *Public Papers of the Presidents of the United States: Richard Nixon, 1971* (Washington, D.C.: Government Printing Office, 1971).

STATEMENT BY RALPH NADER

Hearing before the Joint Congressional Economic Committee
August 20, 1971

I am grateful for the invitation to extend my comments on the aspects of the administration's new economic policies and proposals submitted to Congress.

It is not difficult to penetrate the semantic whirlwind, the facile assurances, and the insupportable economic reasoning which have been issuing from Government spokesmen this week if the administration's package is broken down into its constituent parts, confronted with its alleged objectives and evaluated within this context. First, however it is appropriate I think to comment briefly on the processes of decision-making. Any governmental decision of this scope, Mr. Chairman, has legal aspects, political aspects, economic aspects, value aspects, human value aspects, and I think it is important at times to separate each one of these out insofar as that is possible and see where they add up.

The administration presents a fairly persuasive case against the prior signaling of its move with regard to the dollar, given the rampart speculation thereto in the internal money markets and other well-known variables. There is no excuse, however, for the inordinate secrecy attending its other decisional preliminaries, particularly when there is a great need for public consideration and discussion and fact gathering. As my subsequent observations will illustrate, such preliminaries, both within and outside of Congress, might have restrained the most outrageously special interest features of the package. Beyond that, it is now clear that a number of corporate leaders knew in advance of portions of the package. Judging by its exceptional communiqué to dealers to start selling 1972 model cars with their new price increase immediately on receipt last week, General Motors knew what was coming by way of the price freeze and tried unsuccessfully to slide under the deadline. The public will never know probably what other early alerts there were and what other, if any quid pro quos were agreed to in this ex parte, informal process of government-corporate understanding. . . .

Let me discuss the freeze aspect. First of all, it is, I think, a particularly effective psychological move which is important in any economic policy. I don't think we can make any further favorable judgments on it either as a temporary freeze or what is going to happen afterward until we see what is going to happen afterwards.

I think we can make the following judgments, however, given the facts available to us.

One, it was unnecessarily inequitable. Wages frozen, wages are very easy to freeze; you have an ally in terms of the employer.

Prices are frozen with major gaping loopholes which I will note in a moment, for the consumer. Profits are not frozen, nor is there a substitute of an excess profits tax. . . .

What I am saying is when you freeze prices with loopholes, when you don't freeze interest rates, and you don't freeze profits, and you give a 15-percent tax reduction to corporations you are, in effect, opening the ceiling to profits. You are not even keeping the lid on, you are opening the ceiling. . . .

Let me give you some preliminary loopholes that anybody can notice on a cursory glance. One, raw agriculture produce is exempt. We know why it was exempted at the farm level but it was exempted all the way to the supermarket level, which means that fresh fruits and vegetables, eggs, and other fresh produce that go all the way to the consumer are not going to be frozen. This also means that those companies that sell both processed food goods and fresh fruit goods will be able to in effect camouflage any price increases in the areas that are frozen by increasing them in the fresh produce area.

I might also say that this policy has a dietary effect insofar as elasticity here, the prices of fresh fruits and vegetables and other fresh produce are going to develop a reduced demand by the consumer.

Here is another loophole.

. . . I do want to note that new housing, for example, or products that are considered new are exempted. You know how many products are labeled new and described as new stylistically and by names that are not really new. Many of the all-new cars are about 85 percent exactly what their predecessors were a year before. . . .

Here is another loophole—dental, medical, legal, and other professional fees, they are frozen under the guidelines but if anybody can show me how to freeze those kinds of fees with the enormous flexibility to, in effect, say well, this is a case of one, this is a different situation, quite apart from the administrative difficulties of policing these fees, I would like to see it. . . .

I think what [consumers] should be looking for is last week's prices in their daily newspapers, as a beginning comparison of supermarket prices. They should become much more alert to precisely what kind of brands they are buying, at what rates they are buying in order to avoid the very easy slide that obviously produces a changed price upward.

See U.S. Congress. Joint Economic Committee. *The President's New Economic Program*, Part 1. Hearing, 19, 20, 23 August 1971, 92nd Cong. 1st sess. (Washington, D.C.: Government Printing Office, 1971), p. 77.

NIXON'S TRIP TO CHINA

In 1949, after a four-year civil war, China's nationalist government was swept from power by communist Mao Zedong and his supporters. The loss of American allies in the nationalist government and the fact that China had fallen to a communist power was a shocking blow to the United States, which was deep into its post–World War II anticommunist fervor. Although there were many concerns about China falling into new hands, one of the most pronounced fears was that other Asian nations would also turn communist. President Harry S. Truman had advocated a policy of "containment" with regard to the Soviet Union, hoping to contain communism to that one country, under an assumption that the U.S.S.R. would attempt to pull other countries into its sphere of influence. After China formed a communist government, there was great fear that the Soviet Union and China would join forces in opposition to the United States. This fear did not ultimately materialize.

The fear of communism, however, was bolstered by communist uprisings in Korea and Vietnam in the early 1950s. The Republicans effectively portrayed Truman and the Democrats as too "soft" on communism and were able to recapture the White House in 1952 with the election of Dwight D. Eisenhower. In 1954, President Eisenhower provided the country with an effective, yet fearful, analogy regarding the necessity of fighting communism. He likened Asia to a row of dominoes. When one country falls to communism, it's as if the first domino in a long line of dominoes falls. Each domino eventually falls after the first one is pushed. Thus, the ultimate fear in the United States was that all of Southeast Asia would eventually succumb to communism.

The gripping fear of communism in the United States during the 1950s and 1960s, and the foreign policies that defined anyone labeled a communist as an enemy, did not bode well for productive diplomatic relations with China. The United States refused to recognize the regime of Mao Zedong. In 1964, the fear of China intensified when China tested its first nuclear bomb. Despite his disdain for China along ideological grounds, Richard Nixon recognized the practical necessity of building a relationship with China. The connection between the Soviet Union and China had become increasingly tense and Nixon reasoned that the logical course of action was for the United States to develop positive relations with one of the Soviet Union's largest adversaries. The political risk of alienating anticommunist Americans was not as great as the potential risk of a Soviet and Chinese alliance against the West.

Thus, despite the anticommunist sentiments he expressed throughout much of his political career, President Nixon began making diplomatic overtures to the government in China during the early 1970s. As Nixon stated about this decision, "Both sides recognized that despite our profound philosophical differences we had no reason to be enemies and a powerful reason to be friends: our mutual interest in deterring the Soviet threat."[1] In 1971, a visit to China was planned for President Nixon, the first visit to communist China by an American president. In February 1972, Nixon embarked on the historic visit, cautioning the country not to place too much hope on this first visit, but to recognize it for what it was, a first step. Yet Nixon believed that this visit was his greatest success as president. The statements made before his trip illustrate Nixon's cautious yet hopeful tone.

The visit to China received remarkable media attention. Television crews as well as print journalists followed the president and First Lady Pat Nixon throughout their eight-day visit. Americans were able to watch a great deal of the trip on television, including the many cultural and athletic events scheduled for the entertainment of the American visitors. The entire trip was surrounded with great fanfare and excitement. It was this element of the trip that generated some concern about the president's policy on China. Certainly, there were Americans who opposed the visit to China on purely ideological grounds, arguing that the United States should not build ties with any communist country, but a more pragmatic criticism involved the carnival-like atmosphere of the trip and the impression it gave to other countries with which the United States had ties. In congressional hearings held several months after the president's return from China, Edwin O. Reischauer, a former ambassador to Japan and a professor at Harvard University, testified that this dramatic shift in U.S. policy with regard to U.S. relations with China, coupled with the showy display of the visit, was sure to concern some of our other allies and possibly even constrain relations with them. He believed that a more traditional approach to diplomacy would have served the positive purposes behind the China visit, yet not flouted this growing relationship in the face of other countries, many of which had little affection for China.

NOTE

1. Richard Nixon, *1989: Victory without War* (New York: Pocket Books, 1989), p. 244.

FROM THE PRESIDENT'S NEWS CONFERENCE

Oval Office, February 10, 1972

This trip should not be one which would create very great optimism or very great pessimism. It is one in which we must recognize that 20 years of hostility and virtually no communication will not be swept away by one week of discussion.

However, it will mark a watershed in the relations between the two governments; the postwar era with respect to the People's Republic of China and the United States—that chapter now comes to an end from the time that I set foot on the soil of Mainland China, and a new chapter begins.

Now, how the new chapter is written will be influenced, perhaps influenced substantially, by the talks that will take place. On our side and, we believe, also on their side, we hope that the new chapter will be one of more communication and that it will be a chapter that will be marked by negotiation rather than confrontation and one that will be marked by the absence of armed conflict. These are our hopes.

We, of course, will now see to what extent those hopes can be realized in this first meeting.

See "The President's News Conference" (10 Feb. 1972), p. 349. In *Public Papers of the Presidents of the United States: Richard Nixon, 1972* (Washington, D.C.: Government Printing Office, 1972).

FROM NIXON'S REMARKS ON HIS DEPARTURE FOR A STATE VISIT TO THE PEOPLE'S REPUBLIC OF CHINA

February 17, 1972

Mr. Vice President, Mr. Speaker, Members of the Congress, and Members of the Cabinet:

I want to express my very deep appreciation to all of you who have come here to send us off on this historic mission, and I particularly want to express appreciation to the bipartisan leadership of the House and Senate who are here.

Their presence and the messages that have poured in from all over the country to the White House over the past few days, wishing us well on this trip, I think, underline the statement that I made on July 15, last year, when I announced the visit.

That statement was, as you will recall, that this would be a journey for peace. We, of course, are under no illusions that 20 years of hostility between the People's Republic of China and the United States of America are going to be swept away by one week of talks that we will have there.

But as Premier Chou En-lai said in a toast that he proposed to Dr. Kissinger and the members of the advance group in October, the American people are a great people. The Chinese people are a great people. The fact that they are separated by a vast ocean and great differences in philosophy should not prevent them from finding common ground.

As we look to the future, we must recognize that the government of the People's Republic of China and the government of the United States have had great differences. We will have differences in the future. But what we must do is to find a way to see that we can have differences without being enemies in war. If we can make progress toward that goal on this trip, the world will be a much safer world and the chance particularly for all of those young children over there to grow up in a world of peace will be infinitely greater.

I would simply say in conclusion that if there is a postscript that I hope might be written with regard to this trip, it would be the words on the plaque which was left on the moon by our first astronauts when they landed there: "We came in peace for all mankind."

Thank you and goodbye.

See "Remarks on Departure from the White House for a State Visit to the People's Republic of China" (17 Feb. 1972), p. 367. In *Public Papers of the Presidents of the United States: Richard Nixon, 1972* (Washington, D.C.: Government Printing Office, 1972).

TESTIMONY OF EDWIN O. REISCHAUER, FORMER AMBASSADOR TO JAPAN AND PROFESSOR, HARVARD UNIVERSITY

Hearing before the House Subcommittee on Asian and Pacific Affairs
May 2, 1972

I think we all welcome the recent relaxation of tensions between this country and the People's Republic of China.

It is desirable that we should be moving away from the military containment of China as the core element in our relationships with East Asia. . . .

Still more important is the start of a dialogue between ourselves and the Chinese, because they do constitute something like a quarter of the population of the whole globe, and it is vastly important that a real meaningful dialogue should be developed between our one-third of the world's wealth and the Chinese one-quarter of the world's population if we as a human race are going to be able to address ourselves to the great global problems that are pressing down on us very rapidly.

I heartily endorse the President's initiatives in this direction. I think at long last we are going in the right direction, but I am disturbed by some of the false expectations that have been aroused both in this country and abroad by the histrionics that accompanied this desirable shift in policy and I am appalled by the possible cost to this country and to the world of the apparently thoughtless, one might even say reckless, style in which the policy chance was effectuated.

This style was not necessary, because the results could all have been achieved by a much more sober, more low profile, and more traditional form of diplomacy.

Now, some people might argue that the style is a matter over the dam and we should not concern ourselves with it; however, it seems to me symptomatic of the administration's continued thinking. The administration, I think, is in some sense a victim itself of the false hopes and unrealistic expectations that it has raised, and the blind spots that permitted it to do so much damage through the style of its diplomacy still remain to limit its vision. . . .

Some people have felt that the president's visit to China has achieved a new balance of power in the world, but this, I think, is extremely doubtful. Some people even think that we and the Chinese can somehow settle the problems of that part of the world, but this is mere fantasy.

The president's visit did no more than symbolize a relaxation of tensions between the United States and China—a relaxation which had already occurred and which had grown, I think, primarily out of what we had learned from our Vietnamese fiasco, when we had seen that a half million American troops could not determine the future of Vietnam. Obviously, something new has developed in the world. Outside military power cannot control less developed countries that have been aroused by nationalism to seek to control their own fate. . . .

Whatever the importance of our relationship with China over the long run—and I think over the long run of several decades it is extremely important—other relationships in East Asia will probably prove much more critical for us and the world during the decades ahead.

It was, therefore, unfortunate that, in redirecting our China policy toward new and better goals, the President chose to do this in such a flamboyant style that it seriously damaged some of these other relationships.

Let me explain that point. The United States is by far the richest and strongest country in the world. Most other nations are forced to set their course to some degree in conformity with what they believe to be the path our great ship of state will take. When we shift course, we must do so clearly, firmly, and with unmistakable signals as to our intentions. Otherwise, we will cause great confusion, even consternation, among all those who have set their course by ours. If we appear to be acting in a capricious, unpredictable manner, the confusion will be even greater. But this is exactly what we have seemed to do, twirling the wheel back and forth in bewildering fashion and proclaiming loudly that a presidential visit to China has somehow changed the world.

The dramatic announcement of Dr. Kissinger's trip to Peking and the planned presidential visit to a country with which we did not even have diplomatic relations, much less contacts of trust and amity, while a refreshing surprise to the American public after a couple of decades of Dulles-style inflexibility, seemed to others so entirely unpredictable as to be quixotic and possibly a sign of emotional instability on our part. The high drama and fanfare of the actual visit suggested that there must be more to it than the bland communiqué and social niceties that appeared on the surface—perhaps some Machiavellian big-power deal to "sell the slaves down the river." And, if not that, did not such diplomatic high jinks show that the United States was still, after all, an immature and somewhat flighty nation.

Most of the countries of the world have probably been made a little uneasy by the flamboyant style of our new China policy, but it has been most disturbing for the countries of East and Southeast Asia.

See U.S. House. Committee on Foreign Affairs. *The New China Policy: Its Impact on the United States and Asia.* Hearing, 2–4, 16, 17 May 1972, 92 Cong. 2nd sess. (Washington, D.C.: Government Printing Office, 1972), pp. 4, 5–7.

BUSING

In 1954, the Supreme Court ruled in *Brown v. Board of Education of Topeka, Kansas,* that it was unconstitutional for states to mandate separate schools for white and black children, based on its interpretation of the equal protection clause of the Fourteenth Amendment. This decision predominantly affected states in the South, where legal requirements that African American and white students be segregated by race were common. Primary and secondary schools in non-Southern states also tended to have schools that were segregated by race, but the segregation was largely a consequence of drawing school district lines around predominantly white and black neighborhoods rather than due to state mandate.

The *Brown* case was met with strong, and often violent, opposition in Southern states, and it was not until after Congress passed the Civil Rights Act of 1964 that the majority of Southern African American students attended desegregated schools. Yet, despite the massive opposition in the South, achieving desegregation in the non-Southern states was perhaps even more difficult since the segregation was based on residential patterns, not state law; neither the Congress nor the Supreme Court could require people to live in desegregated neighborhoods to achieve more integrated schools. In 1971, the Supreme Court addressed the continued problem of segregation in urban areas in particular, by ruling in *Swann v. Charlotte-Mecklenburg Board of Education* that school districts could achieve integrated schools by busing students to more distant schools to achieve some racial balance.[1] This policy was advocated primarily by civil rights groups such as the National Association for the Advancement of Colored People (NAACP), which believed that many school districts would continue to violate the civil rights of black students unless specifically prohibited from doing so by the federal courts. Thus, while the *Brown* case had overturned state law regarding state-mandated segregation, the court cases dealing with busing witnessed the Supreme Court playing a much more active role in determining how cities were to accomplish the integration of public schools.

Busing met with massive opposition, primarily by white parents who had a host of complaints and concerns about their children being bused to predominantly black schools, but also by some African American parents, who shared similar concerns for their own children who were being bused to unfamiliar and often distant schools. In line with public opinion, President Nixon did not support busing to achieve integration. While he supported efforts to desegregate the public schools, he did not think that busing was a practical or just solution to the problem. Based on these sentiments, on March 16, 1972, Nixon proposed to Congress a moratorium on busing, which would prevent any new court orders being issued to require busing.

On March 24, 1972, the Subcommittee on Education of the Committee on Labor and Public Welfare in the Senate began holding hearings on the president's proposal. Witnesses testified on the president's proposed moratorium, some supporting the measure while others opposed it. Clarence Mitchell, who was the director of the Washington Bureau of the NAACP, testified vehemently against the moratorium and pointedly claimed that the president was siding with "antiblack" forces. The NAACP's position was that busing was a necessary step to achieve racial equality in education and that to eliminate busing was the first step to reversing much of the progress that had been made toward achieving civil rights for blacks. While busing may not have been the best solution to racial discrimination in education, it was the one solution that was forcing action by school districts that had previously dragged their feet on desegregation.

NOTE

1. *Swann v. Charlotte-Mecklenburg Board of Education*, 402 U.S. 1 (1971).

FROM NIXON'S ADDRESS ON EQUAL EDUCATIONAL
OPPORTUNITIES AND SCHOOL BUSING

Address from the Oval Office, March 16, 1972

Good evening:

Tonight I want to talk to you about one of the most difficult issues of our time—the issue of busing.

Across this nation—in the North, East, West, and South—States, cities, and local school districts have been torn apart in debate over this issue.

My own position is well known. I am opposed to busing for the purpose of achieving a racial balance in our schools. I have spoken out against busing scores of times over many years.

And I believe most Americans, white and black, share that view.

But what we need now is not just speaking out against more busing. We need action to stop it. Above all, we need to stop it in the right way—in a way that will provide better education for every child in America in a desegregated school system. . . .

What we need is action now—not action 2, 3, or 4 years from now. And there is only one effective way to deal with the problem now. That is for the Congress to act. That is why I am sending a special message to the Congress tomorrow urging immediate consideration and action on two measures.

First, I shall propose legislation that would call an immediate halt to all new busing orders by Federal courts—a moratorium on new busing.

Next, I shall propose a companion measure—the Equal Educational Opportunities Act of 1972.

This act would require that every state or locality grant equal educational opportunity to every person, regardless of race, color, or national origin. For the first time in our history, the cherished American ideal of equality of educational opportunity would be affirmed in the law of the land by the elected representatives of the people in Congress. . . .

Let me now go to the heart of the problem that confronts us. I want to tell you why I feel that busing for the purpose of achieving racial balance in our schools is wrong, and why the great majority of Americans are right in wanting to bring it to an end.

The purpose of such busing is to help end segregation. But experience in case after case has shown that busing is a bad means to a good end. The frank recognition of that fact does not reduce our commitment to desegregation; it simply tells us that we have to come up with a better means to that good end.

The great majority of Americans, white and black, feel strongly that the busing of schoolchildren away from their own neighborhoods for the purpose of achieving racial balance is wrong.

But the great majority, black and white, also are determined that the process of desegregation must go forward until the goal of genuinely equal educational opportunity is achieved.

The question, then, is "How can we end segregation in a way that does not result in more busing?" The proposals I am sending to the Congress provide an answer to that question.

One emotional undercurrent that has done much to make this issue so difficult is the feeling that some people have that to oppose busing is to be antiblack. This is dangerous nonsense.

There is no escaping the fact that some people do oppose busing because of racial prejudice. But to go on from this to conclude that "anti-busing" is simply a code word for prejudice is a vicious libel on millions of concerned parents who oppose busing not because they are against desegregation, but because they are for better education for their children. . . .

There are right reasons for opposing busing, and there are wrong reasons—and most people, including large and increasing numbers of blacks, oppose it for reasons that have little or nothing to do with race. It would compound an injustice to persist in massive busing simply because some people oppose it for the wrong reasons.

See "Address to the Nation on Equal Educational Opportunities and School Busing" (16 March 1972), pp. 425, 426, 427, 428. In *Public Papers of the Presidents of the United States: Richard Nixon, 1972* (Washington, D.C.: Government Printing Office, 1972).

STATEMENT FROM CLARENCE MITCHELL, DIRECTOR, WASHINGTON BUREAU, THE NATIONAL ASSOCIATION FOR THE ADVANCEMENT OF COLORED PEOPLE

Hearings before the Senate Subcommittee on Education
March 28, 1972

Under all of the administrations that I have observed during three decades there have been both minor and major officials of Government who have tried to advocate thinly disguised doctrines of white supremacy.

Sometimes, these officials were able to pervert executive power through White House channels and thereby block progress. Never, until March 16, 1972, has the president himself joined with a chorus of anti-black forces who seek to destroy all rights protected by the 13th, 14th, and 15th amendments.

For, make no mistake about it, those who are today attacking the rights of black Americans behind a smokescreen of slogans against busing are, for the most part, the same people who are against equal treatment in all aspects of American life.

When President Nixon took to the airwaves he placed himself on the side of those who have stood in school doorways to bar black children. He gave comfort to those who have applied torches to the school buses to prevent them from being used to achieve desegregation. He aligned himself with the white parents who have fled to the suburbs to escape desegregation in city public schools. . . .

We have considered the president's proposals with great care and grave concern. The following are our conclusions on a point by point analysis.

First, we believe that the so-called student transportation moratorium act is unconstitutional. The president has attempted to justify it on the ground that "there is a substantial likelihood that many local educational agencies will be required to implement desegregation plans that impose a greater obligation than required by the 14th amendment . . ." We do not know what kind of crystal ball the President was using when he sent that wording to Congress but we do reject it as having no basis in fact. So far "busing" has been used only as a tool to protect the rights that are being violated by local school systems, and as we all know after the hearing when Mr. [Elliot] Richardson [Secretary of Health, Education, and Welfare] testified the other day, in response to questioning it was brought out that something about 2 percent of the children who now ride on buses are doing so because of desegregation orders. . . .

The proposed moratorium is no compromise. It is a cruel and savage attempt to use the power of the federal Government to bludgeon the courts into a surrender to mob rule.

The second point, the so-called findings set forth in the president's proposal are palpably misleading. The abolition of the dual school system has not been virtually completed as his bill states.

North and South, the majority of black children of this country still attend segregated schools. It is true that progress has been made, but to pretend that we now have only to eliminate "vestiges" of dual school systems, as the president would have us believe, is to close one's eyes to the conditions in almost all of the major cities of our land that have substantial black populations.

From coast to coast, the NAACP, the NAACP legal defense fund, numerous other groups and even the Department of Justice must still use court action to prod the foot draggers and the opponents of constructive change into compliance with the 1954 school desegregation decisions.

The third point: The financial assistance that the President's bill would offer can be given by full use of Title I of the Elementary and Secondary

Education Act and other legislation now pending in Congress. To use your words, Mr. Chairman, the Nixon bill is a kind of cosmetic treatment which you referred to and the President is trying to pass it off as something new. . . .

The fourth point: Under such innocent sounding terms as "neighborhood schools," "racial balance not required," "transportation of students," "reopening proceedings," and "time limitations on orders," the President has flung the door wide open to a return to the pernicious 1896 doctrine of *Plessy v. Ferguson* [the Supreme Court case in which the principle of "separate but equal" was established].

When we pierce the veil of the administration's rhetoric, we find that old separate neighborhood school for blacks. Of course, it will not appear on the school records as for blacks only. Nor will there be any official word to say that there will be such a thing as a white school.

But make no mistake about it, section 203 of the President's bill says it is not a denial of equal educational opportunity to assign a student to the school nearest his place of residence. It places upon the parents and other persons acting for the student the burden of proving that the true purposes of such assignment is to accomplish and maintain racial segregation. . . .

I think, Mr. Chairman, that the mass of people want their children to go to good schools, and if, as a condition of going to those schools it is necessary to have busing, I think they would be 100 percent in favor of it.

I feel that this whole issue has been distorted, because people get the idea that in order to have a constitutionally sanctioned remedy for wrong, that you have to have a popularity contest to get support for it.

But that is not the way things work in this country. Education is one of the personal rights, as are other constitutional rights, so it would not matter if 99 and $^{44}/_{100}$ths percent were against busing if, as a matter of law, busing would be a constitutionally sanctioned remedy that should be adopted.

See U.S. Senate. Committee on Labor and Public Welfare. *Equal Educational Opportunities Act of 1972.* Hearing, 28 March 1972, 92nd Cong. 2nd sess. (Washington, D.C.: Government Printing Office, 1972), pp. 377–385.

SALT TREATIES

When the Soviet Union tested its first atomic bomb in 1949, the United States quickly lost the strategic advantage it had gained in 1945 when the country first used nuclear weapons against Japan to end World War II in the Pacific. While war had always led to death and destruction, the newly realized prospect that a single weapon could level a city and kill tens of thousands of people was staggering. Once both the United States and the Soviet Union had developed an atomic bomb, there was the realization that a war in which nuclear strikes were exchanged could easily result in the devastation of complete cities, the deaths of possibly millions of people, and the crippling of the world economy. In the United States, it was feared that the Soviet Union would be more inclined to initiate a nuclear war if there was a disparity in the number of weapons held by each country. It was this concern that drove the United States to invest billions of dollars to develop new nuclear weapons, including long-range missiles, which could be guided to locations thousands of miles from the United States, as well as antiballistic missiles that were designed to intercept incoming missiles.

Constitutionally, it is the president's prerogative, through people in his administration, to negotiate treaties with foreign countries. In the spirit of détente, President Nixon was anxious to reach an agreement with the Soviet Union to limit the proliferation of nuclear weapons. Although the initial agreement to begin discussions on a strategic arms limitations treaty was announced near the end of President Johnson's administration, the actual process did not begin until November of President Nixon's first year in office. Negotiations between the two countries extended between November 1969 and May 1972, ending when President Nixon and Soviet Premier Leonid Brezhnev signed the treaty during Nixon's visit to Moscow.

At issue was the limitation of certain types of nuclear weapons. One difficulty of the negotiations process was agreeing to a definition of "strategic arms." The question was raised about whether this term included missiles that could be used in an offensive capacity, such as missiles aimed at another country, or whether it applied to weapons used defensively, such as antiballistic missiles (ABMs), which were designed to intercept incoming missiles. Which missiles were to be limited was difficult to negotiate because each country had its own strengths regarding its nuclear capability. The Soviet Union held the upper hand in land-based intercontinental ballistic missiles (ICBMs), while the United States had focused since 1967 on the development of "multiple independently targeted reentry vehicles" (MIRVS), which allowed a single missile to contain numerous warheads, each with its own target. Both countries had limited ABM systems, although the United States had plans to broaden its defense around key cities and offensive missile sites.

The concept of "mutually assured destruction," was still very much a driving force in SALT negotiations. Mutually assured destruction assumes that any country being attacked with nuclear weapons can inflict just as much damage on the aggressor by using its own nuclear weapons to retaliate. As such, neither country has an incentive to initiate a nuclear attack against the other. In essence, peace is best secured when both countries are able to destroy the other. With this as the underlying assumption of the relationship between the United States and the Soviet Union, it was difficult to come to agreement on limiting offensive weapons, which were seen as guaranteeing a degree of peace between the two countries. It was much easier to find common ground when the negotiations turned to ABMs. Weapons systems, such as antiballistic missiles, that could effectively guard a country against a nuclear attack were seen as a threat to the balance of power between the Soviet Union and the United States, since a country with such a system could initiate an attack without fear of retaliation. These concerns came to light again during the presidencies of Ronald Reagan and George W. Bush, who both wanted to fund antimissile defense systems during their administrations. On December 13, 2001, President George W. Bush officially withdrew the United States from the ABM treaty with Russia in order to pursue a missile defense system.

Because there was considerable agreement between the two countries on ABMs, and considerable disagreement between them regarding offensive weapons, two different agreements were reached. The first, the ABM Treaty, dealt with the limitation of defensive missiles and outlined quite specifically the types of nuclear defense systems each country could have. In addition to the ABM treaty, the two countries reached an Interim Agreement dealing with weapons more offensive in nature. In short, both countries agreed not to increase the number of offensive nuclear weapons for a five-year period and agreed to continue negotiations on limiting these weapons in the future. These issues were considered under SALT II, which was initiated during President Carter's administration.

Although presidents negotiate treaties, it is the constitutional responsibility of the Senate to ratify this type of agreement between the United States and other nations. After the agreements had been reached with the Soviet Union, President Nixon informed the Congress of the results of the negotiations, and specifically requested the Senate to consider and ratify both agreements. In his statements, President Nixon outlined the strengths of the agreements and why he believed they were in the best interest of the United States and the world.

While there was support for arms limitation in the Congress, the most strident criticism was directed at the Interim Agreement. In a statement made before the Senate, Senator Ernest F. Hollings (D-S.C.) expressed his concern over the agreement, basing his criticisms on two points. First, he feared that the United States was placed at a disadvantage by the Interim Agreement since the Soviet Union had a larger number of ICBMs. Second, he voiced a broader concern that the Soviet Union could not be trusted to adhere to the agreement. Ultimately, both the ABM Treaty and the Interim Agreement were ratified.

JOINT COMMUNIQUÉ FOLLOWING DISCUSSIONS WITH SOVIET LEADERS

May 29, 1972

Bilateral Relations

Guided by the desire to place US–Soviet relations on a more stable and constructive foundation, and mindful of their responsibilities for maintaining world peace and for facilitating the relaxation of international tension, the two sides adopted a document entitled: "Basic Principles of Mutual Relations between the United States of America and the Union of Soviet Socialist Republics," signed on behalf of the U.S. by President Nixon and on behalf of the USSR by General Secretary Brezhnev.

Both sides are convinced that the provisions of that document open new possibilities for the development of peaceful relations and mutually beneficial cooperation between the USA and the USSR.

Having considered various areas of bilateral US–Soviet relations, the two sides agreed that an improvement of relations is possible and desirable. They expressed their firm intention to act in accordance with the provisions set forth in the above-mentioned document.

As a result of progress made in negotiations which preceded the summit meeting, and in the course of the meeting itself, a number of significant agreements were reached. This will intensify bilateral cooperation in areas of common concern as well as in areas relevant to the cause of peace and international cooperation.

Limitation of Strategic Armaments

The two sides gave primary attention to the problem of reducing the danger of nuclear war. They believe that curbing the competition in strategic arms will make a significant and tangible contribution to this cause.

The two sides attach great importance to the Treaty on the Limitation of Antiballistic Missile Systems and the Interim Agreement on Certain Measures with Respect to the Limitation of Strategic Offensive Arms concluded between them.

These agreements, which were concluded as a result of the negotiations in Moscow, constitute a major step towards curbing and ultimately ending the arms race.

They are a concrete expression of the intention of the two sides to contribute to the relaxation of international tension and the strengthening of confidence between states, as well as to carry out the obligations assumed by them in the Treaty on the Non-Proliferation of Nuclear Weapons (Article VI). Both sides are convinced that the achievement of the above agreements is a practical step towards saving mankind from the threat of the outbreak of nuclear war.

Accordingly, it corresponds to the vital interests of the American and Soviet peoples as well as to the vital interests of all other peoples.

The two sides intend to continue active negotiations for the limitation of strategic offensive arms and to conduct them in a spirit of goodwill, respect for each other's legitimate interests and observance of the principle of equal security. . . .

See "Joint Communiqué Following Discussions with Soviet Leaders" (29 May 1972), pp. 635–637. In *Public Papers of the Presidents of the United States: Richard Nixon, 1972* (Washington, D.C.: Government Printing Office, 1972).

MESSAGE TO THE SENATE TRANSMITTING THE ANTIBALLISTIC MISSILE TREATY AND THE INTERIM AGREEMENT ON STRATEGIC OFFENSIVE ARMS

June 13, 1972

To the Senate of the United States:

. . . These agreements, the product of a major effort of this administration, are a significant step into a new era of mutually agreed restraint and arms limitation between the two principal nuclear powers.

The provisions of the agreements are explained in detail in the Report of the Secretary of State, which I attach. Their main effect is this: The ABM Treaty limits the deployment of antiballistic missile systems to two designated areas, and at a low level. The Interim Agreement limits the overall level of strategic offensive missile forces. Together the two agreements provide for a more stable strategic balance in the next several years than would be possible if strategic arms competition continued unchecked. This benefits not only the United States and the Soviet Union, but all the nations of the world.

The agreements are an important first step in checking the arms race, but only a first step; they do not close off all avenues of strategic competition. Just as the maintenance of a strong strategic posture was an essential element in the success of these negotiations, it is now equally essential that we carry forward a sound strategic modernization program to maintain our security and to ensure that more permanent comprehensive arms limitation agreements can be reached.

The defense capabilities of the United States are second to none in the world today. I am determined that they shall remain so. The terms of the ABM Treaty and Interim Agreement will permit the United States to take the steps we deem necessary to maintain a strategic posture which protects our vital interests and guarantees our continued security.

Besides enhancing our national security, these agreements open the opportunity for a new and more constructive U.S.-Soviet relationship, characterized by negotiated settlement of differences, rather than by the hostility and confrontation of decades past.

These accords offer tangible evidence that mankind need not live forever in the dark shadow of nuclear war. They provide renewed hope that men and nations working together can succeed in building a lasting peace.

Because these agreements effectively serve one of this Nation's most cherished purposes—a more secure and peaceful world in which America's security is fully protected—I strongly recommend that the Senate support them, and that its deliberations be conducted without delay.

See "Message to the Senate Transmitting the Antiballistic Missile Treaty and the Interim Agreement on Strategic Offensive Arms" (13 June 1972), pp. 674–675. In *Public Papers of the Presidents of the United States: Richard Nixon, 1972* (Washington, D.C.: Government Printing Office, 1972).

STATEMENT OF SENATOR ERNEST F. HOLLINGS (D-S.C.)

September 14, 1972

We have said that we have a bad agreement. We have said that it encompasses inferiority on the part of the United States compared to the U.S.S.R. The administration has gone along with the Jackson amendment, thereby admitting that the agreement is a bad one. The Joint Chiefs of Staff were not consulted on the particular evening that the agreement was entered into and firmed up. The President's advisers did not see this agreement in time. They were told to go ahead and support the agreement and in turn the administration would support all of their requests. This, in turn, instead of stopping the arms race, continued the arms race. That is what happens, Mr. President, when you get a bad agreement. The President made a bad agreement. But he is so popular, it is like the king who wore no clothes. You want to be known as the President who made the breakthrough, and not many are willing to tell you the reality of the situation, that the breakthrough is not a breakthrough at all. In a situation of this kind, instead of being advisory, we should be clear, lucid, and aboveboard, and lay everything on the table, as we did in connection with the ABM agreement.

In antiballistic weaponry we agreed to a 200-missile limitation for the Soviets and 200 ABMs for the United States; 2 sites for the Soviets and 2 sites for the United States, and therein we had an element of equality. That was a good agreement, which would carry forward with it continuing and sustaining validity. Each side was treated alike.

But in the Interim Agreement, we have inequality. Instead of stopping the arms race, it accelerates the arms race; instead of promoting trust, it promotes distrust.

Any freshman law student could look at it and tell you, Mr. President, that it is unequal; any freshman law student seeking approval of this agreement would be called down by the court under the parole evidence rule.

We hear discussions about controls over ICBMs, submarines, and SLBMs. But I ask, what about superiority in technology and superiority in warheads? Well, they are not controlled in this agreement. We may be sure the Soviets will move forward in all these uncontrolled areas. They told our President so. I quote President Nixon on this—"Mr. Brezhnev made it very clear that he intended to go forward in those categories that were not limited."

So there is not doubt about Soviet intentions—none at all.

Of course, on these judgments and prognostications by the Pentagon that we have superiority and that it can be maintained—that is what they told us about the hydrogen bomb; that is what they told us about Sputnik; and their ICBM; and their nuclear sub; and their ABM. And each time we looked around and we found they had not only met us, but they had surpassed us.

Let us proceed on the basis of equality in our agreements. With respect to ICBMs, let us put those in the agreement and have equality in and of itself contained in the agreement. Then when we get to warheads, technology, and other items of armament, they should similarly be agreed to on the basis of equality, because therein is the way we build trust rather than distrust; therein do we begin to disarm rather than arm. . . .

I voted for the President on the Treaty, but I will vote against him on this agreement because careful study has convinced me that this pact accords military superiority, perhaps irreversible military superiority, to the Soviets. I cannot be a party to approving Soviet military superiority over the United States. . . .

Mr. President, the agreement before us falls dismally short on every count. That it would issue from a President who throughout his career has emphasized the necessity to negotiate from strength rather than weakness is nothing short of amazing to me. For years, President Nixon warned against dissipating our advantages, against relinquishing our superiority, and charged that even parity would be damaging to the United States. . . .

Now, the President comes before us, forgoing not only superiority—but parity, too—and asks us to settle instead for inferiority.

Mr. President, I find an agreement deficient when the very delegation charged with the responsibility for negotiating it warns—as the SALT delegation warned on May 9—that if "an agreement providing for more complete strategic offensive arms limitations were not achieved within 5 years, U.S. supreme interests could be jeopardized" and that the United States would then have to withdraw from the agreements. I do not care to play that kind of jeopardy for 5 years, only to find that we have by then fallen permanently behind . . .

Mr. President, I shall vote to reject the agreement. It brings no equality. It offers no guarantees of a more secure world. It brings us not an inch closer to the meaningful reduction in armaments that Americans sincerely desire. Instead, it offers inequality, inferiority, and instability. It is the wrong agreement for all the wrong reasons. We will best serve the cause of peace today by withholding approval of the interim agreement—and then by going forward with a policy and a program which can bring the day of meaningful arms limitations closer to reality.

See Sen. Ernest F. Hollings (S.C.). *Congressional Record* 118, pt. 23 (14 Sept. 1972), pp. 30651, 30654.

PRESIDENTIAL IMPOUNDMENT OF FUNDS

The ability to shape and control federal spending is a significant source of contention between the president and the Congress. Each branch has its own policy priorities and wants those priorities reflected in the budget. Even during times when the majority of Congress and the president are of the same party, it is often a political struggle of wills as to which branch will play the biggest role in shaping the federal budget.

Since 1921, when Congress passed the Budget and Accounting Act, the president has had the duty of preparing the national budget and submitting it to Congress for its consideration. Yet, it remains the constitutional responsibility of Congress to authorize any spending by the national government and appropriate any funds for the budget. As such, the president rarely receives everything he asks for in his budget request and, at times, the budget Congress sends for the president's signature bears little resemblance to his initial proposal. The president can respond to an unfavorable budget in several ways, including an outright veto of the legislation, or impounding some of the more objectionable funds appropriated by Congress. Impoundment is basically a refusal to spend the funds Congress has appropriated for a certain program of the federal government. When funds are impounded in this way, Congress often responds angrily.

Impoundment was widely used before the administration of Richard Nixon, but most observers would agree that Nixon used the strategy to a much greater degree than did previous presidents, refusing to spend billions of dollars appropriated by Congress. These impoundments were primarily directed at domestic policies, including certain farm programs, housing subsidies, and some social welfare policies. Most notably, Nixon impounded over 50 percent of the funds appropriated for waste treatment plants under the Clean Water Act, refusing to spend approximately $6 billion of the $11 billion appropriated for fiscal years 1973 and 1974. His rationale, discussed in several statements made about the nation's economy, was that Congress was irresponsibly spending too much of the taxpayers' money by going on a virtual "spending spree," and it was his responsibility to keep the Congress in check. The following statements were made in the months preceding the 1972 presidential election.

Congress perceived Nixon's use of impoundments differently, believing that the president had violated the separation of powers by not faithfully implementing a budget that had been already approved. Numerous members of Congress believed that Nixon was attempting to unilaterally put in place his national priorities in a manner inconsistent with the Constitution. Congress took several measures to control the executive branch's use of impoundment, including, in the case of some of the more egregious uses of impoundment, filing suit against the administration in the federal courts for the violation of separation of powers, and eventually passing the Impoundment Control Act of 1974 to limit the executive branch's use of impoundments. Senator Frank Church, a Democrat from Idaho who was particularly interested in environmental and water issues, explains his concern regarding Nixon's use of impoundment in an article for *The Nation* magazine.

NIXON'S SPECIAL MESSAGE TO THE CONGRESS ON FEDERAL GOVERNMENT SPENDING

July 26, 1972

This is an urgent appeal for the Congress to join with me to avoid higher taxes, higher prices, and a cut in purchasing power for everyone in the Nation.

Just when we have succeeded in cutting the rate of inflation in half, and just when we have succeeded in making it possible for America's workers to score their largest real spendable income gains in eight years, this tangible, pocketbook progress may be wiped out by proposed excessive spending.

Specifically, Federal spending for the fiscal year 1973 (which began on July 1, 1972) already is estimated to be almost $7 billion higher than was planned in my budget.

That figure by itself is bad enough. But even more spending beyond the budget—and beyond emergency flood relief funds—appears to be on the way.

The inevitable result would be higher taxes and more income-eating inflation in the form of higher prices.

I am convinced the American people do not want their family budgets wrecked by higher prices, and I will not stand by and permit such irresponsible action to undermine the clear progress we have made in getting America's workers off the inflation treadmill of the 1960s.

While specific Federal programs are important to many people and constituent groups, none is more important to all the American taxpayers than a concerted program to hold down the rate of taxes and the cost of living.

In view of this serious threat, I again urge the Congress—in the economic interest of all American citizens—to enact a spending ceiling of $250 billion. I urgently recommended a spending ceiling when I submitted the fiscal 1973 budget earlier this year. . . .

These are the compelling reasons which require me to ask again in the most urgent and explicit language I can frame that the Congress enact at the earliest possible opportunity a spending ceiling—without loopholes or exceptions—to force Government spending back to the $250 billion level in fiscal year 1973.

I again remind the Congress of the situation I cited last January, when I submitted the fiscal year 1973 budget:

"It will be a job-creating budget and a non-inflationary budget only if spending is limited to the amount the tax system would produce if the economy were operating at full employment.

"Those who increase spending beyond that amount will be responsible for causing more inflation."

Since that time, various Congressional actions and indications have heavily underscored all of the reasons I then made for speedy passage of a spending ceiling.

Such a ceiling cannot be completely effective unless the Congress enacts it as I have requested—without exceptions and without loopholes. But if the Congress fails to do this, I do not propose to sit by and silently watch individual family budgets destroyed by rising prices and rising taxes—the inevitable end to spending of this magnitude.

With or without the cooperation of the Congress, I am going to do everything within my power to prevent such a fiscal crisis for millions of people.

Let there be no misunderstanding: If bills come to my desk calling for excessive spending which threatens the Federal budget, I will veto them.

See "Special Message to the Congress on Federal Government Spending" (26 July 1972), pp. 741–743. In *Public Papers of the Presidents of the United States: Richard Nixon, 1972* (Washington, D.C.: Government Printing Office, 1972).

NIXON'S CAMPAIGN STATEMENT ABOUT FEDERAL SPENDING

October 23, 1972

The ABJECT failure of the 92nd Congress to hold to a responsible level of spending casts a long shadow over the glow of a resurging American economy.

Our economy is expanding at a very healthy rate, and it now looks as if our projection of a 6 percent production gain this year will be surpassed.

We have also cut the rate of inflation in half. Here in the New York area, the 1970 inflation increase of 7.4 percent per annum has been trimmed to 4.4 percent. The rate is still too high, but we are making progress here as well as other regions of the country.

We are also creating more new jobs than at any time in more than 16 years. Because so many people are entering the labor market, unemployment is not going down as fast as we would like, but we are confident that it can be brought down to a decent level. Here in the New York area, I am pleased to note, the unemployment rate is already below the national average.

In short, we are on the road to a new prosperity without war and without inflation—something this country has not enjoyed for more than 15 years.

All of this clear pocketbook progress is threatened, however, by the recent congressional spending spree in which the Federal budget was ballooned dangerously by big spenders oblivious to higher prices and higher taxes.

Today I have some news for the big spenders, bad news for them but good news for the taxpayers and consumers.

I am going to use every weapon at my command to hold spending in this fiscal year as close as possible to $250 billion—so that we will not have a new wave of crippling inflation and there will be no need for higher taxes.

Back on my desk in Washington, there are more than 100 pieces of public legislation which the Congress jammed through at the same time it was rejecting my spending ceiling. While at Camp David this past weekend, I studied all of these bills carefully. I found that many of them will serve the public interest, but I am also persuaded that some of them call for spending far in excess of what we can afford. These budget-breakers could only be financed by higher prices or higher taxes, or both.

In the name of the taxpayers and the consumers of America, I say the time has come to stand up to the big spenders. During the coming week there will be a number of vetoes. If there are big spending bills which I must sign for policy reasons, I also promise to exercise my full legal powers to hold down these appropriations, or reduce others to make room for the new programs.

See "Campaign Statement about Federal Spending" (23 Oct. 1972), pp. 1009–1010. In *Public Papers of the Presidents of the United States: Richard Nixon, 1972* (Washington, D.C.: Government Printing Office, 1972).

"IMPOUNDING CONGRESSIONAL POLICY"

The Nation, by Senator Frank Church (D-Idaho) November 22, 1971

The executive branch's insatiable appetite for power is now undermining the last bastion of Congressional strength, control of the purse strings. This development—effected by the impounding of funds—underscores the fact that far too much power is concentrated in the modern Presidency for the good health of constitutional government.

Historically, the rapid growth of Presidential power links directly with the shaping experiences of the 20th century—two World Wars, the Great Depression and a protracted cold war. Unfortunately, the Congress itself has accelerated the trend by tamely yielding its power and responsibility. As a consequence, increasing executive authority has overshadowed the separation of powers prescribed by the Constitution to the point where we must ask whether we are witnessing a permanent decline of constitutional government.

Most authority over foreign policy, including the war-making power that the Constitution vests in Congress, has already passed to the President. Now, on the domestic side, Congress is steadily losing its constitutional grip on the public purse. The disastrous impact of this development can be felt only when one realizes that appropriating money is the most important business assigned to Congress by the Constitution.

The appropriation power, however, lies today as much within the executive domain as within the Congressional. In part, this was inevitable.

The increased complexity of governmental transactions, combined with a concomitant need for flexibility, has understandably led to more executive involvement in budgeting for public spending. However, recent Presidents have reached far beyond these bounds toward unrestricted impoundment of appropriated funds—that is, the outright refusal by the President to expend funds in accordance with the will of Congress. (The money, if blocked, remains in the General Fund at the end of the fiscal period.)

Although Democratic Presidents engaged in impoundment in no small way, the Nixon Administration has gone all out. At last count, impounded funds this year total nearly $13 billion; under Johnson the high was an estimated $10.6 billion; under Kennedy, $6.5 billion. Every day, new stories describe discussions within the Nixon Administration as to whether funds Congress has appropriated for housing, pollution control and health services ought to remain impounded or be released from the executive snare. . . .

There are occasions, certainly, when the impoundment of appropriated funds is legitimate. For example, if only part of an appropriated sum is needed for, say, an irrigation project, then duty dictates that the remainder not be spent. Or, if Congress, as it sometimes does, makes an appropriation permissive, the President is obviously free to spend or save the money as he chooses. Or impoundment may be expressly directed, as in Title 6 of the 1964 Civil Rights Act, where Congress mandates the executive branch to withhold certain funds from localities practicing unlawful discrimination. The area of dispute does not involve such categories but rather executive impoundment made in defiance of Congressional intent.

Obviously the Constitution did not mean to allow the President complete control over spending. It gives him no item veto—if he finds a specific spending item unpalatable, he is obliged to veto the entire appropriation bill in which the item is contained. Furthermore, his veto may be overridden by a two-thirds vote of both bodies of Congress. . . .

It should be understood that a vital ingredient of our democracy is the opportunity afforded diverse political interests—farmers, businessmen, veterans, the elderly and others—to appeal in a meaningful way to Congress on behalf of programs they favor. Once it becomes recognized that any given program may be entombed by the President—even when Congress has authorized it and appropriated the money for it—the American people will sense the futility of turning to their elected representatives. This will compound an already discernible sense of frustration, even helplessness, that many social observers find today among Americans. The public will conclude that the executive branch, largely beyond local reach, is wholly in charge. Confidence and respect for representative government will evaporate and the stage could be set for the coming of an American Cromwell.

What is to be done? Senators of both parties and of differing political outlook have become increasingly concerned. Senator [Mike] Mansfield, the Majority Leader, recently proposed that the House, where appropriation bills customarily begin their legislative journey, institute a court suit to challenge Presidential action. Legal scholars have concluded that no court decisions to date pass directly upon the issue and that decisions of tangential relevance leave the matter in doubt. Some specialists would hesitate to resort to the courts, on the ground that the relationship between the President and Congress is essentially political and not susceptible to judicial remedies.

As for other means, Congressional recourse to the process of impeachment is clearly too harsh to be practical. More realistically, Congress can deny funds requested by the President for programs he may strongly favor, and thus bring pressure on the Chief Executive to implement Congressional intent in other areas. . . .

As a minimum, in any struggle for rectification, Congress must strengthen and regularize its review of executive compliance with Congressional appropriations. . . .

Of course, the most desirable general solution of the problem would be for the executive branch to discipline itself by recognizing that the dominant Presidential initiative in the budgetary process must be matched by meaningful Congressional control. But President Nixon seems insensitive to the problem. In March, when asked about the impoundment issue by Howard K. Smith during an interview on ABC Television, the President replied:

"[w]hen I was a Senator and a Congressman, particularly when I was a Senator and a Congressman with a President of the other party in the White House, I played all of these games, with very little success. These games are going to be played. . . ."

But the issue is not a matter of "games." It goes to the heart of the separation of powers, the principal accomplishment of the founding fathers.

See Senator Frank Church, "Impounding Congressional Policy." *The Nation*, vol. 213, no. 17, November 22, 1971, pp. 519–20.

REVENUE SHARING

Despite the fact that the United States has a federal system of government, with the powers of government divided between the national and state levels, the states have increasingly become reliant on funds from the national government to conduct state business. After the Civil War until approximately 1940, the national government played little role in the operations of the states, limiting itself to the duties outlined by the Constitution as being under the responsibility of the federal government. Part of this strict delineation between the states and the national government was the result of a strict interpretation of the Constitution by the Supreme Court, which essentially prohibited any intrusion by the federal government into responsibilities reserved to the states.

This interpretation began to change after the Great Depression of 1932, however, with the recognition by President Franklin D. Roosevelt and the Congress that the economic crisis was a national problem requiring a national solution, not a problem that could be solved by the disparate policies of each of the individual states. Many of Roosevelt's New Deal policies injected the national government into the affairs of the states and this has proved to be an enduring change, in part reflected by the increasing amount of revenue provided to the state and local governments by the national government.

Policies regarding how these funds, issued in the form of grants, should be disbursed have varied over time. Some grants come with strict instructions as to how the funds should be used while others provide a great deal of discretion to the state or local government to which the grant is made. President Lyndon B. Johnson had relied heavily on "categorical grants," or grants to the states that specified precisely how the funds were to be used. This afforded the federal government some influence over the policy decisions of the states. Conversely, President Nixon supported an approach that gave the states a great deal of latitude in deciding how federal grants were to be used. He believed that the federal government under Presidents Kennedy and Johnson and a Democratically controlled Congress had become too large, unnecessarily interfering in the affairs of state and local governments and interjecting itself into the lives of the American people. He proposed a policy of revenue sharing, which would provide funds to state and local governments for use as these levels of government saw fit. Nixon's plan was approved by Congress in October of 1972, with many members undoubtedly believing this to be a popular move in an election year. Congress eventually approved $16 billion in grants for the 1973–1975 period. The statements from Nixon regarding revenue sharing reflect his ideological stance that the federal government should interfere less with the lower levels of government and give state and local governments more assistance in providing services to the American people.

There were members of Congress, however, who saw revenue sharing as an irresponsible move on the part of the national government. One argument against the program was that revenue sharing gave the false impression that there was "free money" just waiting to be returned to the states. Representative Morris Udall, Democrat of Arizona, explained in a letter to his constituents that this revenue was still coming from tax dollars, and there was some concern that local and state officials would start relying on federal tax dollars to accomplish their goals, rather than just raising the revenue themselves. This would allow these officials to avoid making the difficult decision to raise taxes at the state and local levels. Another argument against the program was based on the fact that the national government was running a deficit, or spending more than it took in from taxes, and that sending more funds back to the states was irresponsible until the national government could achieve a balanced budget.

Representative John W. Byrnes (R-Wisc.) expressed his concern in a statement on the floor of the House of Representatives on June 21, 1972. He explains in his statement that he understands the political attraction of revenue sharing for congressional, state, and local elected officials alike, but he contends that, in the long term, the program is irresponsible for the American taxpayers.

FROM NIXON'S REMARKS ON SIGNING THE GENERAL REVENUE SHARING BILL

October 20, 1972

We stand today on ground in which more history has been made than any place in America. As we stand here, we all realize that the American system of government was born here. We realize, too, that as we stand here the Declaration of Independence, the Constitution, the Bill of Rights—those three great documents—created the federal system. And now by the bill I will soon sign, we have the privilege to renew the federal system that was created 190 years ago.

The Constitution of the United States begins with the words, "We the People," and the bill I shall sign is a demonstration of a principle that we have faith in people, we believe in people, and we believe that government closest to the people should have the greatest support. . . .

The Constitution was a great document, but a constitution made to govern 3 million people in 13 States, 190 years ago, would have been inadequate unless it had within it what is really the genius of the American system: a process by which, through peaceful change, we can take new initiatives to meet the new needs of the country. And so, today, where there are 200 million Americans, there are 50 States, there are great cities and counties and other governments that the Founding Fathers could not possibly have visualized as coming into being, and we have acted. The American Revolution, in other words, is never finished; it must always be renewed, and we are helping to renew it today.

If, as we sign this bill, we proceed on the assumption that it is finished, we will not have met the challenge which is ours. Because, if the 20 or so billion dollars which will be distributed over the years to the States and the cities and the counties will simply mean that more money will go for the same old programs and the same governments and that the people will not benefit, then we will have failed in our task.

What America wants today, at the State level and at the city level and at the county level, and, I believe, at the Federal level, is not bigger government, but better government—and that is what this is about.

And so I would hope that each mayor, each Governor, each county official, would go back to his community or his State or hers, with this dedication in mind: that these funds will be used for the needs of people; that they will mean better schools and better hospitals and better police forces; that they will mean, I would certainly hope, that we will stop the alarming escalation in local and State property taxes, income taxes, and sales taxes. . . .

Today, through this revenue sharing bill, we are giving to the distinguished people here—the mayors, the Governors, the county officials, and your colleagues all across this country—we are giving you the tools, now you do the job. . . .

See "Remarks on Signing the General Revenue Sharing Bill" (20 Oct. 1972), pp. 993–994. In *Public Papers of the Presidents of the United States: Richard Nixon, 1972* (Washington, D.C.: Government Printing Office, 1972).

FROM NIXON'S STATEMENT ABOUT THE GENERAL REVENUE SHARING BILL

October 20, 1972

After many years in which power has been flowing away from those levels of government which are closest to the people, power will now begin to flow back to the people again—a development which can have an enormous impact on their daily existence. . . .

But the most important point is this: In each case it will be local officials responding to local conditions and local constituencies who will decide what should happen, and not some distant bureaucrat in Washington, D.C.

The American people are fed up with government that doesn't deliver. Revenue sharing can help State and local government deliver again, closing the gap between promise and performance.

Revenue sharing will give these hard-pressed governments the dollars they need so badly. But just as importantly, it will give them the freedom they need to use those dollars as effectively as possible.

Under this program, instead of spending so much time trying to please distant bureaucrats in Washington—so the money will keep coming in—State and local officials can concentrate on pleasing the people—so the money can do more good.

See "Statement about the General Revenue Sharing Bill" (20 Oct. 1972), pp. 995–996. In *Public Papers of the Presidents of the United States: Richard Nixon, 1972* (Washington, D.C.: Government Printing Office, 1972).

STATEMENT OF REPRESENTATIVE JOHN W. BYRNES (R-WISC.)

June 21, 1972

Mr. Chairman, I think it has to be recognized that the vote on this [revenue sharing] bill, as far as the House is concerned, was pretty well decided with the adoption of the rule. I am not going to try to kid myself that anything I might say is going to change that situation. I think it ought to be made clear, though, that the principal reason for supporting this bill has been somewhat ignored. It has been somewhat ignored by the chairman of the committee in his discussion of what the bill contains.

This principal reason to which I refer is the appetite of the Governors and mayors, State legislators, city councilmen, and county board members. Their appetite has been whetted for some free money, or new money, from Washington that they can spend as they see fit. Frankly, I cannot blame them too much.

We all know that demands are constantly being made on them for additional services, yet the people are not willing to bear the taxes that those services will cost. And so they are caught in a bind. They apparently envision a "Santa Claus" in Washington saying, "We will send you $30 billion in the next 5 years, and you will be able to take care of some of those requests for services, and you won't have to try to find any way to finance them."

That is a pretty good deal, so I am not criticizing the Governors and the mayors for taking that attitude, even though I must say that it is a pretty selfish one if balanced against the needs and interests of the country. But this is an election year, and it is nice to go home and have the Governor say, "I am with you because you sent me this check from Washington." Or you go to the mayor, and the mayor says, "I am all for you because you sent me a check." I think, frankly, that this reason for supporting the legislation is stronger than any substantive one related to the merits of the bill . . .

This bill is just the beginning, as testimony before the committee demonstrated. Governor [Nelson] Rockefeller [New York], speaking for the National Governor's Conference, said $10 billion "is absolutely essential." Mayor [Roman S.] Gribbs of Detroit, appearing for the U.S. Conference of Mayors, in effect agreed when he stated:

"We feel it should be at the level of $10 billion to meet our needs but that does not mean we would not be pleased to have you pass it at $5 or $6 billion.

"Pleased, but not satisfied."

I would suggest that they are never going to be satisfied. Once we start down this road of financing the general governmental responsibilities of States and localities, the Federal allocation is going to become a line item of revenue in State and local budgets. As they total up their expenditures, and their revenues, if they find a deficit, they will put in a line to balance it out, saying, "We are working in Washington to get this additional amount."

I think anybody who looks at it in a different way is just blinding himself to the true facts of the situation. . . .

As I said when I began, it is not my belief that I am changing any votes on this matter. But I think that there are certain things that must be said before this House starts us on the perilous journey outlined by this bill.

I think it is going to be one that the Congress of the United States will regret, if this program comes to fruition. I think it is one that the executive branch of this country is going to regret. I think it is going to be regretted by the States and by the local units of government as they become more and more dependent upon the Congress of the United States and on the Federal Government for financing their basic governmental services.

But more than anybody else—it is going to be regretted by the American taxpayers who have to pay the bill. No matter where services are incurred, whether they be at the Federal level or the local level, it is the American taxpayer who has to fork out the money.

All we are doing here is adding another level of expenditures and we are going to be turning to these taxpayers for the additional taxes to finance it.

In the process we also will have removed what few restraints—and, frankly, the rather ineffective restraints that we have today—on public spending. By undermining public accountability we undermine the democratic process.

Who is going to suffer in that process? We all will suffer. But in the final analysis, the American taxpayer will suffer the most in order to appease the appetite of State and local officials.

See Rep. John W. Byrnes (Wisc.). *Congressional Record* 118, pt. 17 (21 June 1972), pp. 21709–21710, 21713.

SURRENDER OF WHITE HOUSE TAPES

In June of 1972, five intruders were apprehended in what initially appeared to be a simple burglary of the Democratic National Committee Headquarters in the Watergate office and apartment complex in Washington, D.C. Yet, this event marked the beginning of a series of investigations and revelations that ultimately resulted in the resignation of President Nixon on August 8, 1974. The events collectively referred to as "Watergate" are often seen as a turning point in American politics, when the perceptions of government by both the media and the public turned more distrustful and cynical.

As it would be discovered, the intruders into the Democratic Headquarters had been attempting to wiretap the phones in order to undermine the Democratic Party's campaign activities. This "third-rate burglary attempt," as Nixon's press secretary termed it, would eventually be linked to individuals in the White House largely because of the investigation by two *Washington Post* journalists, Bob Woodward and Carl Bernstein, who discovered that the White House had a secret fund to carry out "dirty tricks" against the president's so-called enemies. Yet the overriding question was whether or not President Nixon was aware of the break-in and the other illegal activities being carried out on his behalf in preparation for the 1972 presidential election. As early as August of 1972, the president had claimed that he had no involvement in the incident.

Once the burglars were irrefutably linked to members of the White House staff, a Senate committee on Watergate began holding hearings in May 1973 to investigate the political abuses of the White House. In addition to the hearings, Archibald Cox was appointed by the attorney general to act as the Justice Department's special prosecutor for the case. It was John Dean, the president's former legal counsel, who first claimed that President Nixon had indeed known of the White House's link to the Watergate break-in, albeit after the fact, and the following cover-up. Initially, there seemed little means of corroborating his assertions against the president, however a former White House aide, Alexander Butterfield, testified ten days later that Oval Office conversations had been recorded since 1971. This startling discovery prompted both the Senate Watergate Committee and Special Prosecutor Cox to request the tapes from the president, who refused to comply. The tapes were subsequently subpoenaed as evidence.

Despite the formal subpoena, which legally required that the tapes be submitted as evidence, President Nixon argued that he did not have to turn over the tapes, citing his "executive privilege." Although, in retrospect, President Nixon clearly avoided turning over the tapes because they did indeed implicate him in the Watergate affair as well as other illegal acts, at the time he asserted that that the tapes contained discussions of issues that, if made public, could harm national security. Thus, he contended that conversations in the Oval Office had to remain confidential, and he refused to comply with the subpoena.

Although Nixon fired Archibald Cox for the intensity of his investigations, the new special prosecutor, Leon Jaworski, continued to press for the tapes, ultimately petitioning the Supreme Court in the matter. Writing for the Court, Chief Justice Warren Burger explained that, while there certainly were instances that might necessitate claims of executive privilege due to national security concerns, the president was not exempt from the law as determined by the judicial branch. Thus, the Supreme Court unanimously ruled in *United States v. Nixon* that the president did have to submit the tapes for any evidence they might contain regarding the criminal investigation surrounding Watergate. On August 5, 1974, President Nixon turned over the tapes to the courts; he resigned three days later on August 8, 1974.

NIXON'S ADDRESS TO THE NATION ABOUT THE WATERGATE INVESTIGATION

Address from the Oval Office, August 15, 1973

Many persons will ask why, when the facts are as I have stated them, I do not make public the tape recordings of my meetings and conversations with members of the White House Staff during this period.

I am aware that such terms as "separation of powers" and "executive privilege" are lawyers' terms, and that those doctrines have been called "abstruse" and "esoteric." Let me state the common sense of the matter. Every day a President of the United States is required to make difficult decisions on grave issues. It is absolutely essential, if the President is to be able to do his job as the country expects, that he be able to talk openly and candidly with his advisers about issues and individuals and that they be able to talk in the same fashion with him. Indeed, on occasion, they must be able to "blow off steam" about important public figures. This kind of frank discussion is only possible when those who take part in it can feel assured that what they say is in the strictest confidence.

The Presidency is not the only office that requires confidentiality if it is to function effectively. A Member of Congress must be able to talk in confidence with his assistants. Judges must be able to confer in confidence with their law clerks and with each other. Throughout our entire history the need for this kind of confidentiality has been recognized. No branch of Government has ever compelled disclosure of confidential conversations between officers of other branches of Government and their advisers about Government business.

The argument is often raised that these tapes are somehow different because the conversations may bear on illegal acts, and because the commission of illegal acts is not an official duty. This misses the point entirely. Even if others, from their own standpoint, may have been thinking about how to cover up an illegal act, from my standpoint I was concerned with how to uncover the illegal acts. It is my responsibility under the Constitution to see that the laws are faithfully executed, and in pursuing the facts about Watergate I was doing precisely that. Therefore, the precedent would not be one concerning illegal actions only; it would be one that would risk exposing private Presidential conversations involving the whole range of official duties.

The need for [confidentiality] is not something confined to Government officials. The law has long recognized that there are many relations sufficiently important that things said in that relation are entitled to be kept confidential, even at the cost of doing without what might be critical evidence in a legal proceeding. Among these are, for example, the relations between a lawyer and his client, between a priest and a penitent, and between a husband and wife. In each case it is thought to be so important that the parties be able to talk freely with each other, that they do not feel restrained in their conversation by fear that what they say may someday come out in court, that the law recognizes that these conversations are "privileged" and that their disclosure cannot be compelled.

If I were to make public these tapes, containing as they do blunt and candid remarks on many subjects that have nothing to do with Watergate, the confidentiality of the Office of the President would always be suspect. Persons talking with a President would never again be sure that recordings of notes of what they said would not at some future time be made public, and they would guard their words against that possibility. No one would want to risk being known as the person who recommended a policy that ultimately did not work. No one would want to advance tentative ideas, not fully thought through, that might have possible merit but that might, on further examination, prove unsound. No one would want to speak bluntly about public figures here and abroad. I shall therefore vigorously oppose any action which would set a precedent that would cripple all future presidents by inhibiting conversations between them and the persons they look to for advice.

This principle of confidentiality in Presidential communications is what is at stake in the question of the tapes. I shall continue to oppose any efforts to destroy that principle, which is indispensable to the conduct of the Presidency.

See "Address to the Nation about the Watergate Investigation" (15 Aug. 1973), pp. 701–702. In *Public Papers of the Presidents of the United States: Richard Nixon, 1973* (Washington, D.C.: Government Printing Office, 1973).

FROM THE MAJORITY OPINION OF THE SUPREME COURT

United States v. Nixon
1974

In the performance of assigned constitutional duties each branch of the Government must initially interpret the Constitution, and the interpretation of its powers by any branch is due great respect for the others. The President's counsel, as we have noted, reads the Constitution as providing an absolute privilege of confidentiality for all Presidential communications. Many decisions of the Court, however, have unequivocally reaffirmed the holding of *Marbury v. Madison*, 1 Cranch 137 (1803), that "[i]t is emphatically the province and duty of the judicial department to say what the law is." . . .

In support of his claim of absolute privilege, the President's counsel urges two grounds, one of which is common to all governments and one of which is peculiar to our system of separation of powers. The first ground is the valid need for protection of communications between high Government officials and those who advise and assist them in the performance of their manifold duties; the importance of this confidentiality is too plain to require further discussion. Human experience teaches that those who expect public dissemination of their remarks may well temper candor with a concern for appearances and for their own interests to the detriment of the decisionmaking process. Whatever the nature of the privilege of confidentiality of Presidential communications in the exercise of [Article] II powers, the privilege can be said to derive from the supremacy of each branch within its own assigned area of constitutional duties. Certain powers and privileges flow from the nature of enumerated powers; the protection of the confidentiality of Presidential communications has similar constitutional underpinnings.

The second ground asserted by the President's counsel in support of the claim of absolute privilege rests on the doctrine of separation of powers. Here it is argued that the independence of the Executive Branch within its own sphere, . . . insulates a President from a judicial subpoena in an ongoing criminal prosecution, and thereby protects confidential Presidential communications.

However, neither the doctrine of separation of powers, nor the need for confidentiality of high-level communications, without more, can sustain an absolute, unqualified Presidential privilege of immunity from judicial process under all circumstances. The President's need for complete candor and objectivity from advisers calls for great deference from the courts. However, when the privilege depends solely on the broad, undifferentiated claim of public interest in the confidentiality of such conversations, a confrontation with other values arises. Absent a claim of need to protect military, diplomatic, or sensitive national security secrets, we find it difficult to accept the argument that even the very important interest in confidentiality of Presidential communications is significantly diminished by production of such material for *in camera* inspection with all the protection that district court will be obliged to provide. . . .

To read the [Article] II powers of the President as providing an absolute privilege as against a subpoena essential to enforcement of criminal statutes on no more than a generalized claim of the public interest in confidentiality of nonmilitary and nondiplomatic discussions would upset the constitutional balance of "a workable government" and gravely impair the role of the courts under [Article] III. . . .

In this case we just weigh the importance of the general privilege of confidentiality of Presidential communications in performance of the President's responsibilities against the inroads of such a privilege on the fair administration of criminal justice. The interest in preserving confidentiality is weighty indeed and entitled to great respect. However, we cannot conclude that advisers will be moved to temper the candor of their remarks by the infrequent occasions of disclosure because of the possibility that such conversations will be called for in the context of a criminal prosecution.

On the other hand, the allowance of the privilege to withhold evidence that is demonstrably relevant in a criminal trial would cut deeply into the guarantee of due process of law and gravely impair the basic function of the courts. A President's acknowledged need for confidentiality in the communications of his office is general in nature, whereas the constitutional need for production of relevant evidence in a criminal proceeding is specific and central to the fair adjudication of a particular criminal case in the administration of justice. Without access to specific facts a criminal prosecution may be totally frustrated. The President's broad interest in confidentiality of communications will not be vitiated by disclosure of a limited number of conversations preliminarily shown to have some bearing on the pending criminal cases.

We conclude that when the ground for asserting privilege as to subpoenaed materials sought for use in a criminal trial is based only on the generalized interest in confidentiality, it cannot prevail over the fundamental demands of due process of law in the fair administration of criminal justice. The generalized assertion of privilege must yield to the demonstrated, specific need for evidence in a pending criminal trial.

See United States v. Nixon, President of the United States, et al. U.S. Reports 418 U.S. 683 (1974): pp. 703, 705–706, 707, 711–713.

THE FIRING OF ARCHIBALD COX

In the United States, it is well accepted that the president is not above the law. Yet in instances where the legality of presidential action has come under scrutiny, the mechanisms for investigating the president have generated much controversy. On the one hand, there is a need to appoint an investigator who will not be swayed by the political pressures that may be exerted by the president or his agents. On the other hand, it can be harmful to the separation of powers as well as to the president's ability to govern if one person is invested with too much power to investigate the president's actions.

This balance between insulating the investigator from political pressures yet preventing the abuse of power is difficult to achieve. In the late 1990s, Kenneth Starr was appointed to investigate President Bill Clinton for his questionable investment activities in the Whitewater real estate development in Arkansas, but his actual investigation extended much further than his original charge, ultimately bringing to light Clinton's relationship with White House intern Monica Lewinsky. His investigation eventually resulted in Clinton's impeachment. Yet despite the seriousness of his allegations, Starr was roundly criticized for having abused the power of his appointment, delving into subjects that fell far beyond his original mission. Yet, investigators must have some independence from the people they are investigating. The experiences of Archibald Cox, who was appointed to the position of special prosecutor during the Watergate investigation, demonstrate this fact.

When evidence was uncovered linking individuals in the White House to the Watergate break-in, President Nixon's Attorney General, Elliot Richardson, appointed a special prosecutor to investigate the events surrounding the Watergate affair. Archibald Cox, as Richardson's appointee, was faced with the difficult situation of being an employee of the Justice Department, officially part of Nixon's administration, who was charged with investigating other officials in that administration, including the president. When it was revealed in congressional Watergate Hearings that the Oval Office was equipped with recording devices, it became Cox's goal to secure the audiotapes as evidence against the administration, a goal he pursued aggressively in the federal court system. Although the president suggested an arrangement which would allow partial disclosure of the tapes to a limited number of senators, Cox refused to accept anything but full disclosure. In response, President Nixon ordered Attorney General Richardson to fire Cox for failing to cooperate with the administration. The decision proved to be embarrassing to Nixon, as both Richardson and Deputy Attorney General William D. Ruckelshaus resigned in protest rather than carry out the president's order. After the resignation of both Richardson and Ruckelshaus, the position of Acting Attorney General fell to Solicitor General Robert H. Bork, who was instructed in a letter from Nixon to carry out the original order to fire Cox. In a brief letter, which explained that Cox was being discharged as directed by President Nixon, Robert Bork officially fired Cox from his position as special prosecutor.

The decision to fire Archibald Cox generated significant criticism. Chesterfield Smith, who was president of the American Bar Association at the time of the dismissal, was forceful in his condemnation of the president's actions, which he claimed flouted the rule of law. In short, the president should not be able to remove an investigator simply because he doesn't like the direction in which the investigation is moving. It was Smith's recommendation that Congress establish a position of "independent prosecutor," which could be utilized when necessary, yet would be removed from the authority of the president. Congress followed this recommendation in 1978 by including a provision for an independent counsel in its Ethics in Government Act. Although this provision was allowed to lapse between 1992 and 1994, President Clinton signed a bill reinstating the office of independent counsel in 1994. This provision was up for renewal in 1999, but due in large part to the controversy over Kenneth Starr's investigation, Congress did not approve its renewal.

NIXON'S LETTER DIRECTING THE ACTING ATTORNEY GENERAL TO DISCHARGE THE DIRECTOR OF THE OFFICE OF WATERGATE SPECIAL PROSECUTION FORCE

October 20, 1973

In his press conference today Special Prosecutor Archibald Cox made it apparent that he will not comply with the instruction I issued to him, through Attorney General Richardson, yesterday. Clearly the government of the United States cannot function if employees of the Executive Branch are free to ignore in this fashion the instructions of the President. Accordingly, in your capacity of Acting Attorney General, I direct you to discharge Mr. Cox immediately and to take all steps necessary to return to the Department of Justice the functions now being performed by the Watergate Special Prosecution Force.

It is my expectation that the Department of Justice will continue with full vigor the investigations and prosecutions that had been entrusted to the Watergate Special Prosecution Force.

Sincerely,

Richard Nixon

See "Letter Directing the Acting Attorney General to Discharge the Director of the Office of Watergate Special Prosecution Force" (20 Oct. 1973), p. 891. In *Public Papers of the Presidents of the United States: Richard Nixon, 1973* (Washington, D.C.: Government Printing Office, 1973).

FROM THE PRESIDENT'S NEWS CONFERENCE

East Room of the White House, October 26, 1973

Also, in consultations that we have had in the White House today, we have decided that next week the Acting Attorney General, Mr. Bork, will appoint a new Special Prosecutor for what is called the Watergate matter. The Special Prosecutor will have independence. He will have total co-operation from the executive branch, and he will have as his primary responsibility to bring this matter which has so long concerned the American people, bring it to an expeditious conclusion, because we have to remember that under our Constitution, it has always been held that justice delayed is justice denied. It is time for those who are guilty to be prosecuted and for those who are innocent to be cleared. And I can assure you ladies and gentlemen, and all of our listeners tonight, that I have no greater interest than to see that the new Special Prosecutor has the cooperation from the executive branch and the independence that he needs to bring about that conclusion. . . .

The matter of the tapes has been one that has concerned me because of my feeling that I have a constitutional responsibility to defend the Office of the Presidency from any encroachments on confidentiality which might affect future Presidents in their abilities to conduct the kind of conversations and discussions they need to conduct to carry on the responsibilities of this office. And of course, the Special Prosecutor felt that he needed the tapes for the purpose of his prosecution.

That was why, working with the Attorney General, we worked out what we thought was an acceptable compromise, one which Judge Stennis, now Senator Stennis, would hear the tapes and would provide a complete and full disclosure, not only to Judge Sirica but also to the Senate committee.

Attorney General Richardson approved of this proposition. Senator Ervin approved of the proposition. Mr. Cox was the only one that rejected it.

Under the circumstances, when he rejected it and indicated that despite the approval of the Attorney General, of course, of the President, and of the two major Senators on the Ervin committee, when he rejected the proposal, I had no choice but to dismiss him.

Under those circumstances, Mr. Richardson, Mr. Ruckelshaus felt that because of the nature of their confirmation that their commitment to Mr. Cox had to take precedence over any commitment they might have to carry out an order from the President.

Under those circumstances, I accepted with regret the resignations of two fine public servants.

Now we come to a new Special Prosecutor. We will cooperate with him, and I do not anticipate that we will come to the time when he would consider it necessary to take the President to court. I think our cooperation will be adequate.

See "The President's News Conference" (26 Oct. 1973), pp. 898–899. In *Public Papers of the Presidents of the United States: Richard Nixon, 1973* (Washington, D.C.: Government Printing Office, 1973).

STATEMENT BY CHESTERFIELD SMITH, PRESIDENT OF THE AMERICAN BAR ASSOCIATION

October 1973

As president of the American Bar Association, I urge in the strongest terms that appropriate action be taken promptly by the courts and, if necessary, by the Congress to repel the attacks which are presently being made on the justice system and the rule of law as we have known it in this country.

The American Bar Association last spring, through its then president, Robert W. Meserve, called for the appointment of an independent prosecutor with responsibility for the investigation and prosecution of the matters which had been revealed by the Senate Select Committee on Presidential Campaign Activities, by the press, and through the federal grand jury, and which are now commonly called the "Watergate Affair." The position of the Association was based upon its Standards for Criminal Justice, which provide that a prosecuting officer should have no conflict of interest or the appearance of a conflict of interest. Thus, under the standards, it would be improper for an investigation of the president himself, of the office of the president, or of the federal government to be conducted by a prosecutor subject to the direction and control of the president.

Based upon assurances made publicly by high officers of the administration, the American Bar Association was most hopeful that, when Archibald Cox was appointed special prosecutor, he would be allowed to pursue justice in all aspects of his investigation without control by those whom he was charged with investigating. Now, the president of the United States, by declaring an intention and by taking overt action to abort the established processes of justice, has instituted an intolerable assault upon the courts, our first line of defense against tyranny and arbitrary power. The abandonment, by presidential fiat, of the time-tested procedures to ensure the equitable distribution of justice constitutes a clear and present danger of compelling significance. The substitution, again by presidential fiat, of a makeshift device—unilaterally improvised and conferring upon one individual functioning in secret, the power to test evidence—may well be acceptable for a congressional investigation, but to insist also that it be utilized by the courts in criminal proceedings is an assault of wholly unprecedented dimension on the very heart of the administration of justice. The absolute gravity of the situation demands the most resolute course on the part of the courts and, if necessary, the Congress.

There can be no menace to our security from within and none from without more lethal to our liberties at home and more fatal to our influence abroad than this defiant flouting of laws and courts. As an American, as a lawyer, and as an officer of the court, in expressing the gravest concern, I express my hope and confidence that the judicial and legislative forces of this nation will act swiftly and decisively to challenge, repeal, and correct this damaging incursion by the president of the United States upon the system of justice, and therefore upon the basic liberties of the citizens of this country.

I continue to hope also that the president of the United States will, upon further reflection, change his course and cease what I believe to be an unprecedented flouting of the rule of law. I also believe that the Congress should, as its first priority, take whatever measures are available to it to re-establish the office of the special prosecutor and to make the special prosecutor independent of the direction and control of those whom he is investigating.

The people of this country will never believe that justice has been done in the "Watergate Affair" until such time as that independent prosecutor is permitted to go into all aspects of the "Watergate Affair" without limitations or controls imposed on him by those whom he has reason to believe are possible participants. At the same time, it is clearly proper that those who are being investigated by the special prosecutor present their objections to his conduct to the courts for a determination as to whether such conduct is legally permissible.

I pledge to do all within my personal power to see that the American Bar Association assists the United States District Court for the District of Columbia and any other federal court in the discharge of its duties and responsibilities in this constitutional crisis.

As a final comment, I applaud—indeed, I am proud of—the action of the three great lawyers, Elliot Richardson, William Ruckelshaus, and Archibald Cox, who, in a most dramatic way, have emphasized to the people of this nation that they are lawyers who honor and cherish the tradition of the legal profession and that they are lawyers who properly and without hesitation put ethics and professional honor above public office.

See "Statement by Chesterfield Smith," *American Bar Association Journal*, vol. 59, December 1973, p. 1391.

VETO OF THE WAR POWERS RESOLUTION

In 1964, the American policy toward the Vietnam War shifted away from merely assisting the South Vietnamese in their efforts against the North Vietnamese, to a policy that involved more direct engagement of American forces against the North Vietnamese. President Johnson argued at the time that the office of the presidency needed more authority to make decisions with regard to military aggression against American forces. In August 1964, Congress approved the Gulf of Tonkin Resolution, which stated in its preamble that "the Congress approves and supports the determination of the President, as Commander in Chief, to take all necessary measures to repel any armed attack against the forces of the United States and to prevent further aggression." In essence, the president was provided with a "blank check" to make whatever decisions he thought were necessary to prevail against the North Vietnamese and these decisions would receive very little scrutiny from the Congress. The Gulf of Tonkin Resolution had the unfortunate consequence of bypassing the constitutional system of checks and balances, which requires that each branch of government share the power of policy making.

With the escalation of the Vietnam War in the latter half of the 1960s, some members of Congress began to believe that the office of the president had acquired too much unchecked power in the area of war making. Both Presidents Johnson and Nixon had critics who believed that each had flouted the constitutional role of the Congress in making critical foreign policy decisions with regard to the Vietnam War. Historian Arthur Schlesinger, Jr., called this period the "imperial presidency," referring to the presidents' seeming belief that they were above the law.

Concerns about the presidents' apparent disregard for congressional involvement came to a head during President Nixon's administration. When Nixon secretly bombed Cambodia, the action was roundly criticized on college campuses and in the halls of government alike as an abuse of power. Suspicions about the president's "imperial" viewpoint were confirmed domestically by his involvement in the Watergate scandal. On June 24, 1970, in response to the bombing of Cambodia, Congress voted to repeal the Gulf of Tonkin Resolution. In addition, the Cooper-Church Amendments were passed, which prohibited the use of U.S. troops outside of Vietnam. Nixon, however, continued the bombing effort in Cambodia. In October of 1973, Congress took more proactive measures to curb the president's war-making powers and reclaim a role for itself in the process by passing the War Powers Resolution.

The War Powers Resolution recognized the need for quick decision making by the president in his constitutional role as commander-in-chief, yet it required the president to confer with the Congress as much as possible in the decision-making process and to inform the Congress within forty-eight hours if troops were deployed. In addition, the commitment of troops could last only sixty days without further authorization by Congress. President Nixon believed that the Act would severely undercut the president's ability to make critical decisions regarding the country's foreign policy. He also believed that the War Powers Resolution was unconstitutional by violating the separation of powers outlined in the Constitution. On October 24, 1973, President Nixon vetoed the Resolution, outlining his reasoning in the veto message sent to Congress.

Interestingly, members of Congress who hoped to override the president's veto argued that the Resolution was necessary to protect the separation of powers, not to thwart it as claimed by Nixon. Both the House and Senate reconsidered the War Powers Resolution on November 7 and voted to override the president's veto. Numerous members of Congress addressed their respective chambers during the debate to override the veto, but the statement made by Representative Michael J. Harrington (D-Mass.) on the floor of the House of Representatives outlines the key arguments particularly well.

The War Powers Resolution did not cease to be a point of contention between presidents and the Congress once it was enacted over the Nixon's veto. Presidents since Nixon have claimed that it places an undue burden on the president's authority as commander-in-chief, yet members of Congress see it as a necessary precaution against presidential abuse of power. Some of these interbranch conflicts have been taken to the federal courts. For instance, President Reagan was challenged in the federal courts on four separate occasions by members of Congress who claimed that the president had violated the War Powers Act in certain military affairs. In such legal challenges, the Supreme Court has generally ruled that the courts are not the appropriate forum for such political conflicts. Since 1973, it has become evident that the War Powers Act has provided little constraint to presidents who have felt it necessary to use military force. Yet, it has served as a reminder of the legitimate congressional claims of authority in the area of foreign policy.

NIXON'S MESSAGE VETOING THE JOINT RESOLUTION CONCERNING THE WAR POWERS OF CONGRESS AND THE PRESIDENT

October 24, 1973

To the House of Representatives:

I hereby return without my approval House Joint Resolution 542—the War Powers Resolution. While I am in accord with the desire of the Congress to assert its proper role in the conduct of our foreign affairs, the restrictions which this resolution would impose upon the authority of the President are both unconstitutional and dangerous to the best interests of our Nation.

The proper roles of the Congress and the Executive in the conduct of foreign affairs have been debated since the founding of our country. Only recently, however, has there been a serious challenge to the wisdom of the Founding Fathers in choosing not to draw a precise and detailed line of demarcation between the foreign policy powers of the two branches.

The Founding Fathers understood the impossibility of foreseeing every contingency that might arise in this complex area. They acknowledged the need for flexibility in responding to changing circumstances. They recognized that foreign policy decisions must be made through close cooperation between the two branches and not through rigidly codified procedures.

These principles remain as valid today as they were when our Constitution was written. Yet House Joint Resolution 542 would violate those principles by defining the President's powers in ways which would strictly limit his constitutional authority.

Clearly Unconstitutional

House Joint Resolution 542 would attempt to take away, by a mere legislative act, authorities which the President has properly exercised under the Constitution for almost 200 years. One of its provisions would automatically cut off certain authorities after sixty days unless the Congress extended them. Another would allow the Congress to eliminate certain authorities merely by the passage of a concurrent resolution—an action which does not normally have the force of law, since it denies the President his constitutional role in approving legislation.

I believe that both these provisions are unconstitutional. The only way in which the constitutional powers of a branch of the Government can be altered is by amending the Constitution—and any attempt to make such alterations by legislation alone is clearly without force.

Undermining Our Foreign Policy

While I firmly believe that a veto of House Joint Resolution 542 is warranted solely in the constitutional grounds, I am also deeply disturbed by the practical consequences of this resolution. For it would seriously undermine this Nation's ability to act decisively and convincingly in times of international crisis. As a result, the confidence of our allies in our ability to assist them could be diminished and the respect of our adversaries for our deterrent posture could decline. A permanent and substantial element of unpredictability would be injected into the world's assessment of American behavior, further increasing the likelihood of miscalculation and war.

If this resolution had been in operation, America's effective response to a variety of challenges in recent years would have been vastly complicated or even made impossible. We may well have been unable to respond in the way we did during the Berlin crisis of 1961, the Cuban missile crisis of 1962, the Congo rescue operation in 1964, and the Jordanian crisis of 1970—to mention just a few examples. In addition, our recent actions to bring about peaceful settlement of the hostilities in the Middle East would have been seriously impaired if this resolution had been in force.

While all the specific consequences of House Joint Resolution 542 cannot yet be predicted, it is clear that it would undercut the ability of the United States to act as an effective influence for peace. For example, the provision automatically cutting off certain authorities after 60 days unless they are extended by the Congress could work to prolong or intensify a crisis. Until the Congress suspended the deadline, there would be at least a chance of United States withdrawal and an adversary would be tempted therefore to postpone serious negotiations until the 60 days were up. Only after the Congress acted would there be a strong incentive for an adversary to negotiate. In addition, the very existence of a deadline could lead to an escalation of hostilities in order to achieve certain objectives before the 60 days expired.

The measure would jeopardize our role as a peace force in other ways as well. It would, for example, strike from the President's hand a wide range of important peace-keeping tools by eliminating his ability to exercise quiet diplomacy backed by subtle shifts in our military deployments. It would also cast into doubt authorities which Presidents have used to undertake certain humanitarian relief missions in conflict areas, to protect fishing boats from seizure, to deal with ship or aircraft hijackings, and to respond to threats of attack. Not the least of the adverse consequences of this resolution would be the prohibition contained in section 8 against fulfilling our obligations under the NATO treaty as ratified by the Senate. Finally, since the bill is somewhat vague as to when the 60-day rule would apply, it could lead to extreme confusion and dangerous disagreements concerning the prerogatives of the two branches, seriously damaging our ability to respond to international crisis.

See "Vetoing House Joint Resolution 542, A Joint Resolution Concerning the War Powers of Congress and the President, Message from the President" (24 Oct. 1973), pp. 893–894. In *Public Papers of the Presidents of the United States: Richard Nixon, 1973* (Washington, D.C.: Government Printing Office, 1973).

COMMENTS BY REPRESENTATIVE MICHAEL J. HARRINGTON (D-MASS.)

November 7, 1973

Mr. Speaker, I rise to urge the House to override the President's veto of the war powers resolution.

President Nixon's veto of House Joint Resolution 542 is the latest step in the erosion of congressional authority with regard to issues of war and peace. For the last 10 years, the American people have witnessed the unilateral commitment of American military forces to hostilities abroad by the President without prior consultation with, or authorization by, the Congress. This expansion of Presidential warmaking power has markedly increased in recent years and is reaching dangerous heights, threatening to undermine the system of checks and balances essential to our constitutional system of government. The time has come for the Congress to reassert its prerogatives and responsibilities to restore the intended balance provided for by the Constitution.

I am alarmed at the growing number of assertions of Presidential authority, both in foreign and domestic affairs. The magnitude of the coverups of illicit military activities in Laos and Cambodia, cloaked and spuriously justified in the name of national security, should impel Congress to assert its legitimate constitutional authority.

It seems to me that some clarification of the implied powers of the

President must be made in the area of warmaking powers. The Founding Fathers were keenly aware of the warmaking powers of the British monarchs and the abuses which stemmed from them. They were explicit in their intent that the power to declare war and to raise armies be left to the legislature; the President would act only as Commander in Chief after hostilities began. The commitment of American forces—except in the most critical situations which directly threaten national survival—should be taken only after full congressional and public discussion. Only through such debate can the national unity necessary to support such commitments be attained.

Mr. Speaker, the war powers resolution would do three things. First, it directs the President to consult with the Congress before and during commitment of American forces to hostilities or to situations in which hostilities may arise, and requires submission of a formal report to Congress when such actions are taken without a declaration of war. Second, the resolution denies the President authority to commit forces for more than 60 days without specific congressional approval, and permits the Congress to order the President to disengage from combat actions any time in the initial 60-day period. Legislation relating to such actions would be entitled to priority congressional consideration. Third, the resolution makes clear that it is not intended to alter the constitutional authority of either the Congress or the President, or to alter existing treaties. The reporting requirements of the resolution would take effect at the time of enactment.

Contrary to the President's position as enunciated in his veto message, I believe that this resolution is constitutional. Rather than taking away from the President's authority which is alleged to be his alone, Congress would be reasserting its intended share of its authority over the warmaking powers of the National Government. Under the Constitution, both the collective judgment of the Congress and that of the President apply to the introduction of American Armed Forces into hostilities, or into situations where there is a clear indication of imminent involvement. . . .

Neither do I believe the resolution would undermine the foreign policy of the United States. The executive branch does not have a monopoly on wisdom in matters affecting national security, and the accumulated experience of Members of Congress should be brought directly to bear on decisions affecting war and peace. By restraining irresponsible executive action, House Joint Resolution 542 is entirely consistent with the Nixon doctrine, which would help foreign nations defend themselves with supporting military aid, but reserve the commitment of American forces only when our national interests are genuinely threatened. The resolution provides the necessary flexibility for Presidential action in the advent of unforeseen circumstances, while assuring that Congress maintains its warmaking authority over the unchecked, unilateral decision of the executive branch.

Each of us has taken an oath to uphold the Constitution. Overriding this veto would help restore the lawful authority of Congress in the process of committing our Nation to war, and in that sense, uphold this oath which we have all taken. As many of our citizens continue to lose faith in our governmental institutions, we in the House must prove ourselves worthy of the trust placed in us by the people. That will require that we assume our responsibilities. For this reason, I urge each of my colleagues to join me in voting to override the President's veto.

See Rep. Michael J. Harrington (Mass.). *Congressional Record* 119, pt. 28 (7 Nov. 1973), pp. 36214–36215.

RECOMMENDED READINGS

Bundy, William P. *A Tangled Web: The Making of Foreign Policy in the Nixon Presidency.* New York: Hill and Wang, 1998.

Emery, Fred. *Watergate: The Corruption of American Politics and the Fall of Richard Nixon.* New York: Times Books, 1994.

Flippen, J. Brooks. *Nixon and the Environment.* Albuquerque: University of New Mexico Press, 2000.

Kimball, Jeffrey P. *Nixon's Vietnam War.* Lawrence: University Press of Kansas, 1998.

Kutler, Stanley I., ed. *Abuse of Power: The New Nixon Tapes.* New York: Free Press, 1997.

Matusow, Allen J. *Nixon's Economy: Booms, Busts, Dollars, and Votes.* Lawrence: University Press of Kansas, 1998.

Miller, Roger LeRoy, and Raburn M. Williams. *The New Economics of Richard Nixon: Freezes, Floats, and Fiscal Policy.* New York: Harper's Magazine Press, 1972.

Thornton, Richard C. *Nixon-Kissinger Years: Reshaping America's Foreign Policy.* St. Paul, Minn.: Paragon House Publishers, 2001.

Gerald Ford

(1974–1977)

INTRODUCTION

The Watergate affair, culminating with the resignation of President Nixon, has long been credited with permanently changing the outlook of Americans toward their government and elected officials. The abuse of power demonstrated by the Nixon administration coupled with the social upheaval of the Vietnam War left the American public less trusting of government and more suspicious of politicians. The media, too, experienced a similar change, demonstrating much greater willingness to scrutinize the actions and motivations of government officials. Unfortunately for Gerald Ford, President Nixon had left the presidency in a weakened position relative to the Congress. After the shame of his resignation, members of Congress were ready to reign in the "imperial presidency" that had expanded out of control during Nixon's tenure in office. This convergence of events and negative sentiments toward the presidency did not bode well for Gerald Ford, who as vice president, had assumed the office after Richard Nixon's resignation.

Ford was inaugurated into office on August 9, 1974. Notwithstanding the events surrounding his assumption of office, President Ford also had the dubious distinction of becoming the only president who had not been elected to the office, further weakening his position relative to the Congress. Ford had been appointed to serve as vice president under Richard Nixon when Spiro Agnew resigned from the office in October 1973 in the midst of his own scandal. Thus, he did not come to the office having won a popular election, which would have conferred the appearance of a public mandate. Thus, given his status as an "appointed" president and a successor to the only president to resign from office, President Ford's hope that the country's "long national nightmare" was over was not fully realized during his administration.

Ford held the office of the presidency for just over three years, which is not much time to set or achieve many policy goals. For the most part, Ford was saddled with "cleaning up" after President Nixon, closing the chapters on both Watergate and Vietnam. In this chapter, eight of Ford's policies will be considered; of these eight, five are directly or indirectly related to either Watergate or Vietnam. These five include the pardon of Richard Nixon, the clemency of Vietnam war resisters, the evacuation of Vietnam, the rescue of the SS *Mayaguez*, and the CIA's use of electronic surveillance techniques against American citizens. The remaining three issues were Ford's anti-inflationary policies ("Whip Inflation Now"), the federal loan program to New York City to prevent the city's bankruptcy, and an international agreement signed at Helsinki, Finland, referred to as the Helsinki Accords.

Ford's first act as president was to pardon Richard Nixon for all offenses against the United States. In his proclamation of pardon, Ford outlined his rationale for pardoning a president who had evidently violated the law while serving in the highest office in the country. He believed the pardon was necessary to bring closure to Watergate. An editorial in the *New York Times* captured the public's disapproval of the decision, arguing that the president needed to demonstrate his commitment to a rule of law rather than making decisions that obviously favor elites. In a related decision, President Ford offered a policy of clemency to resisters of the Vietnam War, including draft dodgers and military deserters. Unlike the absolute nature of Nixon's pardon, the clemency program required all resisters to perform up to two years of community service to "earn" their pardon. The policy satisfied few: some critics believed that the president hadn't gone far enough in his pardon of resisters; others didn't believe resisters should be absolved from their violation of the Selective Service laws at all. Henry Schwarzschild, director of the Project on Amnesty for the American Civil Liberties Union, testified in a hearing in the House of Representatives that the president's policy accomplished very little and that the only just approach was to offer a full pardon.

In August 1974, President Ford presented his plan to address the country's continuing problems with inflation. Ford punctuated his call for reforms with the symbolic gesture of donning a button with the acronym "WIN" emblazoned across the front, standing for "Whip Inflation Now." While the president's plan did involve some substantive proposals, the foundation of the plan was to boost the morale of the country and encourage the public to curb their own actions that were contributing to inflation. This psychological approach to remedying the ills of the economy was criticized by Democrats and Republicans alike. An article in *Newsweek* magazine referred to the president's plan as a "placebo," in that it might make the public feel better, but that it didn't solve any real problems.

Domestic problems, such as the faltering economy, were hardly the only issues faced by President Ford. The events of April and May 1975 demonstrated the demands foreign and defense policy placed on the president. In April, Ford called for the removal of the remaining Americans in South Vietnam when it became evident that the North Vietnamese were taking the capital city of Saigon. The president used American troops to remove the Americans as well as the Vietnamese who were allied with the United States. Because this maneuver came on the heels of congressional passage of the War Powers Resolution in 1973, the Subcommittee on International Security and Scientific Affairs of the House Committee on International Relations met to examine the president's compliance with the Act. Representative Stephen J. Solarz (D-N.Y.) challenged the president, noting that he had previously stated that he would seek congressional approval before using troops in the event of an evacuation. Because Congress had not yet voted on the matter, Solarz argued that the president had overstepped the bound of his office by deciding to deploy troops to the extent that they were used in the evacuation of Saigon. A mere one month later, President Ford's actions were reviewed again in light of the War Powers Resolution, when he used excessive force to rescue the crew of a small commercial ship that was captured by the Cambodians. He argued that the display of force was necessary to quell any other attempts on Americans, but an editorial in *The Nation* magazine argued that the response was overblown and unwarranted.

On August 1, 1975, President Ford offered his support to the Final Act of the Conference on Security and Cooperation in Europe, which he signed in Helsinki, Finland. The Helsinki Accords, as the agreement was called, were designed to create an air of cooperation and security among thirty-three European nations, the United States, and Canada. The two primary considerations were the recognition of Soviet control of the Baltic states of Latvia, Estonia, and Lithuania and the support of human rights in the countries signing the agreement. Yet, while the president signed the agreement, there were those who did not believe that the executive branch did enough to monitor the condition of human rights in other countries, the Soviet Union in particular. Representative Frank Annunzio (D-Ill.) argued that the Congress should take on this responsibility, even if leadership wasn't forthcoming from the president. The House of Representatives also voted for a resolution expressing its unwillingness to recognize the Soviet Union's control over the Baltic States.

Another issue considered in this section is Ford's proposal of a federal loan program to help prevent the bankruptcy of New York City. The case illustrates the president's willingness to change his position in the face of changing circumstances and political pressure. Ford initially had not supported any role for the federal government in assisting New York City with its financial problems. However, when both the state and city of New York demonstrated a willingness to remedy the problem, the president changed his position and advocated that the Congress provide a series on loans to New York to help the city meet its short-term needs. Critics fell on both sides of the issues, with some people wanting to do more for the city and others believing the national government was opening the floodgates to more cities and states asking for a handout. Representative Robert W. Kasten (R-Wisc.) advocated this position in his comments before the House of Representatives.

Finally, the president spearheaded a policy that would place greater restrictions on the Central Intelligence Agency in its use of electronic surveillance against American citizens. When it was discovered that war protestors were routinely spied on by the CIA, the president advanced a proposal that would limit the types of surveillance the CIA could perform and set guidelines for the use of technology against American citizens. Representative Robert F. Drinan (D-Mass.), a Catholic priest, was opposed to the president's plan, arguing that it did not adequately protect Americans and that it left the door open to undesirable spying activities.

PRESIDENT FORD PARDONS RICHARD NIXON

After the humiliating resignation of Richard Nixon, President Ford had the awesome task of serving as president while also attempting to rebuild the nation's trust in the presidency. In his remarks after taking the oath of office on August 9, 1974, in which he claimed that "our long national nightmare is over," he attempted to set the tone for his term of office, praising the rule of law yet also calling for mercy from the American people. Ford, in one of his first acts as president, would discover that these two principles can be hard to reconcile.

On September 8, 1974, less than a month after assuming office, President Ford gave Richard Nixon an absolute pardon for any offenses he may have committed while in office. In short, this meant that Richard Nixon would never have to stand trial for any crimes he may have committed as president and would still receive the benefits of being a former president, such as receiving a presidential pension. Without a pardon, Nixon would likely have stood trial for obstruction of justice and illegal campaign finance activity, among other crimes. In what was certainly an agonizing decision on his part, President Ford had to balance his respect for the rule of law with the need to do what he thought was right in this particular circumstance. Doing what was "right" was not necessarily easy to discern; he had no guidance from past decisions to help him since there were no similar situations on which to model his decision.

Ironically, many other people who were involved in Watergate did stand trial and a number of them served prison terms for their involvement. President Nixon, who served as the country's highest elected official during the time of his misdeeds, was the only person involved in the Watergate affair to be completely exonerated for his involvement. Despite Ford's explanation that a pardon was the best means of achieving justice in this case, many people did not agree with his concept of justice, arguing instead that fairness required Nixon to also stand trial for his offenses. An editorial in the *New York Times* made this argument, stating that as the president, Ford's concerns for justice must be directed toward the American public and that justice, in this case, could only be achieved by following the rule of law.

Ford's calls for mercy appeared to ring particularly hollow when, a mere eight days later, he announced a limited clemency program for Vietnam draft evaders and military deserters, a program that required war resisters to take an oath of allegiance to the United States and perform up to two years of public service in exchange for the grant of clemency. With this decision following the Nixon pardon so closely, it gave the appearance that only a former president warranted full mercy, while mercy for others was bestowed only conditionally, or not at all.

The apparent inconsistency in meting out justice was not the only criticism levied against Ford. There was some concern, which was alluded to in the *New York Times* editorial, that Nixon and Ford had negotiated a deal before Nixon's resignation that would have secured Nixon's pardon after Ford assumed the office. The House Committee on the Judiciary held hearings on this and other issues related to Watergate beginning in late September, less than a month after the pardon was issued. In an unprecedented act, President Ford testified before the Committee where he acknowledged that Alexander Haig, Nixon's chief of staff, had presented him with a deal that would have involved a pardon for Nixon in exchange for his resignation. When asked about his response to this plan, Ford replied, "There was no deal. Period. Under no circumstances." Given Ford's reputation while in Congress and his apparent concern with issues of character, it appears unlikely that the pardon was granted in exchange for Nixon's resignation. However, the questions and doubts raised about the basis of Ford's decision relegated the pardon to the status of being yet another scandalous decision related to Watergate, rather than, as Ford hoped, being its end.

FORD'S REMARKS ON PARDONING RICHARD NIXON

Address from the Oval Office, September 8, 1974

Ladies and Gentlemen:

I have come to a decision which I felt I should tell you and all my fellow American citizens, as soon as I was certain in my own mind and in my own conscience that it is the right thing to do.

I have learned already in this office that the difficult decisions always come to this desk. I must admit that many of them do not look at all the same as the hypothetical questions that I have answered freely and perhaps too fast on previous occasions.

My customary policy is to try and get all the facts and to consider the opinions of my countrymen and to take counsel with my most valued friends. But these seldom agree, and in the end, the decision is mine. To procrastinate, to agonize, and to wait for a more favorable turn of events that may never come or more compelling external pressures that may as well be wrong as right, is itself a decision of sorts and a weak and potentially dangerous course for a President to follow.

I have promised to uphold the Constitution, to do what is right as God gives me to see the right, and to do the very best that I can for America.

I have asked your help and your prayers, not only when I became President but many times since. The Constitution is the supreme law of our land and it governs our actions as citizens. Only the laws of God, which govern our consciences, are superior to it.

As we are a nation under God, so I am sworn to uphold our laws with the help of God. And I have sought such guidance and searched my own conscience with special diligence to determine the right thing for me to do with respect to my predecessor in this place, Richard Nixon, and his loyal wife and family.

Theirs is an American tragedy in which we all have played a part. It could go on and on and on, or someone must write the end to it. I have concluded that only I can do that, and if I can, I must.

There are no historic or legal precedents to which I can turn in this matter, none that precisely fit the circumstances of a private citizen who has resigned the Presidency of the United States. But it is common knowledge that serious allegations and accusations hang like a sword over our former President's head, threatening his health as he tries to reshape his life, a great part of which was spent in the service of this country and by the mandate of its people.

After years of bitter controversy and divisive national debate, I have been advised, and I am compelled to conclude that many months and perhaps more years will have to pass before Richard Nixon could obtain a fair trial by jury in any jurisdiction of the United States under governing decisions of the Supreme Court.

I deeply believe in equal justice for all Americans, whatever their situation or former station. The law, whether human or divine, is no respecter of persons; but the law is a respecter of reality.

The facts, as I see them, are that a former President of the United States, instead of enjoying equal treatment with any other citizen accused of violating the law, would be cruelly and excessively penalized either in preserving the presumption of his innocence or in obtaining a speedy determination of his guilt in order to repay a legal debt to society.

During this long period of delay and potential litigation, ugly passions would again be aroused. And our people would again be polarized in their opinions. And the credibility of our free institutions of government would again be challenged at home and abroad.

In the end, the courts might well hold that Richard Nixon had been denied due process, and the verdict of history would even more be inconclusive with respect to those charges arising out of the period of his Presidency, of which I am presently aware.

But it is not the ultimate fate of Richard Nixon that most concerns me, though surely it deeply troubles every decent and every compassionate person. My concern is the immediate future of this great country.

In this, I dare not depend upon my personal sympathy as a long-time friend of the former President, nor my professional judgment as a lawyer, and I do not.

As President, my primary concern must always be the greatest good of all the people of the United States whose servant I am. As a man, my first consideration is to be true to my own convictions and my own conscience.

My conscience tells me clearly and certainly that I cannot prolong the bad dreams that continue to reopen a chapter that is closed. My conscience tells me that only I, as President, have the constitutional power to firmly shut and seal this book. My conscience tells me it is my duty, not merely to proclaim domestic tranquility but to use every means that I have to ensure it.

I do believe that the buck stops here, that I cannot rely upon public opinion polls to tell me what is right.

I do believe that right makes might and that if I am wrong, 10 angels swearing I was right would make no difference.

I do believe, with all my heart and mind and spirit, that I, not as President but as a humble servant of God, will receive justice without mercy if I fail to show mercy.

Finally, I feel that Richard Nixon and his loved ones have suffered enough and will continue to suffer, no matter what I do, no matter what we, as a great and good nation, can do together to make his goal of peace come true.

Now, therefore, I, Gerald R. Ford, President of the United States, pursuant to the pardon power conferred upon me by Article II, Section 2, of the Constitution, have granted and by these presents do grant a full, free, and absolute pardon unto Richard Nixon for all offenses against the United States which he, Richard Nixon, has committed or may have committed or taken part in during the period from July (January) 20, 1969 through August 9, 1974.

In witness whereof, I have hereunto set my hand this eighth day of September, in the year of our Lord nineteen hundred and seventy-four, and of the Independence of the United States of America the one hundred and ninety-ninth.

See "Remarks on Signing a Proclamation Granting Pardon to Richard Nixon" (8 Sept. 1974), pp. 101–103. In *Public Papers of the Presidents of the United States: Gerald Ford, 1974* (Washington, D.C.: Government Printing Office, 1974).

"THE FAILURE OF MR. FORD"

Editorial in the *New York Times*
September 9, 1974

In giving former President Nixon an inappropriate and premature grant of clemency, President Ford has affronted the Constitution and the American system of justice. It is a profoundly unwise, divisive and unjust act.

Like many lesser public figures who have commented at various stages of the long Watergate controversy, President Ford has sadly confused his responsibilities to the Republic and his understandable sentiments toward one who has inflicted grave damage upon the body politic. Both are valid and compelling but they should be clearly distinguished.

The four reasons that President Ford cites for his decision lay bare this confusion. In summary, he asserts that Mr. Nixon has already suffered enough; an adjudication of his offenses would be divisive; a fair trial would be difficult to achieve; and ultimately, in any event, he—Mr. Ford—would have to decide the matter in the light of his own conscience and sense of compassion.

The adjudication of Mr. Nixon's offenses and the character of the criminal trial in which those offenses would be weighed and argued are one set of concerns. Mr. Nixon's suffering and his claims on President Ford's conscience as a political sponsor, friend and fellow human being are another set of concerns.

President Ford's overriding duty was to his public responsibilities. It is essential that the crimes committed by several of Mr. Nixon's closest associates and apparently by Mr. Nixon himself be determined in a court of law by the same rules of evidence and the same procedures of due process that apply in the American system of justice to every citizen.

Nothing less would satisfy the natural sense of justice of the American people and of a Government founded upon principles of equality and legality. Given the historic significance of Mr. Nixon's offenses that led to his becoming the first President ever to resign, it was essential that the historical record by unmistakably clear.

After the exact nature of the wounds that Mr. Nixon and his associates had inflicted upon the nation had been determined and after the exoneration of conviction of those accused, only then could those wounds begin to heal. Once the processes of justice had run their course, it would be possible and timely for the President and the nation to take into account the personal merits of the offenders and try to mitigate the penalties of law by recourse to the enduring human values of mercy and charity. If clemency had followed conviction rather than preceded it, there would have been wide acceptance of President Ford's exercise of his power to pardon.

As it is, by recklessly pushing aside special prosecutor Leon Jaworski and the grand jury and the trial jury as well, President Ford has failed in his duty to the Republic, made a mockery of the claim of equal justice before the law, promoted renewed public discord, made possible the clouding of the historical record, and undermined the humane values he sought to invoke.

His duty was to see that the law was enforced and wrongdoers punished. His duty was to see to it that those who have already served time in prison for their crimes such as E. Howard Hunt, Donald Segretti and Egil Krogh; those now serving their sentences such as Charles Colson and John W. Dean, 3d; and those who stand accused of grave crimes such as H.R. Haldeman, John N. Mitchell and Mr. Nixon himself would all be treated the same.

Instead, he has laid American jurisprudence open to the severe and lingering accusation that there is one kind of justice for the agents and underlings and another for the ex-President in whose name and for whose supposed benefit the misdeeds were committed.

President Ford speaks of compassion. It is tragic that he had no compassion and concern for the Constitution and the Government of law that he has sworn to uphold and defend. He could probably have taken no single act of a non-criminal nature that would have more gravely damaged the credibility of this Government in the eyes of the world and of its own people than this unconscionable act of pardon.

Rather than calm public passions and restore a fundamental sense of national unity, Mr. Ford has ignited fresh controversy. How bitter that controversy is sure to become was shown by the immediate resignation in protest of the President's own press secretary, J. F. terHorst, acting as "a matter of conscience." It might have stirred less public outrage if the President, in what amounted to secret and discreditable plea bargaining with his predecessor, had insisted on a frank and forthright confession of guilt. Instead he settled for an unctuous, guileful statement from Mr. Nixon in which the former President admits nothing specific and skillfully blurs the issues. The Justice Department's deal with former Vice President Agnew last year was seriously questionable; yesterday's arrangement sinks below even that poor precedent. . . .

In a time when the nation has been repeatedly dismayed by so many acts of corruption, intrigue and deceit, President Ford has signally failed to provide courageous and impartial moral leadership.

See "The Failure of Mr. Ford," *New York Times*, September 9, 1974, p. 34.

CLEMENCY FOR VIETNAM DRAFT EVADERS AND MILITARY DESERTERS

It is an understatement to say that the Vietnam War was a tremendously divisive issue in the United States. The war itself, plus the question of whether or not the United States should be involved in Southeast Asia at all, was the overarching issue that plagued the country, but other related issues arose that contributed to the controversy over the war. In particular, the draft system, which required young men to serve in the military when there were not enough volunteers, came under harsh criticism from various fronts. Between 1964 and 1973, all men between the ages of 18 and 26 were required to register with the Selective Service System for potential service in Vietnam. In all, 1,766,910 men were drafted during this period to serve in the war.

While all young men had to register, not all had to serve. A lottery system was instituted in December 1969 to determine the order of draft selection. The lottery consisted of a random drawing of every date of the year, with every date being assigned a number in the order in which it was selected, and men between the ages of 18 and 26 whose birthday was on that date were required to report for service. The dates were considered in the order of their drawing until the military had the necessary number of men. The process of drawing the dates was quite dramatic, with each date secured in a small, blue plastic capsule, drawn from a jar one by one, and announced over the national radio and television stations. The later a particular birthdate was drawn, the less chance a man born on that date had of being drafted. This process was repeated every year until 1973.

Not all people drafted ultimately served in Vietnam. For instance, there were numerous legal exceptions afforded in the Selective Service regulations, such as exemptions for conscientious objectors and deferments for college students. There were others who were drafted yet refused to serve. Often opposition to the draft fell along moral lines, arguing that both the war itself and the draft system were immoral acts of the U.S. government and that compliance with these acts was tantamount to approval. Although resistance was a violation of the law, for most war resisters it was preferable to participating in the injustice they witnessed, both at home and in Southeast Asia. Draft cards were burned in protest and many resisters moved to Canada to avoid being sent to Vietnam.

While many people sympathized with the sentiments of the resisters, others believed that they were shirking their duty to the country. There was considerable resentment among those people who had been drafted and chosen to serve. Veterans' groups opposed any leniency, portraying resisters as being spoiled and in need of punishment for their lack of patriotism and service. Opposition to the war had grown, however, among the American public, and opponents' disillusionment with the war and the American government in general manifested itself in a call for leniency for the resisters. The extreme views on the issue ranged from prosecuting resisters to the president providing a complete pardon for their crimes. President Ford, in his desire to balance these two views, settled on a middle ground: clemency for the resisters.

President Ford's clemency plan allowed draft dodgers and military deserters to earn their clemency by performing up to two years of community service. Individuals seeking clemency were also required to take an oath of allegiance to the United States, an act critics noted was not required of President Nixon for him to receive a complete pardon. It was President Ford's hope that a clemency program with a service component would strike a balance between those people who advocated a complete pardon for military resisters and those who favored no leniency at all shown toward resisters. What it accomplished, instead, was criticism from both sides. It did not bring the reconciliation to the American people that Ford had hoped.

By most measures, the policy was not a success. Of the approximately 130,000 people who were declared eligible to receive clemency, only 23,000 even applied. Henry Schwarzschild, director of the Project on Amnesty for the American Civil Liberties Union, testified before a subcommittee of the House Committee on the Judiciary about the limitations and problems associated with the president's plan. It was his argument that the plan provided very little incentive for resisters to seek clemency, due to the very limited nature of the policy and the fact that clemency was granted with "strings" attached. In addition to the obvious failure of the plan based on the small numbers of people applying for clemency, he also argued that the plan was a failure morally. He asserted that true healing after the Vietnam War would come only if a complete amnesty were granted to resisters. In January 1977, President Jimmy Carter did grant a complete amnesty to war resisters.

PRESIDENT FORD'S REMARKS ANNOUNCING A PROGRAM FOR THE RETURN OF VIETNAM-ERA DRAFT EVADERS AND MILITARY DESERTERS

White House, September 16, 1974

Good Morning:

In my first week as President, I asked the Attorney General and the Secretary of Defense to report to me, after consultation with other Governmental officials and private citizens concerned, on the status of those young Americans who have been convicted, charged, investigated, or are still being sought as draft evaders or military deserters.

On August 19, at the national convention of Veterans of Foreign Wars in the city of Chicago, I announced my intention to give these young people a chance to earn their return to the mainstream of American society so that they can, if they choose, contribute, even though belatedly, to the building and the betterment of our country and the world.

I did this for the simple reason that for American fighting men, the long and divisive war in Vietnam has been over for more than a year, and I was determined then, as now, to do everything in my power to bind up the Nation's wounds.

I promised to throw the weight of my Presidency into the scales of justice on the side of leniency and mercy, but I promised also to work within the existing system of military and civilian law and the precedents set by my predecessors who faced similar postwar situations, among them Presidents Abraham Lincoln and Harry S. Truman.

My objective of making future penalties fit the seriousness of each individual's offense and of mitigating punishment already meted out in a spirit of equity has proved an immensely hard and very complicated matter, even more difficult than I knew it would be.

But the agencies of Government concerned and my own staff have worked with me literally night and day in order to develop fair and orderly procedures and completed their work for my final approval over this last weekend.

I do not want to delay another day in resolving the dilemmas of the past, so that we may all get going on the pressing problems of the present. Therefore, I am today signing the necessary Presidential proclamation and Executive orders that will put this plan into effect.

The program provides for administrative disposition of cases involving draft evaders and military deserters not yet convicted or punished. In such cases, 24 months of alternative service will be required, which may be reduced for mitigating circumstances.

The program also deals with cases of those already convicted by a civilian or military court. For the latter purposes, I am establishing a clemency review board of nine distinguished Americans whose duty it will be to assist me in assuring that the Government's forgiveness is extended to applicable cases of prior conviction as equitably and as impartially as humanly possible.

The primary purpose of this program is the reconciliation of all our people and the restoration of the essential unity of Americans within which honest differences of opinion do not descend to angry discord and mutual problems are not polarized by excessive passion.

My sincere hope is that this is a constructive step toward a calmer and cooler appreciation of our individual rights and responsibilities and our common purpose as a nation whose future is always more important than its past.

At this point, I will sign the proclamation [4313] that I mentioned in my statement, followed by an Executive order [11803] for the establishment of the Clemency Board, followed by the signing of an executive order [11804] for the Director of Selective Service, who will have a prime responsibility in the handling of the matters involving alternate service.

Thank you very much.

See "Remarks Announcing a Program for the Return of Vietnam-Era Draft Evaders and Military Deserters" (16 Sept. 1974), pp. 136–137. In *Public Papers of the Presidents of the United States: Gerald Ford, 1974* (Washington, D.C.: Government Printing Office, 1974).

STATEMENT OF HENRY SCHWARZSCHILD, DIRECTOR, PROJECT ON AMNESTY, AMERICAN CIVIL LIBERTIES UNION

Hearings before the House Subcommittee on Courts, Civil Liberties, and the Administration of Justice of the Committee on the Judiciary
April 18, 1975

The Clemency Program instituted by President Ford by his Proclamation of September 16, 1974, is not an amnesty and was not intended to be an amnesty. It is, to the very contrary, an expression of the war policies of this and the prior Republican and Democratic administrations. With its punitive and demeaning provisions, its exclusion of most of those who need amnesty, its morass of conflicting standards and procedures, its administration by four governmental agencies that are hostile to the fundamental moral commitments of the war resisters, the Presidential Clemency Program is designed to reaffirm that the war in Southeast Asia was right and that those who refused to participate in it are the criminals of the Vietnam era. The Clemency Program says that the government, in its generous humanity, will lessen the punishment due to the war resisters below what the law otherwise might have imposed, but it insists upon punishment so that the horrible past shall stand validated. It permits the government that inflicted the horrors of that war upon Asians and Americans alike the self-satisfaction of claiming to be generous and humane. The Clemency Program is rather like the spectacle of the Vietnamese children, who were made into orphans by us, being virtually kidnapped to the United States in a demonstration of the benign humanity of the American government.

The Clemency Program offers its peculiar remedies only to a very small proportion of those in need of amnesty: to some of the draft violators, to some of the military deserters, to some few of those with less-than-honorable discharges, and to none of the other categories of people at all. Of the estimated 750,000 people in need of a post-Vietnam amnesty, perhaps 130,000 were declared eligible for the Presidential Clemency. Of those who were eligible, 80% chose not even to apply for clemency, despite massive publicity and persuasion. Of the 23,000 that did apply, most stand to gain absolutely nothing whatever from the Program, as we shall show in a moment.

The Clemency Program is a failure, not only in terms of statistics. Its failure lies fundamentally in the moral and political assumptions that gave birth to it, and its failure lies in the unresolved problem of war resistance and the lives of thousands of men and women who had the courage to defy the might and power of the United States by saying NO to what they saw then—as we all see now—to be a monumental national and international disaster.

No extension, no tinkering with the Clemency Program's mechanism, no self-serving statements from its administrators about their fairness will change that failure into success. A universal and unconditional amnesty would not accomplish much. Such a true amnesty would not end poverty or racial bigotry or war. It would not even restore to GIs their lives or their limbs or the years they gave to that war not would it give back to the war resisters the years spent in prison or exile or underground, the pain of separation from family and friends. But amnesty would be doing what we can do—and therefore must do—to end hurt and victimization arising from the war among ourselves and it would say that this country will live in peace with those who wanted it to live in peace with the world. That would be a noble act. We have not had many noble acts from our government in a long time. We would be well served by such an amnesty.

See U.S. House. Committee on the Judiciary. *Presidential Clemency Program.* Hearing, 14, 17, 18 April 1975, 94th Cong. 1st sess. (Washington, D.C.: Government Printing Office, 1975), pp. 134–135.

"WHIP INFLATION NOW"

In spite of President Nixon's efforts to curb inflation using wage and price controls during his administration, rising inflation continued to plague the nation's economy through President Ford's term in office. Unfortunately, the economy was also still in a recession, with high unemployment rates and a related slowdown in the construction of new houses and automobile purchases between 1973 and 1976. As the new president, Ford was faced with having to recommend policies to address these economic problems, yet as had been the case with President Nixon, remedies to such wide-ranging problems were not easy to develop.

One tactic considered by Ford was to rein in some of the more costly programs funded by Congress. President Nixon had attempted to do this by impounding the funds already appropriated by Congress, but his use of impoundment had provoked controversy among lawmakers and had been deemed unconstitutional by the federal courts, at least to the extent that Nixon had impounded funds. Ford wanted to distance himself from his ill-fated predecessor, however, and chose instead to use his veto power to curtail congressional spending. When Congress submitted bills that included appropriations above the level Ford thought was prudent for the American economy, he would simply veto the bill, refusing to sign it into law.

The veto is a powerful tool at the president's disposal. Theoretically, it should only be used as a last resort. The president's ultimate objective is to persuade Congress to adopt his policy goals as legislation is drafted, so that by the time a bill reaches his desk, he has already had some influence on its creation and final shape, and can sign it into law. When Congress chooses to disregard the president's objectives, the president must either sign a bill he doesn't particularly like or veto it, sending it back to Congress with an explanation as to why the bill was rejected. If a president vetoes legislation often, it may signal that the president has little influence in Congress. In his attempt to keep inflation down and cut government spending, President Ford chose to veto over fifty pieces of legislation in his two and a half years as president.

Although he was forced to use his veto power often, Ford did submit an economic recovery plan to the Congress in an attempt to curb the rising rate of inflation and stimulate new economic growth, including tax increases and cuts in federal spending. While much of the plan was aimed at the federal budget and tax structure, one portion of the proposal relied more heavily on the good will of the American people to adjust their behavior in ways that would bring down inflation. In a televised address, President Ford requested that the American people send in ideas to help cut government spending and inflation, and in an appeal to the public to "Whip Inflation Now," Ford donned a lapel pin emblazoned with the acronym, "WIN" to represent his new slogan. The pins were made available to the public, but the White House only received requests from 100,000 people, leaving unclaimed a vast majority of the 12 million pins produced for the campaign.

On its best face, Ford's proposals seemed folksy and naive, while at worst, it appeared to be a public relations stunt. The simple appeal to the "American spirit" to counter the country's significant economic travails appeared incompetent and ineffectual and both Republicans and Democrats criticized his proposals, claiming that something more specific and ambitious was needed to put a dent in the rate of inflation. The media, too, was not kind to Ford's proposal. An editorial in the *New York Times* likened Ford's proposals to a placebo, in that any effect it would have on the economy would be caused simply by people believing it would have an effect, not because the plan itself actually had any influence on the economy. Ford did not appear particularly wedded to his plan, either. Only months later, in his State of the Union address, Ford advocated substantial tax cuts, a complete reversal of the plan he had proposed in September of 1974.

FORD'S CONCLUDING REMARKS AT THE SUMMIT CONFERENCE ON INFLATION

September 28, 1974

The most important weapon in the fight against inflation is the spirit of the American people. This spirit is no secret weapon; it is renowned all over the world. And I call on each of you in this room, but more urgently, on each of you at home watching on television and all the other Americans across this vast land who either hear or read my words, I urge them, as I know they will, to join with all of us in a great effort to become inflation fighters and energy savers.

I know all across our country the question everyone asks me is, "What can I do to help?"

I will tell you how we can start. Right now, make a list of some 10 ways you can save energy and you can fight inflation. Little things that become habits—they do become habits—they don't really affect, in some instances, your health and happiness. They are habits that you can abandon if we are all faced with this emergency.

I suggest that each person exchange your family's list with your neighbors, and I urge you and ask you to send me a copy. Some of the best ideas come from your home rather than from the White House. The success or failure of our fight against inflation rests with every individual American. Our country is above all a union, and you and I can make it a more perfect union as our fathers did.

One of our delegates yesterday, Sylvia Porter, the well-known newspaper columnist on economics, has kindly consented to help me get this voluntary citizens program organized and underway, and I thank you very, very much, Sylvia.

It was dramatically pointed out here yesterday that inflation strikes our society very unevenly. Government must concern itself with those on whom the burden falls excessively. For instance, we must provide productive work for those without jobs. We must adjust our tax system to encourage savings, stimulate productivity, discourage excessive debt, and to correct inflation-caused inequities. And I can assure the American people that the executive branch and the Congress working together will effectuate and implement such a program . . .

See "Remarks Concluding the Summit Conference on Inflation" (28 Sept. 1974), pp. 208–209. In *Public Papers of the Presidents of the United States: Gerald Ford, 1974* (Washington, D.C.: Government Printing Office, 1974).

ADDRESS TO A JOINT SESSION OF THE CONGRESS ON THE ECONOMY

October 8, 1974

My fellow Americans, 10 days ago I asked you to get things started by making a list of 10 ways to fight inflation and save energy, to exchange your list with your neighbors, and to send me a copy.

I have personally read scores of the thousands of letters received at the White House, and incidentally, I have made my economic experts read some of them, too. We all benefited, at least I did, and I thank each and every one of you for this cooperation.

Some of the good ideas from your home to mine have been cranked into the recommendations I have just made to the Congress and the steps I am taking as President to whip inflation right now. There were also firm warnings on what Government must not do, and I appreciated those, too. Your best suggestions for voluntary restraint and self-discipline showed me that a great degree of patriotic determination and unanimity already exists in this great land.

I have asked Congress for urgent specific actions it alone can take. I advised Congress of the initial steps that I am taking as President. Here is what only you can do: Unless every able American pitches in, Congress and I cannot do the job. Winning our fight against inflation and waste involves total mobilization of America's greatest resources, the brains, the skills, and the willpower of the American people.

Here is what we must do, what each and every one of you can do: To help increase food and lower prices, grow more and waste less; to help save scarce fuel in the energy crisis, drive less, heat less. Every housewife knows almost exactly how much she spent for food last week. If you cannot spare a penny from your food budget—and I know there are many—surely you can cut the food that you waste by 5 percent.

Every American motorist knows exactly how many miles he or she drives to work or to school every day and about how much mileage she or he runs up each year. If we all drive at least 5 percent fewer miles, we can save, almost unbelievably, 250,000 barrels of foreign oil per day. By the end of 1975, most of us can do better than 5 percent by carpooling, taking the bus, riding bikes, or just plain walking. We can save enough gas by self-discipline to meet our 1 million barrels per day goal.

I think there is one final thing that all Americans can do, rich or poor, and that is share with others. We can share burdens as we can share blessings. Sharing is not easy, not easy to measure like mileage and family budgets, but I am sure that 5 percent more is not nearly enough to ask, so I ask you to share everything you can and a little bit more. And it will strengthen our spirits as well as our economy.

See "Address to a Joint Session of the Congress on the Economy" (8 Oct. 1974), pp. 236–237. In *Public Papers of the Presidents of the United States: Gerald Ford, 1974* (Washington, D.C.: Government Printing Office, 1974).

"FORD'S RX: A PLACEBO"

Newsweek
October 21, 1974

From his arrival in the White House, Gerald Ford had known that inflation could be his toughest problem—"public enemy No. 1." In a long drum roll of conferences ending with a mass meeting in Washington of nearly everybody on the economic scene, Ford sought counsel on what to do. And when he went before a joint session of Congress last week to announce his long-awaited economic program, he paraphrased Franklin D. Roosevelt in the depths of the 1933 crisis. "Our constituents want leadership," he said. "Our constituents want action."

The results hardly justified the rhetoric. What Ford offered was a committee-designed package of economic compromises with something for everybody and, in the final analysis, very little hard action against inflation. As expected, he proposed a 5 percent surtax on corporations and middle to upper-income individuals and said that revenue would be used to offset investment incentives and pay for extended unemployment benefits and a limited WPA-style public-service jobs program. He asked Congress to pare back the current Federal budget to $300 billion. In the crucial field of energy conservation, he offered up a series of largely voluntary measures ranging from cold-water laundering to bicycling. And he led a cheer for his new economic game plan, pinning to the Presidential lapel a red-and-white button lettered WIN—an acronym for Whip Inflation Now.

There was one loud answering cheer from Wall Street, where the Dow Jones industrials soared 45.45 points in the next two days and brokers exulted, "The bear is dead!" But nobody else seemed satisfied. Democrats roundly denounced the program for its dearth of fresh ideas—"The button should have said PUNT," complained [Democratic] Sen. Walter Mondale of Minnesota—and Republicans joined them in condemning the tax surcharge as an unfair burden on the middle class. Economists gave the program mixed reviews. The New York Times's James Reston suggested that Ford had "nibbled the bullet," and The Wall Street Journal stated flatly that it was now up to Federal Reserve chairman Arthur Burns to dampen inflation. The voters had yet to express themselves, but Congress was certain to take its cue from the Nov. 5 election returns.

Caution: White House aides defended the package as a "relatively ambitious program from a guy as cautious as Ford." But in fact, it was designed to be weak—a placebo to ease the pain of stagflation while the tight-money and spending policies begun by Richard Nixon do their work. "All of Ford's policies provide the appearance of action which can at best be only marginal in economic effect," a top government economist said frankly. "But if they buy us time to let us pursue the basic work of belt-tightening, then they are probably worth it." Other aides hinted that there might be two more, successively tougher programs in store—one soon after next month's election and another in the State of the Union Message in January. And Ford himself gave warning that he might invoke sterner measures if the old-time religion failed . . .

The package drew immediate fire from both sides of the aisle. "The nation needed a strong, specific program," added Sen. James Abourezk, a South Dakota Democrat. "It got an uncoordinated mishmash of public-relations gimmickry and precious few concrete ideas." The program was so inadequate, said New Jersey's Republican Sen. Clifford Case, that "even if Congress took every action the President requests, we would be little, if at all, nearer the solution than we are today."

See "Ford's Rx: A Placebo," *Newsweek*, vol. 84, no. 17, October 21, 1974, pp. 33–34.

VIETNAM EVACUATION

By April 1975, the chances for victory in Vietnam looked dim. Although the communist North Vietnamese had not yet gained control of all of Vietnam, the fall of the country to a communist regime appeared inevitable. The number of options left to the United States was quickly waning. While the possibility of sending more money for the military support of the South Vietnamese still existed, the political environment in Washington rendered that option unlikely. The only course of action that seemed inevitable was the eventual evacuation of the remaining Americans and some Vietnamese from the country. March 30 had already witnessed a large sea-lift evacuation mission of Vietnamese refugees from the coastal area around Danang, and by early April, it seemed apparent that the evacuation of the remaining Americans was imminent.

By April 10, President Ford still had hopes that the complete fall of Vietnam could be forestalled and that a political settlement could be reached with the North Vietnamese. In an address before a joint session of Congress, he outlined what he thought were the options left for the United States. In the address, he requested that Congress consider appropriating additional funds to support the military efforts of the South Vietnamese, at the very least to stabilize their effort enough to warrant calls for a political settlement. He also requested an increased amount for the humanitarian relief of the Vietnamese as well as for the evacuation of Vietnamese supporters of the United States, the Vietnamese family members of Americans, and many of the children left orphaned by the war. Lastly, he asked that Congress grant him the authority to deploy American troops, if necessary, for the sole purpose of aiding an evacuation of Americans and the Vietnamese to whom the United States had an obligation. Given his appraisal of the situation in Vietnam, he asked that Congress quickly deal with these requests by April 19.

Speed, however, is not characteristic of the legislative process. While both the Senate and the House of Representatives did consider bills that provided additional funds for military and humanitarian assistance, the final vote on a compromise bill did not occur in the House until May 1, three days after the evacuation. The president's proposal failed, not because there was opposition to humanitarian aid, but largely because the bill included a provision that would have allowed the president to use troops in the event of an evacuation, a provision that was largely irrelevant after April 29.

When it became evident that Saigon was lost, President Ford had to act, with or without congressional authority to use troops. Ford ordered the evacuation of all remaining Americans—over 1,300 people—plus approximately 5,600 Vietnamese, using seventy military helicopters and 865 Marines to carry out the mission. Americans viewed television images of people pushing and struggling to board helicopters, even as the craft were lifting off the roofs of the American embassy and apartment buildings in Saigon. In an address to the American public, President Ford commented that the "action closes a chapter in the American experience." As is often the case with politics, however, there was a political epilogue to the closing chapter.

On May 7, 1975, the Subcommittee on International Security and Scientific Affairs of the House Committee on International Relations held the first day of hearings on President Ford's compliance with the War Powers Resolution in his use of troops in the Saigon evacuation and other cases. The hearings were held in large part as an evaluation of the War Powers Act, but the overarching question was President Ford's record in complying with the law. The Honorable Monroe Leigh, legal advisor to the Department of State, was asked to testify at the hearing to explain the position of the executive branch and to demonstrate whether and how the president had fulfilled the notification and consultation requirements in the law. Leigh explained that the president, as commander-in-chief, did have the constitutional authority to use troops for evacuation purposes, even without legislation from Congress authorizing the action.

There was no appreciable criticism of Ford's decision to evacuate Saigon; most people recognized that as a necessity, given the circumstances. However, there was criticism that the president had appeared less than forthright in his decision to use troops to evacuate such a large number of Vietnamese, as well as to evacuate at least eighty-five individuals from third countries. Representative Stephen J. Solarz (D-N.Y.) asked numerous questions of Mr. Leigh, making the point that the president had crossed the line of constitutionality and legality in using troops to the extent that they were used in the evacuation of non-Americans. Solarz also questioned the logic of Leigh's argument that the president had acted constitutionally, asking him time and again why the president had asked Congress on April 10 to grant him authority to use troops, when, after the evacuation was already accomplished, the president then claimed that he had the power to do so, even in absence of legislation. While discussion in the hearing remained courteous and largely framed in terms of the legality of the president's actions, there were other members of Congress who spoke much more pointedly about their opposition to the large number of Vietnamese refugees who were removed in the evacuation, many of whom were brought to the United States.

FORD'S ADDRESS ON U.S. FOREIGN POLICY BEFORE A JOINT SESSION OF THE CONGRESS

April 10, 1975

The situation in South Vietnam and Cambodia has reached a critical phase requiring immediate and positive decisions by this Government. The options before us are few and the time is very short.

On the one hand, the United States could do nothing more; let the Government of South Vietnam save itself and what is left of its territory, if it can; let those South Vietnamese civilians who have worked with us for a decade or more save their lives and their families, if they can; in short, shut our eyes and wash our hands of the whole affair—if we can.

Or, on the other hand, I could ask the Congress for authority to enforce the Paris accords with our troops and our tanks and our aircraft and our artillery and carry the war to the enemy.

There are two narrower options:

First, stick with my January request that Congress appropriate $300 million for military assistance for South Vietnam and seek additional funds for economic and humanitarian purposes.

Or, increase my requests for both emergency military and humanitarian assistance to levels which, by best estimates, might enable the South Vietnamese to stem the onrushing aggression, to stabilize the military situation, permit the chance of a negotiated political settlement between the North and South Vietnamese, and if the very worst were to happen, at least allow the orderly evacuation of Americans and endangered South Vietnamese to places of safety.

Let me now state my considerations and my conclusions.

I have received a full report from General Weyand, whom I sent to Vietnam to assess the situation. He advises that the current military situation is very critical, but that South Vietnam is continuing to defend itself with the resources available. However, he feels that if there is to be any chance of success for their defense plan, South Vietnam needs urgently an additional $722 million in very specific military supplies from the United States. In my judgment, a stabilization of the military situation offers the best opportunity for a political solution.

I must, of course, as I think each of you would, consider the safety of nearly 6,000 Americans who remain in South Vietnam and tens of thousands of South Vietnamese employees of the United States Government, of news agencies, of contractors and business for many years whose lives, with their dependents, are in very grave peril. There are tens of thousands of other South Vietnamese intellectuals, professors, teachers, editors, and opinion leaders who have supported the South Vietnamese cause and the alliance with the United States to whom we have a profound moral obligation. . . .

I have therefore concluded that the national interests of the United States and the cause of world stability require that we continue to give both military and humanitarian assistance to the South Vietnamese.

Assistance to South Vietnam at this stage must be swift and adequate. Drift and indecision invite far deeper disaster. The sums I had requested before the major North Vietnamese offensive and the sudden South Vietnamese retreat are obviously inadequate. Half-hearted action would be worse than none. We must act together and act decisively.

I am therefore asking the Congress to appropriate without delay $722 million for emergency military assistance and an initial sum of $250 million for economic and humanitarian aid for South Vietnam.

The situation in South Vietnam is changing very rapidly, and the need for emergency food, medicine, and refugee relief is growing by the hour. I will work with Congress in the days ahead to develop humanitarian assistance to meet these very pressing needs.

Fundamental decency requires that we do everything in our power to ease the misery and the pain of the monumental human crisis which has befallen the people of Vietnam. Millions have fled in the face of the Communist onslaught and are now homeless and are now destitute. I hereby pledge in the name of the American people that the United States will make a maximum humanitarian effort to help care for and feed these hopeless victims.

And now I ask Congress to clarify immediately its restrictions on the use of U.S. military forces in Southeast Asia for the limited purposes of protecting American lives by ensuring their evacuation, if this should be necessary. And I also ask prompt revision of the law to cover those Vietnamese to whom we have a very special obligation and whose lives may be endangered should the worst come to pass.

I hope that this authority will never have to be used, but if it is needed, there will be no time for Congressional debate. Because of the gravity of the situation, I ask the Congress to complete action on all of these measures not later than April 19. . . .

See "Address before a Joint Session of the Congress Reporting on United States Foreign Policy" (10 Apr. 1975), pp. 462–464. In *Public Papers of the Presidents of the United States: Gerald Ford, 1975* (Washington, D.C.: Government Printing Office, 1975).

FORD'S STATEMENT FOLLOWING EVACUATION OF U.S. PERSONNEL FROM THE REPUBLIC OF VIETNAM

April 29, 1975

During the past week, I had ordered the reduction of American personnel in the United States mission in Saigon to levels that could be quickly evacuated during an emergency, while enabling that mission to continue to fulfill its duties.

During the day on Monday, Washington time, the airport at Saigon came under persistent rocket as well as artillery fire and was effectively closed. The military situation in the area deteriorated rapidly.

I therefore ordered the evacuation of all American personnel remaining in South Vietnam.

The evacuation has been completed. I commend the personnel of the Armed Forces who accomplished it as well as Ambassador Graham Martin and the staff of his mission, who served so well under difficult conditions.

This action closes a chapter in the American experience. I ask all Americans to close ranks, to avoid recrimination about the past, to look ahead to the many goals we share, and to work together on the great tasks that remain to be accomplished.

See "Statement Following Evacuation of United States Personnel from the Republic of Vietnam" (29 Apr. 1975), p. 605. In *Public Papers of the Presidents of the United States: Gerald Ford, 1975* (Washington, D.C.: Government Printing Office, 1975).

COMMENTS BY REPRESENTATIVE STEPHEN J. SOLARZ (D-N.Y.)

Hearings before the House Subcommittee on International Security and Scientific Affairs of the Committee on International Relations
May 7, 1975

Hearings Seen as Enormously Valuable

I want to say at the outset that while I understand the desire to retroactively justify actions which were taken, perhaps more on the basis of moral and statutory considerations that in the course of attempting to do so, I think we still have an obligation because of the fact that it created precedents for the future not to throw consistency and rationality to the winds.

I must say, Mr. Leigh [legal advisor to State Department], with all due respect for your constitutional acumen and learning, that I am deeply disturbed by some of what, I think, are rather dangerous doctrines which you have advanced in the course of your testimony and I would like to explore the implications of several of them. . . .

First of all, as I understand your testimony today, you said, in effect, that in your judgment the President has the authority, without advanced statutory action on the part of the Congress, for a declaration of war to use American troops not only to evacuate American citizens from other lands and not only to evacuate American citizens incidental to the evacuation of American citizens, but he can evacuate foreign nationals as well. Also, in your judgment you felt the President had the authority to use troops solely for the purpose of evacuating foreign nationals.

Now if, in fact, this is the case, I am not sure what the necessity was for the legislation specifically authorizing the President to evacuate not only American citizens but foreign nationals as well. Based on your testimony, I gather you were suggesting this was requested largely for political rather than constitutional purposes because the President wanted, I gather, broad-based constitutional support for the action he was taking. Yet, if in fact, that was the underlying rationale for the request, I must tell you as one member of the International Relations Committee I feel I was misled because during the course of the testimony and debates on the floor of the House, the argument was made not simply that the President wanted political legitimation of his efforts but rather this authority was specifically needed. Did he or didn't he need the authority, and if he didn't need the authority, why were we told that he did need the authority? . . .

Let me say if in fact it was the President's position that he lacked such authority—and I am not sure what his position is either—but if he felt he lacked such authority, then the bill that was reported out by the Senate and the bill that was reported out by the conference committee conferred no additional authority on him that he didn't already have because the language of that legislation specifically limited the duration for which such troops could be used to the amount of time necessary to evacuate the Americans. According to your statement, it was the President's position all along that with respect at the very least to American citizens and those Vietnamese nationals that could be taken out at the same time that he already had the authority in the absence of such legislation. . . .

As I understand your interpretation of the President's constitutional authority to use troops for evacuation, it would appear that if the legislation which was reported from the conference had been adopted by both the House and the Senate prior to the final evacuation that the limitations in that legislation on the manner in which the President could deploy the troops for this purpose were, if I understand you correctly, inherently constituted as a violation of the President's inherent constitutional authority. . . .

This is to say, the legislation, by limiting the number of troops that could be used to the number necessary to evacuate Americans and their dependents and the limitation on the amount of time during which the troops could be deployed to the amount of time necessary to evacuate the Americans—if your interpretation of the President's constitutional authority is correct—in and of themselves were unconstitutional; and if the President has determined that he wanted to keep the troops in longer than the amount of time necessary to evacuate Americans, he would have been constitutionally justified in doing so, the restrictions in the bill notwithstanding, and if the President decided that he needed only, say, 5,000 troops to evacuate the Americans but for whatever the reasons he wanted to send in 10,000 or 15,000 for the purposes of an evacuation, that he would have been within his constitutional authority as Commander in Chief to do so with restrictions in this bill notwithstanding.

See U.S. House. Committee on International Relations. *War Powers: A Test of Compliance, Relative to the Danang Sealift, the Evacuation of Phnom Penh, the Evacuation of Saigon, and the* Mayaguez *Incident.* Hearing, 7 May, 4 June 1975, 94th Cong. 1st sess. (Washington, D.C.: Government Printing Office, 1975), pp. 25, 26, 34, 35–36.

RECOVERY OF SS *MAYAGUEZ*

On May 12, 1975, the U.S. merchant ship SS *Mayaguez* was stopped by a Cambodian gunboat and boarded by members of the Cambodian Navy. Based on their suspicions that the *Mayaguez* might be carrying military cargo, the Cambodians stopped the ship and ordered the captain to take it to the island of Koh Tang where it could be searched. Over the next two days, the captain and crew of thirty-nine were removed from the ship, placed on a fishing boat, and ferried to Kompong Som on the Cambodian mainland where they were questioned about any involvement with the FBI or CIA.

In response to the incident, President Ford ordered the U.S. military to intervene in an attempt to rescue the American hostages and retake the *Mayaguez.* The plan was to prevent the Cambodians from removing the *Mayaguez* crew from Koh Tang, with the thought that a rescue would be easier off the island than from the mainland. Although several Cambodian boats were sunk or harassed as they were leaving the island, the U.S. military was unaware that the crew had indeed been removed from Koh Tang and, on May 14, U.S. Marines invaded the island. There, they were met with fierce resistance from Khmer Rouge troops, with forty-one Marines being killed during the invasion and the subsequent rescue of the American troops. Three Marines were inadvertently left on the island during the rescue and are presumed to have been killed by the Khmer Rouge. Ironically, at the time of the invasion, members of the *Mayaguez* crew were no longer on the island but had, in fact, already been released by their captors and were en route to an American destroyer ship, the USS *Wilson*.

While relations between the United States and Cambodia had been tense throughout the Vietnam War, the relationship had made a marked turn for the worse in April of 1975, when the communist Khmer Rouge took control of the Cambodian capital, Phnom Penh. Given the events of April 1975, it seems likely that the president was very sensitive to any assault on the United States, which helps explain the scale of the military response. It had only been a few weeks since the remaining Americans had been hastily evacuated from Vietnam, and it was now evident that both Vietnam and Cambodia had fallen to communist regimes. From President Ford's point of view, it was imperative that the United States not suffer another blow to its national pride nor allow another country to insult the nation's resolve to protect itself and its people. President Ford outlined his reasoning behind the military response in an address to the nation on May 15, 1975; the response was overwhelmingly positive.

It's difficult to say whether Ford's decision was ultimately a success or failure. In a sense, the answer is that both are correct. On the one hand, the captain and crew of the *Mayaguez* were released unharmed within a few days of their capture, and that was the ultimate goal of the mission. On the other hand, forty-one Marines were killed in the operation, more than the number of the *Mayaguez* crew they were sent to rescue. Twenty-three men were killed on May 13 in a helicopter crash, with the additional deaths being related to the invasion of Koh Tang. In addition to the deaths, there were some significant problems in the execution of the Marine operation. First, it was incorrectly assumed that the crew was still on the island of Koh Tang, and second, crew members had already been released and were on their way to the USS *Wilson* before the Marines were deployed to Koh Tang.

While the response in the United States was generally quite positive, there were some who criticized the president for using such a heavy-handed approach in what could be seen as a relatively minor event. An editorial in *The Nation* magazine termed the president's decision "machismo diplomacy" and countered the public's enthusiasm with a charge that the scale of the military response had been irresponsible and immature on the part of the United States. In short, the question posed in the editorial was whether the United States will always use force to address the inevitable conflicts that arise with other countries.

FORD'S LETTER TO THE SPEAKER OF THE HOUSE AND THE PRESIDENT PRO TEMPORE OF THE SENATE ON U.S. ACTIONS IN THE RECOVERY OF THE SS *MAYAGUEZ*

May 15, 1975

On 12 May 1975, I was advised that the SS *Mayaguez*, a merchant vessel of United States registry en route from Hong Kong to Thailand with a U.S. citizen crew, was fired upon, stopped, boarded, and seized by Cambodian naval patrol boats of the Armed Forces of Cambodia in international waters in the vicinity of Poulo Wai Island. The seized vessel was then forced to proceed to Koh Tang Island where it was required to anchor. This hostile act was in clear violation of international law.

In view of this illegal and dangerous act, I ordered, as you have been previously advised, United States military forces to conduct the necessary reconnaissance and to be ready to respond if diplomatic efforts to secure the return of the vessel and its personnel were not successful. Two United States reconnaissance aircraft in the course of locating the *Mayaguez* sustained minimal damage from small firearms. Appropriate demands for the return of the *Mayaguez* and its crew were made, both publicly and privately, without success.

In accordance with my desire that the Congress be informed on this matter and taking note of Section 4(a)(1) of the War Powers Resolution, I wish to report to you that at about 6:20 A.M., 13 May, pursuant to my instructions to prevent the movement of the *Mayaguez* into a mainland port, U.S. aircraft fired warning shots across the bow of the ship and gave visual signals to small craft approaching the ship. Subsequently, in order to stabilize the situation and in an attempt to preclude removal of the American crew of the *Mayaguez* to the mainland, where their rescue would be more difficult, I directed the United States Armed Forces to isolate the island and interdict any movement between the ship or the island and the mainland, and to prevent loss of life or injury to the U.S. captives. During the evening of 13 May, a Cambodian patrol boat attempting to leave the island disregarded aircraft warnings and was sunk. Thereafter, two other Cambodian patrol craft were destroyed and four others were damaged and immobilized. One boat, suspected of having some U.S. captives aboard, succeeded in reaching Kompong Som after efforts to turn it around without injury to the passengers failed.

Our continued objective in this operation was the rescue of the captured American crew along with the retaking of the ship *Mayaguez*. For that purpose, I ordered late this afternoon [May 14] an assault by the United States Marines on the island of Koh Tang to search out and rescue such Americans as might still be held there, and I ordered retaking of the *Mayaguez* by other Marines boarding from the destroyer escort *Holt*. In addition to continued fighter and gunship coverage of the Koh Tang area, these Marine activities were supported by tactical aircraft from the Coral Sea, striking the military airfield at Ream and other military targets in the area of Kompong Som in order to prevent reinforcement or support from the mainland of the Cambodian forces detaining the American vessel and crew.

At approximately 9:00 P.M. EDT on 14 May, the *Mayaguez* was retaken by United States forces. At approximately 11:30 P.M., the entire crew of the *Mayaguez* was taken aboard the *Wilson*. U.S. forces have begun the process of disengagement and withdrawal.

This operation was ordered and conducted pursuant to the President's constitutional Executive power and his authority as Commander-in-Chief of the United States Armed Forces.

Sincerely,
Gerald R. Ford

See "Letter to the Speaker of the House and the President Pro Tempore of the Senate Reporting on United States Actions in the Recovery of the SS *Mayaguez*" (15 May 1975), pp. 669–670. In *Public Papers of the Presidents of the United States: Gerald Ford, 1975* (Washington, D.C.: Government Printing Office, 1975).

"MACHISMO DIPLOMACY"

**Editorial in *The Nation*,
May 31, 1975**

By far the most troublesome aspect of the *Mayaguez* action has been the jubilant, backslapping response it evoked. Congress was virtually unanimous in its approval (there were some conspicuous exceptions, Sen. Gaylord Nelson for one); it took the Senate four hours to voice its commendations, with the conservatives being the most laudatory. As for the public, it has been almost as enthusiastic as Ford and Kissinger, who have been filmed congratulating each other and patting themselves on the back in a manner reminiscent of a team of freshmen wrestlers after their first intercollegiate victory. The reaction suggests that we have learned little from our experience in Indochina; on the contrary, the defeat of United States policy in Vietnam seems to have evoked a jingoistic mood which, as long as it lasts, is likely to encourage future follies.

Commentators have attempted to separate the *Mayaguez* action from the Administration's self-serving characterizations of it in order to praise the former while remaining only mildly critical of the latter. But the severance is dubious. Seizure of the ship was a reckless act on the part of the Cambodians but, in the context, it was not piracy. Allowance must be made for the understandable jumpiness of the new regime and also for its claim that the ship was not on the high seas when it was seized, but in Cambodian territorial waters.

The same allowance for uncertainty and confusion must be granted the Ford Administration, although to a lesser degree. Even so, the rescue action, which had distinct overtones of a punitive expedition, was anything but brilliant in conception and execution. There appears to have been a multiple failure of intelligence. The crew of the *Mayaguez* was not on Tang Island, where the Marines invaded, but on another island 25 miles away. Ten minutes before the assault on Tang, Phnom Penh had radioed an offer to release the ship. Also ignored were similar seizures of a South Korean and a Panamanian ship in the same waters—for inspection—some days before the seizure of the *Mayaguez*. The appearance of the ship with its on-deck vans or containers suggested that it might be carrying military cargo, although in fact it was not. Contrary to intelligence reports, Tang Island was heavily defended. Casualty figures change from hour to hour, and were not firm as this issue went to press, but according to the latest Defense Department figures, fifteen Americans are dead, three missing in action and fifty wounded.

Crew members of the *Mayaguez*, as we now know, were treated courteously; even acts of kindness were shown them. Once the Cambodians were convinced that the ship was not carrying "arms, ammunition, or bombs," Captain Miller was assured that he and his crew would be released. Sixteen minutes before the men were released, the first air strikes against the mainland began. A second series followed thirty-seven minutes after the crew members were safely aboard an American destroyer (the excuse being that this attack was necessary to protect the Marines). Attempting to prevent the crew's removal from the island to the mainland, American planes harassed the fishing boat to which they had been transferred. For four hours, jets bombed close to it, strafed it and dropped tear gas, but did not succeed in turning it back. Fortunately these firings were accurate, but the lives of the entire crew were in danger throughout the prolonged assault; they could easily have been sacrificed as a consequence of the Administration's indulgence in *machismo* diplomacy. If the safety of the crew and the return of the ship were the sole considerations—as Administration spokesmen insist—then the action can be condemned as foolhardy and arrogant and still another example of military overkill and trigger-happiness.

But the military action is far less significant than the hoopla about it.

Kissinger and Ford were obviously itching to clobber some safe target by way of demonstrating that they had passed their tests as tough statesmen and that the United States was still addicted to the use of military force as a substitute for diplomacy. The enthusiasm which greeted the action has been explained as a pardonable reaction to national frustration over Vietnam, but it is also a sign that we have not yet learned to think of American power in terms of present-day world realities. We continue to see ourselves as we want to see ourselves and not as others see us. Senator Goldwater's reference to "little half-assed nations" attempting to push us around was not only offensive but stupid; it will be quoted by national leaders around the world for a long time, as an example of precisely what is wrong with this country's conception of its role in the world. . . .

Worst of all, the popular enthusiasm with which the *Mayaguez* action has been greeted has flashed a signal to Kissinger and Ford that they can continue to use military force in reckless and stupid ways as a substitute for realistic diplomacy. Forget about the restrictions on the President's power to wage war. In this instance, the "consultation" with Congress was perfunctory and came after the fact, but there were not audible objections, not even fro the authors of the War Powers Act. Reports James Wieghart in the New York *Daily News*: "When Ford entered the Cabinet room . . . to inform the assembled Congressional leaders of his decision to use force to free the *Mayaguez*, the legislators—all veterans of similar sessions held by Presidents Johnson and Nixon during the Vietnam years—rose to their feet and applauded before Ford opened his mouth. They are like the goose in the barnyard, honking at the rising sun, lacking memories and foresight. It is as if yesterday never happened and tomorrow will never come."

In this instance, as Sen. Alan Cranston [D-Calif.] observed, we were fortunate enough to "luck out" but what about the next time? and the next? and the next?

See "Machismo Diplomacy," *The Nation* vol. 220, no. 21, May 31, 1975: pp. 642–643.

HELSINKI ACCORDS

Although most countries consider the governments of other states sovereign, meaning they are free to make decisions within their own territorial boundaries, countries do at times agree collectively to promote or constrain certain types of policies or actions. These agreements can come in the form of treaties and other types of less formal agreements, but they all rest on the premise that countries that signal their approval will be bound by the provisions in the agreement. Although not a treaty, the

Final Act of the Conference on Security and Cooperation in Europe, also known as the Helsinki Accords, is an example of an international agreement that was designed to influence the behavior of governments signing the document. In this case, the behavior involved how signatory governments would treat their own citizens.

In November 1972, thirty-five nations began meeting in Helsinki, Finland, to discuss issues of security and cooperation among the countries of Europe as well as the United States and Canada. Discussions took place for three years, with the Helsinki Accords being signed by all thirty-five participants on August 1, 1975. Because numerous topics were considered, the accords were divided into three main sections, called "baskets," in which cooperative efforts in the areas of technology, security, economics, science, and human rights were outlined. Two of the issues considered in Helsinki generated significant controversy in the United States. The first was the issue of human rights and the skepticism that countries like the Soviet Union would actually adhere to the agreement. Some of the specific concerns regarding human rights were freedom from religious persecution and the freer movement of people across political boundaries. The second issue involved the recognition of Soviet control over the Baltic states of Estonia, Latvia, and Lithuania, countries that had been controlled by the Soviet Union since World War II.

At the signing of the Helsinki Accords, President Ford addressed the conference to express his own support of the agreement, explaining that the goals of the accords were consistent with the values of the United States. Although his speech was general in nature, he explained that the provisions of the agreement would allow the participating countries to continue the process of achieving peace in Europe. Yet, in the United States, the Helsinki Accords were subjected to very close scrutiny, particularly with regard to the human rights provisions and the recognition of the Soviet Baltic states. In a hearing before the House Subcommittee on International Political and Military Affairs of the Committee on International Relations, Representative Frank Annunzio (D-Ill.) expressed his grave concern that the human rights provision of Basket III was being ignored by the Soviet Union. He wasn't persuaded that the Ford Administration was doing enough to guarantee that the Soviet Union and other countries were honoring the agreement. He also made reference to an earlier House Resolution that had restated the commitment of the House of Representatives not to recognize Soviet control of the Baltic states. That resolution had demonstrated the House's convictions that the Soviet Union had illegally taken control of the Baltic states and that the United States should in no way condone its actions.

FORD'S ADDRESS IN HELSINKI BEFORE
THE CONFERENCE ON SECURITY AND
COOPERATION IN EUROPE

August 1, 1975

The nations assembled here have kept the general peace in Europe for 30 years. Yet there have been too many narrow escapes from major conflict. There remains, to this day, the urgent issue of how to construct a just and lasting peace for all peoples.

I have not come across the Atlantic to say what all of us already know—that nations now have the capacity to destroy civilization and, therefore, all our foreign policies must have as their one supreme objective the prevention of a thermonuclear war. Nor have I come to dwell upon the hard realities of continuing ideological differences, political rivalries, and military competition that persist among us.

I have come to Helsinki as a spokesman for a nation whose vision has always been forward, whose people have always demanded that the future be brighter than the past, and whose united will and purpose at this hour is to work diligently to promote peace and progress not only for ourselves but for all mankind.

I am simply here to say to my colleagues: We owe it to our children, to the children of all continents, not to miss any opportunity, not to malinger for one minute, not to spare ourselves or allow others to shirk in the monumental task of building a better and a safer world.

The American people, like the people of Europe, know well that mere assertions of good will, passing changes in the political mood of governments, laudable declarations of principles are not enough. But if we proceed with care, with commitment to real progress, there is now an opportunity to turn our people's hopes into realities.

In recent years, nations represented here have sought to ease potential conflicts. But much more remains to be done before we prematurely congratulate ourselves.

Military competition must be controlled. Political competition must be restrained. Crises must not be manipulated or exploited for unilateral advantages that could lead us again to the brink of war. The process of negotiation must be sustained, not at a snail's pace, but with demonstrated enthusiasm and visible progress.

Nowhere are the challenges and the opportunities greater and more evident than in Europe. That is why this Conference brings us all together. Conflict in Europe shakes the world. Twice in this century we have paid dearly for this lesson; at other times, we have come perilously close to calamity. We dare not forget the tragedy and the terror of those times.

Peace is not a piece of paper.

But lasting peace is at least possible today because we have learned from the experiences of the last 30 years that peace is a process requiring mutual restraint and practical arrangements.

This Conference is a part of that process—a challenge, not a conclusion. We face unresolved problems of military security in Europe; we face them with very real differences in values and in aims. But if we deal with them with careful preparation, if we focus on concrete issues, if we maintain forward movement, we have the right to expect real progress.

The era of confrontation that has divided Europe since the end of the Second World War may now be ending. There is a new perception and a shared perception of a change for the better, away from confrontation and toward new possibilities for secure and mutually beneficial cooperation. That is what we all have been saying here. I welcome and I share these hopes for the future.

The postwar policy of the United States has been consistently directed toward the rebuilding of Europe and the rebirth of Europe's historic identity. The nations of the West have worked together for peace and progress throughout Europe. From the very start, we have taken the initiative by stating clear goals and areas for negotiation.

We have sought a structure of European relations, tempering rivalry with restraint, power with moderation, building upon the traditional bonds that link us with old friends and reaching out to forge new ties with former and potential adversaries. . . .

I profoundly hope that this Conference will spur further practical and concrete results. It affords a welcome opportunity to widen the circle of those countries involved in easing tensions between the East and the West.

See "Address in Helsinki before the Conference on Security and Cooperation in Europe" (1 Aug. 1975), pp. 1074–1076. In *Public Papers of the Presidents of the United States: Gerald Ford, 1975* (Washington, D.C.: Government Printing Office, 1975).

STATEMENT OF REPRESENTATIVE FRANK ANNUNZIO
(D-ILL.)

**Hearings before the House Subcommittee on International
Political and Military Affairs of the Committee on
International Relations
November 18, 1975**

The Final Act of the Conference on Security and Cooperation in Europe was signed on August 1, 1975, in Helsinki, Finland, and contains provisions designed to guarantee basic human rights and to allow for the free movement of people, information, and ideas between East and West. Unfortunately, the record of compliance, to date, with the Helsinki final act can be called mixed at best. The Soviet Union and some East European countries have been exceedingly slow in implementing the provisions of the agreement.

Personally, I was opposed to the signing of this document because it was interpreted to mean official U.S. endorsement of the absorption of the three Baltic States and other territories into the Soviet Union. On December 2, 1975, the House passed my resolution to put the House of Representatives on record that there has been no change in the long-standing policy of the United States on nonrecognition of the illegal seizure and annexation by the Soviet Union of the three Baltic nations of Estonia, Latvia, and Lithuania, and that it will continue to be the policy of the United States not to recognize in any way the annexation of the Baltic States.

Moreover, the Soviets considerably watered down their original promise to include in the Helsinki document strong guarantees for wider dissemination of information and freer movement of peoples. The Soviet response to applications for immigration by Latvians, Lithuanians, Estonians, Jews, Ukrainians, and many other non-Russian peoples, and also to efforts at liberalization of the press in Czechoslovakia and other countries is ample evidence of the emptiness of such promises. However, I believe that the Congress should insist on strictly monitoring Soviet compliance with their weak promises to allow the freer movement of peoples and the wider dissemination of information.

History has shown that agreements are mere scraps of paper unless accompanied by a resolve to translate them into reality. Clearly, if we now do not insist that the Helsinki accords be implemented, there is little hope of compliance by the other side on matters reluctantly conceded at the conference. If we relax our efforts to carry out the results of the final act, our citizens will be justified in asking why we bothered to labor so long and hard for each concession or why we dignified the document with the highest stamp of approval.

The administration, of course, has primary responsibility for securing implementation of the Helsinki agreement. However, Congress can also perform a useful role in monitoring compliance with the provisions of the final act. The proposed Commission on Security and Cooperation in Europe would bring together Members of the Congress with representatives from the executive branch, selected by the President. The Commission's role would be to inform Congress and the American people of developments relating to compliance with the Helsinki agreement. We are convinced that systematic public exposure of the record will encourage all participating states to take seriously their pledges—pledges which, if implemented, could truly strengthen peace and security in Europe while satisfying the most basic human rights and aspirations.

See U.S. House. Committee on International Relations. *Conference on Security and Cooperation in Europe*, Part II. Hearing, 18 November 1975, 4 May 1976, 94th Cong. 1st sess. (Washington, D.C.: Government Printing Office, 1975), p. 75.

FEDERAL LOANS TO NEW YORK CITY

By the mid-1970s, numerous large cities in the United States were experiencing financial difficulties. These difficulties arose largely because cities' tax revenue was decreasing as the nation's economy worsened and city industries increasingly moved to the suburbs. The problem in New York City was significant enough that the city was close to bankruptcy by 1975.

Until November 1975, President Ford kept contending that the federal government should not contribute in any way to New York's recovery. The president certainly did not want New York to bankrupt itself, but he also didn't want to set a precedent that the national government would "bail out" any major city that was threatened with financial hardship. He made it clear that the responsibility lay with the local and state government to take care of their own problems, and that the city should not look for handouts from Washington, D.C. The president's position generated quite a bit of controversy. While there were those who agreed with him, there was also a great deal of concern about the potential economic consequences of letting the most populous city in the country go bankrupt. Another related issue made the president's stance look hypocritical: The government had recently bailed out some large corporations on the verge of bankruptcy. The rationale behind assisting corporations was that it was in the public's interest to support a large corporation, primarily because it made a contribution to the American economy by providing employment and goods. Those wanting to help out New York argued that the same case could be made for a city as large as New York.

Interestingly, by November 26, the president had changed his position on the matter. Certainly, political pressure regarding the issue may have prompted him to reconsider his position. The New York *Daily News*, for instance, condemned the president's earlier decision not to loan the city funds with the headline, "Ford to City: Drop Dead." Yet it was Ford's contention that his opinion changed because the situation had changed. Both the city and state of New York had taken steps to diminish their financial difficulties. The plan included the difficult decision to raise taxes, cut spending, and restructure the pension plan of municipal employees, among other steps. Yet, while the plan would significantly improve the city's financial prospects in the long term, it was not enough to completely rule out bankruptcy because of the immediate spending needs of the city. After seeing the determination of New York to put its own financial house in order, the president concluded that the federal government could make a series of loans to New York to cover its day-to-day expenses until its own plan could go ito effect. Because the president's proposal involved the appropriation of federal funds to make the loans, he had to rely on Congress to pass legislation for the loans to be made. In his speech of November 26, he asked Congress to extend a line of credit to New York, explaining that there would be stringent repayment conditions attached to the loans.

Just as there were opponents and supporters of the president's prior stance on providing assistance to New York, by changing his position, Ford created an entirely new set of opponents and supporters. Many people who were adamantly opposed to federal assistance for New York found their own positions shifting from support to opposition as the president's positions changed. There were concerns that other city governments might be less likely to practice fiscal responsibility if they thought they could simply turn to the national government for a financial bailout. As the House considered the Seasonal Financial Assistance Act of 1975, Representative Robert W. Kasten (R-Wisc.) spoke out in opposition to the lending legislation. He argued that New York had not taken the steps necessary to decrease its financial problems, and that the federal government should not use taxpayers' money to bail out what was, essentially, irresponsible spending on the part of New York. Ultimately, the legislation did pass, and New York City was able to effectively weather its financial crisis.

FORD'S STATEMENT ON MEASURES TAKEN TO IMPROVE
THE FINANCIAL SITUATION OF NEW YORK CITY

November 26, 1975

I would like to comment briefly on recent developments in New York. Since early this year, and particularly in the last few weeks, the leaders of New York State and of New York City have been working to overcome the financial difficulties of the city which, as a result of many years of unsound fiscal practices, unbalanced budgets, and increased borrowing, threaten to bring about municipal bankruptcy of an unprecedented magnitude.

As you know, I have been steadfastly opposed to any Federal help for New York City which would permit them to avoid responsibility for managing their own affairs. I will not allow the taxpayers of other States and cities to pay the price of New York's past political errors. It is important to all of us that the fiscal integrity of New York City be restored and that the personal security of 8 million Americans in New York City be fully assured.

It has always been my hope that the leaders of New York, when the chips were down, face up to their responsibilities and take the tough decisions that the facts of the situation require. That is still my hope, and I must say that it is much, much closer to reality today than it was last spring.

I have, quite frankly, been surprised that they have come as far as they have. I doubted that they would act unless ordered to do so by a Federal court. Only in the last month, after I made it clear that New York would have to solve its fundamental financial problems without the help of the Federal taxpayer, has there been a concerted effort to put the finances of the city and the State on a sound basis. They have today informed me of the specifics of New York's self-help program.

This includes: Meaningful spending cuts have been approved to reduce the cost of running the city. Two, more than $200 million in new taxes have been voted. Three, payments to the city's noteholders will be postponed and interest payments will be reduced through the passage of legislation by New York State. Four, banks and other large institutions will have agreed to wait to collect on their loans and to accept lower interest rates. Five, for the first time in years members of municipal unions will be required to bear part of the cost of pension contributions and other reforms will be made in union pension plans. Six, the city pension system is to provide additional loans of up to $2.5 billion to the city.

All of these steps, adding up to $4 billion, are part of an effort to provide financing and to bring the city's budget into balance by the fiscal year beginning July 1, 1977.

Only a few months ago we were told that all of these reforms were impossible and could not be accomplished by New York alone. Today they are being done.

This is a realistic program. I want to commend all of those involved in New York City and New York State for their constructive efforts to date. I have been closely watching their progress in meeting their problem.

However, in the next few months New York will lack enough funds to cover its day-to-day operating expenses. This problem is caused by the city having to pay its bill on a daily basis throughout the year while the bulk of its revenues are received during the spring. Most cities are able to borrow short-term funds to cover these needs, traditionally repaying them within their fiscal year.

Because the private credit markets may remain closed to them, representatives of New York have informed me and my Administration that they have acted in good faith, but they still need to borrow money on a short-term basis for a period of time each of the next 2 years in order to provide essential services to the 8 million Americans who live in the Nation's largest city.

Therefore, I have decided to ask the Congress when it returns from recess for authority to provide a temporary line of credit to the State of New York to enable it to supply seasonal financing of essential services for the people of New York City.

There will be stringent conditions. Funds would be loaned to the State on a seasonal basis, normally from July through March, to be repaid with interest in April, May, and June, when the bulk of the city's revenues come in. All Federal loans will be repaid in full at the end of each year.

There will be no cost to the rest of the taxpayers of the United States.

This is only the beginning of New York's recovery process, and not the end. New York officials must continue to accept primary responsibility. There must be no misunderstanding of my position. If local parties fail to carry out their plan, I am prepared to stop even the seasonal Federal assistance.

I again ask the Congress promptly to amend the Federal bankruptcy laws so that if the New York plan fails, there will be an orderly procedure available. A fundamental issue is involved here—sound fiscal management is an imperative of self-government. I trust we have all learned the hard lesson that no individual, no family, no business, no city, no State, and no Nation can go on indefinitely spending more money than it takes in.

As we count our Thanksgiving blessings, we recall that Americans have always believed in helping those who help themselves. New York has finally taken the tough decisions it had to take to help itself. In making the required sacrifices, the people of New York have earned the encouragement of the rest of the country.

See "Statement on Measures Taken to Improve the Financial Situation in New York City, News Conference" (26 Nov. 1975), pp. 1902–1904. In *Public Papers of the Presidents of the United States, Gerald Ford, 1975* (Washington, D.C.: Government Printing Office, 1975).

STATEMENT OF REPRESENTATIVE ROBERT W. KASTEN, JR. (R-WISC.)

December 2, 1975

Mr. Chairman, in October, I stated my firm opposition to a Federal bailout for New York City. Today, I reiterate my position. I will vote against H.R. 10481 for one basic reason: The $2.3 billion Federal loan proposal does not get at the root of New York City's problem. It treats only the symptoms.

Excessive spending is the problem. New York City, while taking steps to increase tax revenues, has demonstrated insufficient resolve to substantially reduce the city's lavish spending level.

A favorable vote for the Federal loan proposal is a refusal to let the lessons of profligate spending be learned from New York City's example. The city has not yet taken the necessary actions to warrant Federal aid. New York City has not bailed itself out.

I share President Ford's surprise that New York City's leaders have come as far as they have in trying to put the city's finances in order— but they have not come far enough.

New York City runs 18 municipal hospitals. On an average day, 25 percent of the hospital beds are empty. The city spends millions to pay the hospital expenses of those who use private hospitals.

Yet, the city has offered no plan to cut back on the services of its municipal hospital system, or to consolidate and reorganize its public hospital system to maximize its use, or to compel those on public assistance to use municipal hospitals.

New York is the only U.S. city which runs a university system free of a charge for tuition. It is one of the largest university systems in the world.

Yet, the city has offered no plan to charge tuition or set up a scholarship fund for poor students, which would cost the city only a fraction of what the city pays for tuition-free education to all.

Although apartments are a third of New York's tax base, rent-control laws have reduced the growth of the tax base. Ownership of buildings becomes unprofitable when a landlord cannot raise rents to cover costs. As a result, last year about 36,000 apartments were abandoned—enough to house the population of Waukesha, West Bend, and Watertown, Wis.

Yet, no attempt has been made to end rent control.

Instead of drastically cutting the city's expenses by making these necessary reforms, the city's leaders boast of raising taxes by $200 million to pay its bills, as if there were no limit.

The city's leaders seem to forget that low taxes are not the problem. New York taxes are already high. Spending is the problem.

Simply raising taxes is unacceptable as a long-term strategy to end the city's financial difficulties. Increased taxes, among other consequences, will drive more people and businesses from the city, which will act to further erode the city's tax base.

Welfare spending in New York is expensive and out of control. One in 10 New York welfare recipients may be legally ineligible for welfare assistance. New York City's lavish welfare-related spending annually amounts to $3.5 billion, about one-third of the city's total expenditures.

Yet, no proposal has been offered to reduce the city's welfare budget.

The President has been quoted as saying not long ago that if New York City submitted a believable plan to balance its budget by 1978, "It hardly seems necessary for the Federal Government to get involved." I agree.

The people of Wisconsin and elsewhere in the Nation should not be expected to support the President's high-risk proposal to aid a city which spends at the rate of $1,223.68 per resident per year. According to the Tax Foundation, that spending rate is more than four times the average annual per capita spending of $295.48 for all other American cities.

The people of Wisconsin should not be expected to risk their hard-earned dollars to help a city beleaguered and teetering on the edge of insolvency—so it can continue its massive university system where tuition is free, and shoot more money into its massive municipal hospital system.

It is said that the Federal Government will make money from interest on loans to New York City. Yet, it is the Federal Government—with the taxpayers' money—that will be taking a risk for New York City, assuming for all Americans a burden that is not their own. Our Nation, itself deep in debt, will be granting a high-risk loan to a city that even the most financially solvent banks will not assist.

The Nation will be risking billions of dollars, gambling that it may make a little, and assuming that a lesson will be learned.

Federal loans will achieve only an easing of seasonal variations in the city's receipts and spending, and some have asserted that the $2.3 billion level is inadequate to realistically guarantee the objectives of H.R. 10481.

And let us not forget that the precedent for Federal loans to New York City will be remembered when other municipalities throughout the Nation face similar circumstances.

H.R. 10481 poses yet another problem. It does not include the revisions in bankruptcy laws recently approved by the House Judiciary Committee. And Federal loans should be incorporated in one measure with a bankruptcy provision to indicate the total Federal response which may be expected in the New York City situation.

The State of New York is attempting a legislated default providing by statute for a moratorium on city payments on its notes. If this approach fails to survive a legal challenge, an actual default would occur. We could then expect another plea by the city for further Federal aid. Coupling the loan and bankruptcy provisions would help to define the parameters of Federal aid which could be anticipated by the State and the city in the event that the present legislated default becomes a legal default.

Again, New York City has not bailed itself out—it has not done enough to earn Federal assistance. And what little it has done is certainly not enough for any important lessons to be learned. Passage of the bill would serve only to demonstrate that Congress will reward a city that creates the illusion of fiscal responsibility.

See Rep. Robert W. Kasten, Jr. (Wisc.). *Congressional Record* 121, pt. 29 (2 Dec. 1975), pp. 38170–38171.

THE CIA CONTROVERSY

In order to maintain national security against threats posed by other countries or groups, the U.S. government has established several agencies to obtain intelligence, or information, about potential threats. Both the Federal Bureau of Investigation (FBI) and the Central Intelligence Agency (CIA) play roles in gathering and using intelligence to protect the United States and its people from, among other things, terrorist acts and the acts of countries hostile to the United States. The FBI, as part of the Department of Justice, is responsible for upholding federal law as well as protecting the country from internal threats to its security. The CIA, on the other hand, is an independent agency, responsible to the president. The agency provides intelligence services to the president, the National Security Council, and others in the government who are involved in foreign policy matters. Its responsibility falls more in the area of foreign intelligence, spying on other countries, and protecting the United States from espionage by others. Only with a great deal of information can foreign policy decisions be made that best reflect the reality of U.S. relationships with other countries.

Striking a balance between the collection of necessary information to maintain national security and the protection of citizens' constitutional rights has been difficult, however. This concern has been particularly acute with the increased use of technology in intelligence gathering since the mid-1900s. While intelligence gathering is still largely dependent on the use of people to infiltrate organizations or governments and secretly collect and convey information, the use of electronic devices has increased substantially since World War II. In many ways, this has made intelligence gathering an easier process, but it can also be abused more easily as well.

In a democracy, there is the expectation that the public will be protected from abuses of power by the government and, further, that people have rights that are to be protected by government. One way this is accomplished is through a system of checks and balances, whereby potential abuses by one part of government are kept in check by other parts of government. The difficulty in achieving this in the area of intelligence is that secrecy is fundamentally important to the success of the operation. For intelligence agencies to be held accountable for their actions, other government officials must be aware of these actions. Yet, the more people who are informed of intelligence operations, the greater the likelihood that secrets will be disclosed.

The need for additional accountability by the intelligence community became painfully apparent in late 1974, when illegal acts conducted by the CIA during the Nixon administration were revealed. In December of 1974, two articles were published in the *New York Times* that brought to light substantial abuses by the CIA. The agency had, in short, been spying on American citizens, including Vietnam War protesters, civil rights activists, and political opponents of President Nixon. There was also evidence that the CIA had engaged in assassination plots against foreign leaders. Although the articles did not delve into the actions of agencies other than the CIA, there is substantial evidence that Presidents Johnson and Nixon had also used the FBI to gather information about their political adversaries. The public was outraged by these charges and on January 4, 1975, President Ford responded to these disclosures by creating a presidential commission to study the intelligence operations of the United States and to make recommendations regarding the oversight of these operations. The commission's report was released to the public on June 10, 1975.

The respective responses by both the president and the Congress illustrate the different interests and perspectives each branch brings to bear on a single issue. Political scientist Kenneth Kitts claims that it was in the best interest of President Ford to take quick action on the CIA scandal before Congress was able to develop any means of overseeing the authority of the intelligence community.[1] From the perspective of the executive branch, it was important to protect the public from illegal activities by the CIA, but it was also fundamentally important that the agency be allowed to continue gathering useful intelligence for national security. Further, it was important to the president that any involvement by Congress not endanger the useful roles these agencies play. Conversely, from a congressional perspective, it was important that the Congress not be omitted from any process of oversight for these agencies, given the greater representative nature of the legislative branch. With this in mind, select committees from both the House of Representatives and the Senate held lengthy investigative hearings on intelligence gathering to determine what reforms would best serve both the protection of rights and the protection of national security. As a result of these and other proceedings, both the House of Representatives and the Senate formed permanent select committees on intelligence to maintain a congressional presence in this policy area.

In partial response to the recommendations of his commission on CIA activities, President Ford released Executive Order 11905 in February of 1976, which took steps to reorganize portions of the CIA. In his announcement of February 18, he also made several legislative recommendations to Congress that reflected his view of the proper and welcome role of Congress in matters of intelligence. Critics argued that these recommendations maintained a pronounced presence for the executive branch in the operations of the CIA and did not go far enough in protecting the public from overzealous intelligence agencies. The heightened use of technology by intelligence agencies and its unique threat to constitutional rights were of particular concern. In a hearing held to specifically consider the use of electronic surveillance equipment in intelligence gathering, Representative Robert F. Drinan (D-Mass.) criticized the president's recommendations for providing too much leniency to U.S. intelligence agencies, stating that appeals to protect national security should not be used by these agencies as a shield to justify the violation of rights.

NOTE

1. Kenneth Kitts, "Commission Politics and National Security: Gerald Ford's Response to the CIA Controversy of 1975," *Presidential Studies Quarterly* 26 (fall 1996) p. 1081–98.

FORD'S EXECUTIVE ORDER 11905

February 18, 1976

By virtue of the authority vested in me by Article II, Section 2 and 3 of the Constitution, and other provisions of law, I have today issued an Executive Order [11905] pertaining to the organization and control of the United States foreign intelligence community. This order establishes a clear line of accountability for the Nation's foreign intelligence agencies. It sets forth strict guidelines to control the activities of these agencies and specifies as well those activities in which they shall not engage.

In carrying out my Constitutional responsibilities to manage and conduct foreign policy and provide for the Nation's defense, I believe it essential to have the best possible intelligence about the capabilities, intentions, and activities of governments and other entities and individuals abroad. To this end, the foreign intelligence agencies of the United States play a vital role in collecting and analyzing information related to the national defense and foreign policy.

It is equally as important that the methods these agencies employ to collect such information for the legitimate needs of the government conform to the standards set out in the Constitution to preserve and respect the privacy and civil liberties of American citizens.

The Executive Order I have issued today will insure a proper balancing of these interests. It establishes government-wide direction for the foreign intelligence agencies and places responsibility and accountability on individuals, not institutions.

I believe it will eliminate abuses and questionable activities on the part of the foreign intelligence agencies while at the same time permitting them to get on with their vital work of gathering and assessing information. It is also my hope that these steps will help to restore public confidence in these agencies and encourage our citizens to appreciate the valuable contribution they make to our national security.

Beyond the steps I have taken in the Executive Order, I also believe there is a clear need for some specific legislative actions. . . .

My first proposal deals with the protection of intelligence sources and methods. The Director of Central Intelligence is charged, under the National Security Act of 1947, as amended, with protecting intelligence sources and methods. The Act, however, gives the Director no authorities commensurate with this responsibility.

Therefore, I am proposing legislation to impose criminal and civil sanctions on those who are authorized access to intelligence secrets and who willfully and wrongfully reveal this information. This legislation is not an "Official Secrets Act," since it would affect only those who improperly disclose secrets, not those to whom secrets are disclosed. Moreover, this legislation could not be used to cover up abuses and improprieties. It would in no way prevent people from reporting questionable activities to appropriate authorities in the Executive and Legislative Branches of the government.

It is essential, however, that the irresponsible and dangerous exposure of our Nation's intelligence secrets be stopped. The American people have long accepted the principles of confidentiality and secrecy in many dealings—such as with doctors, lawyers and the clergy. It makes absolutely no sense to deny this same protection to our intelligence secrets. Openness is a hallmark of our democratic society, but the American people have never believed that it was necessary to reveal the secret war plans of the Department of Defense, and I do not think they wish to have true intelligence secrets revealed either.

I urge the adoption of this legislation with all possible speed. . . .

I will meet with the appropriate leaders of Congress to try to develop sound legislation to deal with a critical problem involving personal privacy—electronic surveillance. Working with Congressional leaders and the Justice Department and other Executive agencies, we will seek to develop a procedure for undertaking electronic surveillance for foreign intelligence purposes. It should create a special procedure for seeking a judicial warrant authorizing the use of electronic surveillance in the United States for foreign intelligence purposes.

I will also seek Congressional support for sound legislation to expand judicial supervision of mail openings. The law now permits the opening of United States mail, under proper judicial safeguards, in the conduct of criminal investigations. We need authority to open mail under the limitations and safeguards that now apply in order to obtain vitally needed foreign intelligence information.

This would require a showing that there is probable cause to believe that the sender or recipient is an agent of a foreign power who is engaged in spying, sabotage or terrorism. As is now the case the criminal investigations, those seeking authority to examine mail for foreign intelligence purposes will have to convince a federal judge of the necessity to do so and accept the limitations upon their authorization to examine the mail provided in the order of the court. . . .

Congress should seek to centralize the responsibility for oversight of the foreign intelligence community. The more committees and subcommittees dealing with highly sensitive secrets, the greater the risks of disclosure. I recommend that Congress establish a Joint Foreign Intelligence Oversight Committee. Consolidating Congressional oversight in one committee will facilitate the efforts of the Administration to keep the Congress fully informed of foreign intelligence activities. . . .

Both the Congress and the Executive Branch recognize the importance to this Nation of a strong intelligence service. I believe it urgent that we take the steps I have outlined above to insure that America not only has the best foreign intelligence service in the world, but also the most unique—one which operates in a manner fully consistent with the Constitutional rights of our citizens.

See "Executive Order 11905" (18 Feb. 1976), pp. 362–364, 365. In *Public Papers of the Presidents of the United States: Gerald Ford, 1976* (Washington, D.C.: Government Printing Office, 1976).

STATEMENT BY REPRESENTATIVE ROBERT F. DRINAN (D-MASS.)

Hearing before the Senate Subcommittee on Intelligence and the Rights of Americans of the Select Committee on Intelligence July 1, 1976

Mr. Chairman and members of the Committee, I am pleased to appear before you regarding a matter of utmost importance to the national security: the Foreign Intelligence Surveillance Act of 1976 (S. 3197). If this bill becomes law in its present form, it will indeed pose a very serious threat to the security of this nation. In my judgment this proposal is offensive to the Fourth Amendment and allows unwarranted intrusions into the privacy of all persons within the jurisdiction of the United States.

When this bill was first introduced in the Congress last March, I was happy to see, at first glance, that the Administration had finally accepted the idea that court orders must be obtained to secure foreign intelligence information through electronic surveillance. For the past several years, the Department of Justice and the White House have steadfastly opposed any legislation which would require court approval before engaging in such surveillance in so-called "national security" cases. Upon further examination, however, I have concluded that the bill still gives the Executive Branch too much power to use wiretaps and other electronic devices to obtain foreign intelligence information.

I continue to believe that any electronic surveillance, whether approved by a court or not, violates the Fourth Amendment because such interceptions of private conversations can never satisfy its particularity requirement. It should be recalled that, to obtain a warrant for such surveillance under the Fourth Amendment, the applicant must submit a sworn statement, "particularly describing the place to be searched, and the persons or things to be seized." Invariably an application for a bug or a tap cannot be that specific; it cannot describe with particularity all the persons to be overheard or all the conversations to be recorded.

I also question the value of the information obtained from such surveillance. It is instructive to examine the annual reports of the Director of the Administrative Office of the United States Courts prepared under Title III of the 1968 Act. The reports show that, in 1973 for example, Federal agents listened to 112,314 conversations involving about 5,500 individuals. Less than half of these intercepts contained any relevant or allegedly incriminating information. The operations cost the taxpayers over $1.5 million. Furthermore these statistics do not include the data on warrantless surveillance, which need not be reported under the 1968 Act.

But we should remember that Title III surveillance at least is directed at criminal conduct. Before any tap or bug can be authorized the judge must find, among other things, "probable cause for belief that an individual is committing, has committed, or is about to commit a particular offense" enumerated in Title III. S. 3197 has no such limitation. It is, pure and simple, an authorization to obtain information unrelated to crime or criminal conduct. This is a fundamental defect in the bill. Senator [John V.] Tunney [of *California*] has said it represents the first time in American history that Congress would permit intrusions into the lives of aliens and citizens alike for activities having nothing to do with unlawful conduct.

Thus, the underlying premise of the bill must be called into question: Is the authority sought in this proposal really needed? Has the Department of Justice or any of the bill's proponents presented hard evidence of the value of intelligence surveillance? For too long we have assumed the necessity of the intelligence gathering function through electronic surveillance. The extensive congressional hearing record—the impeachment proceedings in the House, the inquiries of the Church Committee, and hopefully the examination of S. 3197 by this Committee—demonstrates the very tenuous base upon which that assumption rests . . .

In short, Mr. Chairman, S. 3197 is an attempt to give the American people the impression that adequate steps are now being taken to protect their privacy in communications that may involve alleged foreign intelligence information. But upon close examination, the bill is quite deficient. It does very little, even after amendment by the Judiciary Committee, to control the discretion of the Executive Branch to engage in this kind of electronic surveillance. Unsupported appeals to "national security" should not determine whether this bill becomes public law. "The security of the Nation is not at the ramparts alone. Security also lies in the value of our free institutions," as the District Judge in the Pentagon Papers case cogently observed. And an integral part of our free institutions is the security of the people from intrusions by government agents into their privacy. I urge this Committee, in the strongest words I can, to reject this cosmetic proposal.

See U.S. Senate. Select Committee on Intelligence. *Electronic Surveillance within the United States for Foreign Intelligence Purposes.* Hearing, 29 June, 1 July, 6, 10, 24 August 1976, 94th Cong. 2nd sess. (Washington, D.C.: Government Printing Office, 1976), pp. 112–115.

RECOMMENDED READINGS

Brittan, David. *The Mayaguez Incident.* Cambridge, Mass.: Kennedy School of Government, 1983.

Congressional Quarterly, Inc. *President Ford: The Man and His Record.* Washington, D.C.: Congressional Quarterly, Inc., 1974.

Firestone, Bernard J., and Alexej Ugrinsky, eds. *Gerald R. Ford and the Politics of Post-Watergate America.* Westport, Conn.: Greenwood Press, 1993.

Mollenhoff, Clark R. *The Man Who Pardoned Nixon.* New York: St. Martin's Press, 1976.

3

JIMMY CARTER

(1977–1981)

INTRODUCTION

Jimmy Carter's election to the presidency was probably more a reflection of the public's dissatisfaction with the previous presidencies of Nixon and Ford than it was a clear message of support for this previously little known, former governor of Georgia. However, if the public had hoped for change in the presidency, Jimmy Carter certainly delivered, bringing the perceptions and goals of one who is new to Washington, D.C. Unlike the previous four presidents, Carter had no experience in Congress before assuming the office of the president. While this "outsider" status was probably one of Carter's appeals, it did not bode well for his relations with Congress, possibly because Carter was unable or unwilling to play by Washington's "rules of the game."

A publicly professed Christian, Carter firmly believed that United States should take the high road when making policies, injecting an element of morality into both domestic and foreign policy decisions. This approach, however, did not always win supporters, even among members of his own Democratic Party. Numerous policies advocated by Carter demonstrate his perception that government should be used for good. However, "good" is subjective; what one sees as being good, another sees as detrimental or harmful. Several of Carter's policies reveal this moralistic approach to policy making, including the linkage of American foreign policy to issues of human rights and the condemnation of the Soviet invasion of Afghanistan, which prompted Carter to withhold American grain from the Soviets and to boycott the Moscow Olympics in 1980. Similarly, he also didn't want the United States to be perceived as taking advantage of less fortunate countries, as witnessed by his desire to turn over operations of the Panama Canal to the Panamanians.

Carter was also plagued with the continuing economic trials experienced by Nixon and Ford. He employed a variety of policies to remedy the problems, including the deregulation of the trucking and airline industries, an anti-inflation package of legislation, and a series of energy policies attempting to minimize American reliance on imported oil. As with all presidents, Carter had other domestic goals he hoped to achieve. His first act as president was to pardon Vietnam War resisters, and he demonstrated his commitment to social policies by persuading Congress to create the Department of Education and passing landmark environmental legislation.

A marked difference between Carter and his two predecessors was the shift in the country's attention away from Southeast Asia and toward the Middle East. While the Soviet Union continued to loom large in American foreign policy, demonstrated by Carter's completion of the SALT II agreement, many of his policies reflected the changing status of the Middle East for the United States. Carter's policies included efforts to achieve peace by bringing Egyptian and Israeli leaders together at Camp David, as well as promoting the interests of the United States, outlined in the Carter Doctrine. The political upheaval in the Middle East as well as the growing resentment against the United States for its involvement in the region manifested itself very visibly when fifty-two people were held hostage in Iran for fourteen months, which was prompted by the U.S. acceptance of the Shah of Iran for medical treatment. Carter's ill-fated rescue attempt effectively opened the door to his 1980 defeat by Ronald Reagan.

In this section, fourteen of Carter's key policies will be addressed. The first four deal with issues that arose in 1977, the first year of his presidency. The first action Carter took after his inauguration was to pardon resisters of the Vietnam War. Both in his Proclamation of Pardon on January 21 and during a question-and-answer period with employees of the Department of Defense, Carter explained his decision to pardon war resisters, claiming it was a just response to their honest opposition to the war. Representative John T. Myers (R-Ind.) disagreed, proposing a successful amendment to the Department of Defense appropriations bill that prevented any appropriations from being spent to carry out the president's pardon. The second issue in this section came to the fore in March 1977, when President Carter sent a letter to Congress expressing his desire to link foreign policies such as military or economic aid with the receiving country's commitment to human rights. A group of ten men and women in the House of Representatives expressed their concern over the president's proposal in a committee report to the full House. It was their contention that the president's plan would be applied inequitably by the United States, in that human rights violations would more likely be considered a variable in providing aid for some countries than others.

One of the president's most successful policies was the deregulation of the nation's airline industry, the third issue of this section. In a letter to the Senate written in July 1977, he urged senators to pass his proposal, arguing that it would help decrease the costs of air travel and would increase competition among air carriers. He reiterated his beliefs at the United Steelworkers of America Convention. While small air carriers were supportive of the president's policy, larger companies opposed it. C.E. Meyer, president of Trans World Airlines (TWA), testified at a Senate hearing that deregulation would actually hurt the airline industry and that airfares had been kept low because of regulation.

In September 1977, Carter turned his attention south to Latin America, where resentment had been brewing against the United States for years because of its control of the Panama Canal Zone. In a show of good will toward Panama, Carter finalized the details of a treaty with Panama that would turn over control of the Canal Zone to Panama by December 31, 1999. Carter expressed his support of the treaty both in a White House briefing and in the signing ceremony for the treaty. Ronald Reagan expressed the concerns of Carter's critics that the United States should not relinquish control of the canal on the chance that Panama would associate at some future time with U.S. enemies, limiting the country's access to this vital waterway.

The fifth issue considered, energy taxes, was one part of a much larger package of energy legislation designed to diminish U.S. reliance on Middle Eastern oil, in particular, and nonrenewable resources, in general. Carter wanted to deregulate the price of domestic oil, but to tax any windfall profits domestic oil producers would gain as a result of setting higher prices. The president attempted to build support for his policies by speaking in Bangor, Maine, about the need for conservation and alternative energy sources. Harold B. Scoggins, Jr., a representative of the Independent Petroleum Association of America, testified against the tax portion of the president's plan in a hearing held by a Senate committee, although his organization supported the deregulation of domestic oil prices.

In September 1978, President Carter made history by bringing the leaders of two warring nations together to negotiate a peace treaty. At the Camp David presidential retreat, Egyptian President Anwar al-Sadat and Israeli Prime Minister Menachim Begin met to work through their fundamental disagreements over rights to certain territories around Israel. President Carter praised the two leaders during comments at the close of the meetings. While there did appear to be some progress made toward peace, the Camp David Accords were not an unqualified success.

An article in *The Economist* made the point that very little communication took place between Sadat and Begin, and that the two men spent more time talking at each other than to each other. But the peace, although a cold peace, has endured.

A month after the Camp David Accords were signed, President Carter addressed the nation in a televised speech about the economic woes of the country. Although he offered some policies to address the continued high rate of inflation, his tone was pessimistic and foreboding. Senator Harrison Schmitt (R-N.M.), in his opening statements before Senate hearings on the president's anti-inflation package, accused the president of failing to provide moral leadership to the country with regard to the economy.

President Carter tackled another domestic issue in February 1979, when he proposed the creation of the Department of Education. In his message to Congress transmitting the proposal, Carter explained the need for a centralized body to deal with education at the national level, rather than incorporating education into the missions of other federal departments. Monsignor Wilfrid H. Paradis, secretary for education of the U.S. Catholic Conference, expressed his opposition to the new department in a Senate hearing, explaining that a greater federal role in education policy threatened to diminish the influence of local governments and parents in the education of children.

On June 18, 1979, attention turned once again to the relationship between the United States and the Soviet Union with the signing of SALT II. Negotiations on the treaty began shortly after SALT I was signed, considering the difficult issue of offensive weapons that had been addressed only in the Interim Agreement of SALT I. Carter helped complete the negotiations, and in remarks to the Annual Convention of the American Newspaper Publishers' Association, he explained how SALT II would help limit the number of offensive nuclear weapons for each country, better assuring peace between the two superpowers. Senator Sam Nunn (D-Ga.) well-known for his expertise in the area of foreign affairs and a member of the president's own party, expressed concern over the treaty in remarks made during a Senate hearing. He claimed that unless the president increased the defense budget, SALT II placed the United States at a disadvantage and he could not support it.

The changing political environment of the Middle East prompted Carter to adopt a policy specifically addressing U.S. interest in the region. In his State of the Union Address on January 21, 1980, Carter outlined what was referred to as the Carter Doctrine, in which the United States would intervene on behalf of Middle Eastern countries that were threatened or invaded by outside forces. Marvin Zonis, a professor at the University of Chicago, testified to the House committee that the president's policy was largely misguided, in that the biggest threat to the Middle

East did not come from outside the region, but from the political instability within the region.

The Carter Doctrine was largely prompted by the Soviet invasion of Afghanistan at the end of 1979, and two of Carter's early policies in 1980 were reactions to the invasion. In another section of the State of the Union address on January 21, Carter explained that the United States was obligated to respond to the Soviets' invasion of a neighboring country, and that his first policy in that regard was to withhold the sale of American grain to the Soviet Union. The Soviets were anticipating a difficult winter and a shortage of grain, and Carter hoped that the grain embargo would pressure the Soviets into reconsidering their invasion. U.S. farmers were hit hard by the policy, however; they were left with a large surplus of grain and lowered prices. An editorial in *Farmer's Digest* offered the farmers' perspective of the embargo. The second policy made in response to the Soviet invasion was to boycott the summer Olympics, which were to be held in Moscow. President Carter discussed his decision in March 1980 with representatives of the U.S. Olympic team. To many, this response, which was designed to embarrass the Soviet Union, seemed trite when compared to the magnitude of the Soviets' aggression. Humorist George Plimpton wrote a column in *Newsweek* magazine, poking fun at the president's response to the military invasion.

Carter's most significant failure as president occurred in April 1980, when he authorized a rescue attempt of the hostages held in Iran. When the plan failed, the president was forced to address the nation to explain that the hostages had not been freed, and that eight Marine and Air Force members had died in the attempt. Because Congress guards its role in defense policy quite jealously, hearings were soon held in the Senate to consider whether or not the president had violated the War Powers Act in his use of troops in the rescue attempt. Senator Richard G. Lugar (R-Ind.) accused the president of withholding information from Congress prior to the attempt, for fear that Congress would not have approved.

Last, the president accomplished a significant success in the area of environmental policy in December 1980, a month following his defeat for reelection. In anticipation of Ronald Reagan taking over the office of the president, Carter and the Democrats in Congress were able to pass major legislation regarding the cleanup of hazardous waste sites. As Carter commented in Jacksonville, Florida, the Superfund, as it was called, would help protect the environment by providing a means for the cleanup of these sites. Because chemical manufacturers were required to help finance the restoration of these sites, the industry was adamantly opposed to Superfund. Robert A. Roland, president of the Chemical Manufacturers Association, testified before a House hearing that the Superfund unfairly singled out the chemical industry and that there were better ways to finance the cleanup of hazardous wastes.

PARDON FOR VIETNAM WAR RESISTERS

One of the president's most unambiguous constitutional powers is the power to pardon individuals convicted of crimes. Despite the clear language of the Constitution, using this power can often be controversial. The two controversies that typically surround the pardon relate to whom the president pardons and the reasons for the pardon. When the person pardoned is well-known or when the pardon appears to have political motivations, criticism is quick to follow. Gerald Ford's pardon of Richard Nixon and Bill Clinton's pardon of fugitive billionaire Marc Rich are examples of the types of pardons that generate a great deal of controversy. Because the potential for controversy always exists with the pardon, most presidents choose to make the majority of their pardons at the end of their term as president.

Like Gerald Ford before him, Jimmy Carter chose to extend a pardon almost immediately after taking office. After he assumed the presidency, Ford pardoned Richard Nixon for all crimes he may have committed during the Watergate affair, yet he only offered a limited clemency to Vietnam War resisters. The pardon of Nixon would have generated controversy in its own right, but the controversy was compounded by the realization that ordinary citizens were not provided with the same benefits as a former president. During Carter's presidential campaign, he stated that he would correct the incomplete and unfair clemency policy of President Ford by offering a complete pardon to Vietnam War resisters.

On January 21, 1977, in his first act as president, Carter issued the pardon to individuals who had violated the Selective Service Act between August 4, 1964 and March 28, 1973. The decision was controversial. There seemed to be very little middle ground among the American public on the issue, with some believing the president had acted justly, and others vehemently opposing the pardon. The president addressed the issue in a question and answer session he held with Department of Defense employees, an audience that was not particularly supportive of the pardon. Because the pardon is a power specifically granted to the president by the Constitution, the other branches of government can do little about a pardon they oppose. Short of amending the constitution, the only check on the president's decision to offer pardons is public opinion and if the president waits until the end of his term, concern even for public approval is largely removed. In the case of Carter's pardon of Vietnam War resisters, opponents of the pardon were frustrated that there was nothing they could do to block the decision.

Members of Congress who were opposed to the president's decision were determined to limit the effect of the pardon in whatever way they could. One power the Congress has is to appropriate funds for the various programs administered by the national government and it was to the appropriations power that these opponents turned in their effort to undermine the pardon. Added to a defense department appropriations bill in June 1977 was an amendment offered by Representative John T. Myers (R-Ind.), which would have prevented any appropriations from being used to administer Carter's pardon. The amendment had been proposed before in a supplemental appropriations bill, and had passed, and Myers inserted it again in the major appropriations bill then under consideration. The amendment was adopted a second time. The actual effect this provision would have on the pardon was negligible. The administration of the pardon was essentially a costless exercise, but Myers offered the amendment largely as a symbolic gesture in opposition to the president's decision. He included in his statement that neither he nor his constituents supported the pardon, and although he knew the president did have the authority to make the decision, the Congress did not have to support it financially.

CARTER'S PRESIDENTIAL PROCLAMATION OF PARDON

Granting Pardon for Violations of the Selective Service Act, August 4, 1964 to March 28, 1973
January 21, 1977

Acting pursuant to the grant of authority in Article II, Section 2, of the Constitution of the United States, I, Jimmy Carter, President of the United States, do hereby grant a full, complete and unconditional pardon to: (1) all persons who may have committed any offense between August 4, 1964 and March 28, 1973 in violation of the Military Selective Service Act or any rule or regulation promulgated thereunder; and (2) all persons heretofore convicted, irrespective of the date of conviction, of any offense committed between August 4, 1964 and March 28, 1973 in violation of the Military Selective Service Act, or any rule or regulation promulgated thereunder, restoring to them full political, civil and other rights.

This pardon does not apply to the following who are specifically excluded therefrom:

(1) All persons convicted of or who may have committed any offense in violation of the Military Selective Service Act, or any rule or regulation promulgated thereunder, involving force or violence; and

(2) All persons convicted of or who may have committed any offense in violation of the Military Selective Service Act, or any rule or regulation promulgated thereunder, in connection with duties or responsibilities arising out of employment as agents, officers or employees of the Military Selective Service system.

In Witness Whereof, I have hereunto set my hand this 21st day of January, in the year of our Lord nineteen hundred and seventy-seven, and of the Independence of the United States of America the two hundred and first.

See "Presidential Proclamation of Pardon, Proclamation 4483" (21 Jan. 1977), p. 5. In *Public Papers of the Presidents of the United States: Jimmy Carter*, 1977 (Washington, D.C.: Government Printing Office, 1977).

RESPONSE TO A QUESTION REGARDING THE PARDON

Question-and-Answer Session with Department of Defense Employees
March 1, 1977

I know that my own position on granting a pardon to the violators of the Selective Service laws during the Vietnam conflict was not a popular decision for many Americans to accept. But I don't believe that the patriotism of American service men and women, now or in the future, is predicated on whether or not the pardon was granted.

And I believe that we can count on the full support of Americans in time of trial or time of danger to defend our country. My own son went to Vietnam. He served there voluntarily and came back home. I served in two wars. And I believe that in the future, we can count on American citizens to serve their country without any doubt.

I have also a historical perspective about this question. I come from the South. I know at the end of the War Between the States, there was a sense of forgiveness for those who had been not loyal to our country in the past, and this same thing occurred after other wars as well.

I also felt that those who had left our country during the Vietnam war and had been living overseas for 10, 12, 15 years, had been punished enough. It was a matter of judgment. I made my judgment clear during the campaign. I never misled anyone. I made the major announcement of my plan to grant this pardon at an American Legion convention in Seattle, perhaps one of the most antagonistic audiences that I could have chosen. But I didn't want to mislead anyone about it, and I was elected either because of it or in spite of it.

Now, the other consideration for those who have been guilty of military offenses will be handled completely within the Department of Defense. The Attorney General, the Secretary of Defense, and their representatives are trying to deal with other violators of military regulations and laws on an individual case basis. This was another part of my commitment to the American people during the campaign.

I don't have any apology to make about it. I made my decision clear before the election. The first week I was in office, I carried out my commitment. And I believe that the patriotism and support of the American Government and its people, in times of crisis in the future, will be met by courageous people as they have been in the past, regardless of what my decision was on the pardon question.

See "Department of Defense: Remarks and Question and Answer Session with Department Employees" (1 Mar. 1977), pp. 266–267. In *Public Papers of the Presidents of the United States: Jimmy Carter, 1977* (Washington, D.C.: Government Printing Office, 1977).

AMENDMENT OFFERED BY REPRESENTATIVE JOHN T. MYERS (R-IND.)

June 13, 1977

Mr. Chairman, I offer an amendment.

The Clerk read as follows:

"Amendment offered by Mr. Myers of Indiana: . . . None of the funds appropriated or otherwise made available in the Act shall be obligated or expended for salaries or expenses in connection with the dismissal of any pending indictments for violations of the Military Selective Service Act alleged to have occurred between August 4, 1964 and March 28, 1973, or the termination of any investigation now pending alleging violations of the Military Selective Service Act between August 4, 1964 and March 28, 1973, or permitting any person to enter the United States who is or may be precluded from entering the United States under 8 U.S.C. 1182(a) (22) or under any other law, by reason of having committed or apparently committed any violation of the Military Selective Service Act."

. . . Mr. Chairman, this is the same limitation amendment which was offered by the Member and passed the House on the supplemental back in March. It is a limitation on the expenditures relative to the pardon of the evaders, those who left the service of the country during the Vietnam era. It has nothing to do so far as challenging or questioning the constitutional authority of the President of the United States to Executive orders of pardon. The pardon does stand. The President does have that authority. I am not questioning that for a moment. It is simple exercise of the authority of the House of Representatives and this Congress to decide how the public's money shall be spent.

Mr. Chairman, I have found that the great majority of the people in my congressional district oppose having their tax money spent to carry out the pardon. After receiving mail from all over the United States when this amendment was offered back in March, it is certainly the view of a great majority of the people in this country that they do not want to see any of their tax dollars spent to further the pardon or bring back those who were not forced out of the country but left of their own volition.

Mr. Chairman, if we go back for the just a moment to examine the cases of these pardoned people. We are considering—again not considering the pardon, because the pardon has already been issued and it is already standing—these people during the Vietnam era did have an opportunity not to have to serve in a frontline or carry a rifle if they were serious, honest, conscientious objectors. The law provided for those people for an alternative service. There were a great many ways in which an individual might serve his country without evading the laws and the draft system. They chose to evade and violate the law.

This is a simple exercise of the right of this House to deny that funds can be used to carry out the pardon. It was passed overwhelmingly in March. Again, because of every public opinion poll I have been shown and by the mail received concerning this amendment, I am quite sure that this amendment will be accepted again today.

See Rep. John T. Myers (Ind.). *Congressional Record* 123, pt. 15 (13 June 1977), p. 18575.

HUMAN RIGHTS AND FOREIGN POLICY

Although foreign aid has never been a particularly popular program with the American people, it has played an important role in building positive relationships between the United States and other countries. Certainly, the United States conveys an economic benefit to those countries on the receiving end, but in providing aid, both in the form of economic and military assistance, the United States conveys a symbolic message as well. In deciding which countries receive aid and which do not, which countries receive more and which receive less, the U.S. government can communicate its support for or opposition to the policies or actions of other countries. On the positive side, aid may be used as means of persuasion to encourage countries to take a course of action supported by the United States, or as a reward to a country that has made decisions favored by the United States. Conversely, aid may be discontinued if a nation pursues a course of action not supported by the United States. In essence, foreign aid may be used both as the proverbial carrot and stick to influence the actions of other countries.

While other presidents have used foreign aid to communicate their support for other countries, few have interjected as much idealism into the process as President Carter. During his administration, Carter was very much of the opinion that policies regarding foreign aid should be closely linked with furthering the American ideals of freedom and equality in other parts of the world. As such, he believed that countries routinely violating basic human rights should not receive the same benefits as countries attempting to protect the individual rights of its citizens.

Carter expressed his position on the American commitment to human rights numerous times. In a letter transmitting foreign aid legislation to Congress in March 1977, Carter explained that human rights should be one consideration when devising American policy toward other countries. Yet there was an element of flexibility in his message to Congress, adding that he didn't want Congress to pass legislation that would hinder current relationships with other countries. Other statements regarding human rights and foreign policy were not always as tempered as were those to Congress. In comments to the European Broadcast Journalists, for instance, his position seemed much firmer and absolute in tone. He expressed his "undeviating commitment" to the pursuit of human rights around the world. The flexibility that had appeared in his letter to Congress was not evident in the later statement.

This inconsistency can be attributed to the different audiences the president must address. In both statements, a commitment to human rights was expressed, but his letter to Congress reflected the political realities of passing foreign aid legislation. The fact of the matter is, there are countries with which the United States needs to maintain positive relations, despite their record of human rights violations. For instance, the United States has been criticized, often by Americans, for maintaining relations with China because of that country's treatment of its own citizens. Yet, the United States has to consider whether it is prudent to disregard or sanction a country of over 1 billion people that has become a primary trading partner. Carter's message to the European Broadcast Journalists appears to reflect the more idealistic aspects of his position, rather than the political compromise of those ideals.

Although the differences in the president's messages were more a matter of degree than actual substance, they did open the door to criticism by members of Congress who were considering his foreign assistance legislation. In a report by the House Committee on Appropriations, a group of representatives provided a dissenting view of the legislation being considered by the House of Representatives. They were broadly concerned with the very attempt to link foreign policy with human rights, implicitly characterizing this as an extremist approach to foreign policy. They were also more specifically concerned with the inequitable manner in which foreign aid was being appropriated. The representatives claimed that in an attempt to provide the flexibility the president desired, the legislation would only serve to embitter the countries that were singled out for cuts in aid. Because of these two concerns, they could not support the legislation.

TRANSMITTING PROPOSED FOREIGN AID LEGISLATION

Letter from President Carter to the Speaker of the House and the President of the Senate
March 28, 1977

I am transmitting today a bill to authorize security assistance programs for the fiscal years 1978 and 1979. I consider these programs essential to the attainment of important United States foreign policy goals throughout the world, and to reassure our friends and allies of the constancy of our support.

The programs authorized by this legislation include both military and economic forms of security assistance, with approximately two-thirds of the funds requested intended for nonmilitary programs. In addition, the bill provides for the continuation of our important international narcotics control efforts.

The authorizations I am proposing reflect downward adjustments this Administration has made in several programs in light of the human rights situations in the countries concerned. We are committed to a continuing effort to ensure that human rights considerations are taken fully into account in determining whether our security assistance programs serve our national security and foreign policy objectives.

I am not at this time proposing major changes in the authorities and statutory procedures which now govern security assistance and arms export controls. I have made clear on several occasions my deep concern over the burgeoning international traffic in arms. I am firmly resolved to bring greater coherence, restraint and control to our arms transfer policies and practices. To this end, I have ordered a comprehensive review of our policies and practices regarding both governmental and commercial arms exports.

Our goal is to develop, in close consultation with the Congress, policies which respect our commitments to the security and independence of friends and allies, which reflect fully our common concern for the promotion of basic human rights, and which give substance to our commitment to restrain the world arms race.

The completion of this process within the next few months will give both the Executive Branch and the Legislative Branch a sound foundation on which they can base a thoughtful reexamination of existing law and fashion needed legislative revisions which will complement our common policy objectives, ensure appropriate participation and oversight by the Congress, and provide clear authority for the efficient conduct of approved programs.

In the meantime, I urge the Congress to avoid legislative initiatives which could disrupt important programs or would hinder a future cooperative effort based on a thorough evaluation of the facts and policy considerations.

See "Letter from President Carter to the Speaker of the House and the President of the Senate Transmitting Proposed Legislation" (28 Mar. 1977), pp. 522–523. In *Public Papers of the Presidents of the United States: Jimmy Carter, 1977* (Washington, D.C.: Government Printing Office, 1977).

EUROPEAN BROADCAST JOURNALISTS' QUESTION-AND-ANSWER SESSION WITH PRESIDENT CARTER

May 2, 1977

My stand on human rights is compatible with the strong and proven position taken by almost all Americans. We feel that the right of a human being to be treated fairly in the courts, to be removed from the threat of prison, imprisonment without a trial, to have a life to live that's free is very precious. In the past this deep commitment of the free democracies has quite often not been widely known or accepted or demonstrated.

Our policy is very clear. It doesn't relate just to the Soviet Union. I've always made it clear that it doesn't. It relates to our own country as well. It relates to all those with whom we trade or with whom we communicate.

It's an undeviating commitment that I intend to maintain until the last day I'm in office. And through various means, either public statements or through private negotiations, through sales policies, we are trying to implement a renewed awareness of the need for human rights in our dealing with all countries.

See "European Broadcast Journalists Question and Answer Session" (2 May 1977), pp. 765–766. In *Public Papers of the Presidents of the United States: Jimmy Carter, 1977* (Washington, D.C.: Government Printing Office, 1977).

FOREIGN ASSISTANCE PROGRAMS

Statement of Minority Views of Representatives C. W. Bill Young (R-Fla.), Clarence E. Miller (R-Ohio), William L. Armstrong (R-Colo.), Robert H. Michel (R-Ill.), Jack F. Kemp (R-N.Y.), J. Kenneth Robinson (R-Va.), John T. Myers (R-Ind.), Virginia Smith (R-Nebr.), Clair W. Burgener (R-Calif.), and Robert C. McEwen (R-N.Y.) House Committee on Appropriations, June 15, 1977

Although the foreign aid program of the United States has never really been popular with the American people, since they have had little recourse anyway they have reluctantly swallowed their objections and provided assistance all over the world. This bill has items in it which we can support. There are however a number of features in this bill and the whole foreign aid program which we feel are not representative of the goals and values of the United States. It is not our intention to destroy the foreign aid program, but rather we are trying to make it a better program, one we can support and one we believe the people of our country can support. It is our hope that necessary changes can be made in this program so not only will we be able to support it, but the American people will be able to give it their support as well. . . .

Human Rights

The issue of human rights played a major role in the Committee's consideration of military aid programs. Programs were reduced or eliminated, totaling $22,500,000 in Nicaragua, Argentina, Brazil, El Salvador, Guatemala, Ethiopia, and the Philippines because of alleged human rights violations. However, other countries who are also considered violators of human rights are still treated generously in this bill. Some of these countries include Indonesia, Thailand, Ghana, Bangladesh, Senegal, Liberia, and Haiti. This is clearly an inconsistent policy. The issue of human rights should be addressed uniformly rather than on a selective hit or miss basis. The subcommittee did adopt effective language on this, but then insisted on selectively picking certain countries for program cuts while ignoring others. It's hard to know which countries are the worst violators of human rights, since the Committee held specific hearings on human rights violations for only Nicaragua and the Philippines. Much of the information made available to the Committee concerning human rights violations came from special interest groups. The reliability of this information should be questioned, and the wisdom of basing U.S. foreign policy on this type of information is a dangerous precedent.

The President has expressed his position on this issue on several occasions. He does not want Congress to tie his hands in this matter. The President wants flexibility so that he can work with these countries, maintaining good relations with our allies and at the same time seeking improved relations with other countries. Selectively reducing aid to one of our allies, like the Philippines, or publicly embarrassing them, will serve no useful purpose. In fact, it is our concern that friendly countries like the Philippines might feel inclined to save face by taking some action against the United States in response to this obvious slap in the face this Committee action gives them.

While there are some in our government who have said they believe Communists are a stabilizing factor in certain parts of the world, there are also those who believe that stopping military aid based on human rights conditions in certain countries who are friendly to us, is in our national interest. We do not agree with these people on either account. If a government needs military equipment or training, it is going to obtain that assistance whether we provide it or not. What we are in fact doing is telling them to find another source for their defense needs. We are opening the door for the Soviets to come into our own backyard. No matter how we arrive at this point—if we lose our allies we will become a very isolated and lonely island in a rather hostile world. . . .

As stated in our opening remarks, we are not opposed to all of the programs in this bill. But, as we have shown, there are many programs that raise very serious questions concerning the value of our participation in them. We have not been satisfied with many of the answers we have received so far. The President has stated on numerous occasions his intention to balance the budget by 1981, and we strongly support him in this effort. However, we are unable to see how the large increase in this bill or any plan to double foreign aid can be consistent with our goal to balance the budget. It is our hope that a restructuring of the foreign aid program can take place and the objectionable portions of the program be eliminated so that eventually we can develop a foreign aid program which will enjoy the support of the American people rather than their opposition.

See U.S. House. Committee on Appropriations. *Foreign Assistance and Related Programs, Appropriations Bill 1978* (H. Rpt. 95–417) (Washington, D.C.: Government Printing Office, 1977), pp. 67, 71, 75.

AIRLINE DEREGULATION

Generally speaking, when the government makes public policy, some segments of society benefit from the decision, and others bear the cost of that policy. Because a single policy can affect various groups in very different ways, certain policies generate a great deal of conflict and controversy, while others face much less opposition. People and groups specifically disadvantaged by a policy have a real incentive to speak out in opposition to that policy, consequently making the policy-making process more contentious. One type of policy that can spark tremendous controversy is regulatory policy, which is a policy by which the government attempts to regulate or control behavior—usually the actions of industry or business groups. Regulatory policies may be passed to protect the public from dangerous business practices, such as the dumping of hazardous chemicals, but regulations may also protect industries that are deemed vital to the economy from excessive or harmful competition. Both types of regulation garner a great deal of attention from the industries specifically affected by the policies.

Until 1978, the airline industry was heavily regulated, both to protect the interests of consumers of air travel and the airline industry itself. Until the mid-1920s, the commercial airline industry was used primarily by the U.S. Postal Service, which would contract with private carriers to ship domestic mail. To supplement their income, these carriers also began offering passenger service, and in 1926, the industry had grown to the point that the federal government was compelled to regulate air traffic routes through the Air Commerce Act. However, Congress was well aware of the industry's strong desire to branch out into passenger air service, so in 1925 and 1926 congressional leaders debated how the federal government could help promote commercial air travel. Air carriers were largely supportive of regulation, such as rules governing air traffic routes, because it was perceived to make air travel safer. In 1958, Congress passed the Federal Aviation Act, placing responsibility for commercial airline regulation in the hands of the Federal Aviation Agency, which was also created by the Act. The FAA was renamed the Federal Aviation Administration in 1967, when it was moved into the Department of Transportation. The FAA had broad responsibilities, including the creation of a system of air traffic control, the development of safety requirements, the licensing of airline carriers, and the regulation of airfares for passengers.

Thus, regulation of the airlines was originally perceived as a necessity to protect and promote the airline industry, an industry considered crucial to the country's economy, and as a means to protect consumers from hazardous equipment or slipshod aviation practices. There was also concern that the relatively few airline companies would practice collusion to set unreasonably high airfares, so the FAA regulated the fares that could be set. While there were certainly valid reasons for regulating the airline industry so intensively, the policy was criticized in the 1970s for preventing competition in the airline industry. Because airfares were established by the Federal Aviation Administration, the typical forces driving competition in most businesses were largely absent.

This regulatory policy was not universally endorsed by airline companies, either. Smaller companies complained that it kept newcomers out of the industry, and they argued that airfares would actually decrease if more competition were injected into the industry. Regulations limiting entry into certain routes were hampering the growth of the industry. Larger airline companies, however, were satisfied with government regulation, largely because they benefited from a system that effectively controlled competition. President Carter endorsed the idea that more competition and less government interference would benefit the industry. He proposed legislation to Congress that would remove some of the barriers to smaller airline companies and would allow each company to set its own fares, rather than having all companies adhere to the same rates. When the Senate held hearings on the bills dealing with deregulation, representatives from various airlines testified about the expected effect deregulation would have on the industry. The testimony broke down along size lines: The large companies were opposed to the president's deregulation proposal; smaller, commuter carriers were generally in favor of it. The testimony of C.E. Myer, Jr., president of TWA, exemplifies the arguments made against the proposal, primarily reflecting the interests of large companies. Despite the opposition expressed by these companies, the president's proposal was ultimately approved, opening the door to the creation of many low-fare airline companies.

AIRLINE INDUSTRY REGULATION

President Carter's Letter to Members of the Senate Committee on Commerce, Science, and Transportation July 28, 1977

To Members of the Senate Committee on Commerce, Science, and Transportation:

Reducing regulation of the airline industry is the first major opportunity to meet our shared goal of eliminating outdated and excessive government regulation. Sound regulatory reform is a top priority of my Administration. I commend you for the progress you and your colleagues have made in working toward that goal.

I urge you to speed the pace of your deliberations so that a bill can be acted upon by the Senate this year. You have already made significant decisions on many parts of the bill. But the most important decisions still lie ahead. I would like to elaborate upon the principles I set forth in my Message to Congress on March 4, 1977, and share with you my views on pricing and entry.

1. *Automatic Route Entry*. Pricing flexibility must be accompanied by strong entry provisions. It is entry, or the realistic threat of it, that prevents price flexibility from being abused. Automatic route entry is especially important in keeping prices low, and I consider it to be one of the most important elements of a reform bill. The current provision in the bill allows carriers to enter a very limited number of new markets each year without having to undergo the costly process of obtaining Board approval. The record developed by your Committee clearly supports even greater automatic entry than is provided by the current draft.

2. *Presumption in Favor of Entry*. Retention of the provision in the bill that would reverse the burden of proof in entry proceedings is essential. The presumption should be that competition is consistent with the public interest. Anyone who is against new competition should have to show that it would be harmful to the public—not the other way around. Indeed, I would prefer a provision reversing the burden of proof immediately upon enactment of the bill, rather than delaying its effectiveness of this provision for three years, as in the current draft.

3. *Unused Route Authority*. If a carrier has authority to serve a market but has chosen not to use it, a new carrier who would like to serve the public in that market should be given the opportunity to do so. There is simply no justification for preventing new carriers from serving markets that other carriers are not using. The draft bill makes entry against a carrier holding unused authority more difficult than entry into markets where no such unexercised grants of authority are outstanding. I recommend that this provision of the current bill be strengthened.

4. *Pricing Flexibility*. One of the major aims of reform is to allow carriers to lower their prices wherever possible. The current regulatory scheme permits lower fares only by means of heavily regulated and highly restricted price discounts. I urge you to support the provisions in the bill which take meaningful steps to remove the artificial regulatory barriers to lower prices.

I believe that entry provisions and upward pricing flexibility are intimately related. To the extent that the automatic entry and dormant authority provisions are strengthened, and the burden of proof is reversed at an earlier date, some limited upward pricing flexibility may be warranted. But if these changes are not made, then I would support a move to limit carriers' price increases only where they are justified by rising costs. Alternatively, you might wish to consider explicitly tying entry to pricing; that is, providing for some easing of the bill's entry limitations in those instances where prices have been significantly increased.

There are many aspects of this complex reform legislation, but the value which the ordinary citizen ultimately gains from our efforts mainly depends on the Congress' resolution of these four basic issues.

Sincerely,

Jimmy Carter

See "Airline Industry Regulation" (28 July 1977), pp. 1379–1380. In *Public Papers of the Presidents of the United States: Jimmy Carter, 1977* (Washington, D.C.: Government Printing Office, 1977).

CARTER'S REMARKS AT THE UNITED STEEL WORKERS OF AMERICA CONVENTION

September 20, 1978

Another example of important anti-inflation legislation is airline deregulation. Many of you flew in here by commercial airline service. One price that has gone down in the last year substantially is the price of an airline ticket on domestic and overseas flights. At first, the airline industry screamed that this would be devastating to them. Many airplanes on which I flew as a candidate for President would only have 25 percent or less of the seats filled. Now, because of reduced fares, those same planes are averaging 75 percent occupancy. Travel to other countries is increasing rapidly. The average working people of our country can travel in speed and comfort. And the profits of the airline companies have gone up substantially. It's been good all around.

This has mostly been done by regulatory action, the Civil Aeronautics Board, my own decisions, particularly in overseas flight. But shortly, perhaps even today, the House will vote on an airline deregulation bill that will put these enormously improved practices into law and make them permanent. We need to let those policies be embedded in the law, so that domestic airline fares can also be reduced by competition under the American free enterprise system. Government, of course, cannot do jobs like this alone in holding down unnecessary prices.

See "Atlantic City, New Jersey: Remarks at the United Steel Workers of America Convention" (20 Sept. 1978), p. 1549. In *Public Papers of the Presidents of the United States: Jimmy Carter, 1978* (Washington, D.C.: Government Printing Office, 1978).

STATEMENT OF C.E. MEYER, JR., PRESIDENT AND CHIEF
AIRLINE EXECUTIVE, TRANS WORLD AIRLINES

**Hearings before the Senate Subcommittee on Aviation of
the Committee on Commerce, Science, and Transportation
March 24, 1977**

I very much appreciate the opportunity to present my views on the critical issue of airline regulation as I believe it is a subject on which considerable additional attention must be focused.

After months of study and a series of comments from a wide range of interested parties, I believe the consequences at issue have yet to be adequately defined in practical economic and social terms. There continue to be a number of contradictions and questions for which satisfactory answers have not been provided.

Therefore, I am obliged to register TWA's opposition in the proposed changes in the rules governing the airline industry as contained in S. 689 and S. 292—particularly in regard to the entry and pricing provisions.

In addition, I must express deep concern that one of the major stated purposes of the proposed legislation is a desire to increase competition in what has been and increasingly is a highly competitive industry. The airlines have long suffered from the unfortunate conflict of being highly regulated and, at the same time, highly competitive. The proposed legislation simply worsens that condition.

There are a number of fundamental questions that I believe you must resolve before you enact any program of the scope now before you. I'd like to hear the answers and I believe those directly affected by the changes should hear them, too. Among these are:

One: What will be the impact on the communities now served? You have heard the argument about cross-subsidization and I will not burden you with further comments in that area, except to note that no one has effectively described what will happen to service to smaller communities, other than noting that where needed it will be subsidized by Federal funds.

When I consider that Amtrak, which originally was a 2-year experiment, is now in its 6th year of existence, that it cost the taxpayers $360 million in fiscal year 1976 and [we] expect to spend an additional $6.2 billion between 1976 and 1980, I suggest that additional study must be given to identifying the cost to the Nation's taxpayers of new, subsidized service to small communities as a substitute for existing service.

Two: What impact will the proposed legislation have on the 300,000 employees directly involved in the airline industry? I believe the effect will be severe. . . .

Three: What happens to the hundreds of thousands of employees who are involved in supporting the airline industry in the production of aircraft and related equipment if the industry cannot attract the capital necessary to place future orders?

During the more prosperous years of the 1960s, aircraft design made great technological advances. A variety of new planes appeared that grew progressively quieter, more efficient in their use of fuel, and generally more productive in their response to a variety of service requirements.

But with the decline of airline profitability and of new orders in the years since, those advances have slowed to a halt for lack of demand. There has, in fact, been no significant new design in passenger aircraft in this country since 1968. . . .

Four: Will the long-term effect of the open competition be an increased number of airlines, or will it produce, as it did in California, a limited number of survivors? I believe history has demonstrated rather clearly the likelihood of the survival of a few large, financially powerful carriers which will dominate the industry. Is that really what the proponents of regulatory change want?

Five: What will be the impact on fuel consumption of increased competition over a sustained period of time?

The airlines have been very diligent in responding to the Nation's energy crisis and the escalating cost of fuel. Last year, for example, while carrying 21 million more passengers than they did in 1973, they used 800 million gallons less fuel, as the result of various conservation measures in scheduling and operating procedures. . . .

My company's main objections to many of the proposed changes before you can be summarized in terms of what seems to be a series of serious contradictions—contradictions between what the bills say they want to do and what they probably will do in fact, and also between their probable impact and the stated national policy objectives enunciated by the administration.

See U.S. Senate. Committee on Commerce, Science, and Transportation. *Regulatory Reform in Air Transportation.* Hearing, 21–24 March 1977, 95th Cong. 1st sess. (Washington, D.C.: Government Printing Office, 1977), pp. 467–469, 471.

PANAMA CANAL TREATIES

The Panama Canal has been a vital route between the Atlantic and Pacific oceans since 1906. In 1903, President Theodore Roosevelt reached an agreement with the newly independent Panama to fund the construction of a canal along a 10-mile strip of land across Panama. The canal would shave 8,000 miles off the voyage between the Atlantic and Pacific. In the agreement, the United States paid the Panamanian government $10 million and received an ongoing lease for $250,000 a year. While the United States did not actually own the canal, the 10-mile-wide Canal Zone was under the sovereignty and administrative authority of the United States.

While the canal had originally been perceived by the Panamanians as a welcome investment in their country's economy, by the 1960s, it was seen as yet another symbol of American intervention in Latin America. Resentment was running high in Panama during the 1970s, and several riots broke out against Americans in the Canal Zone. As a step toward rebuilding support for the United States in the region, President Carter agreed to negotiate a new Panama Canal Treaty with government leaders from Panama, which would provide a greater role for Panama in the canal's operation and administration. In short, it would turn over administration of the Canal Zone to Panama by December 31, 1999.

From President Carter's perspective, this was the right course of action for several reasons. First, it would serve to diminish the anti-American sentiments in Latin America by demonstrating the country's trust in the abilities of Panama to run the canal. Second, the new treaty would set right the wrong that was inflicted on Panama in the 1903 treaty, which was hastily signed during the aftermath of Panama's declaration of independence from Columbia. The United States held the clear advantage in the 1903 treaty. In his remarks of August 30, 1977, regarding the treaty, Carter makes one point that becomes a lightning rod for conflict with those opposing the treaty. In his defense of the treaty, Carter claims that while the United States did maintain control over the Canal Zone, it did not, in fact, maintain a sovereign, or ruling, presence around the canal. As can be seen in the statement made by then-California governor Ronald Reagan in opposition to the treaty, the question of whether the United States did or did not have sovereignty becomes an important one.

Critics of the treaty contended that it was not in the national interest of the United States to relinquish control over the canal because the United States could not be sure that the government of Panama would adhere to the tenets of the treaty, especially when it came to the canal's neutrality. The canal was too strategic an asset to be turned over to Panama. Yet, the president does have the constitutional authority to negotiate treaties, and as long as two-thirds of the Senate ratifies it, the treaty is approved. Critics, like Ronald Reagan, wanted to discredit the treaty before it was approved. In his testimony before a Senate hearing, Reagan concentrated on the issue of American sovereignty over the Canal Zone. If indeed the United States *owned* the Canal Zone, as he claimed, the transferral of land to the Panamanian government could simply be negotiated in a treaty and ratified by the Senate. Instead, the entire Congress would have to pass legislation to transfer land to Panama. Despite some significant opposition to the treaty, it was ultimately ratified by the Senate.

CARTER'S REMARKS DURING A BRIEFING ON THE PANAMA CANAL TREATY

For Business and Political Leaders and State Officials from Florida and Georgia
August 30, 1977

Our Secretary of Defense, former Secretary of State, present Secretary of State, President Ford, Secretary Kissinger, and others who have studied this treaty in detail have concluded that many of the legitimate concerns faced about the treaty 2 years ago or 5 years ago, 10 years ago, 14 years ago, have been alleviated. And all those who in the past have been against the treaty and who would have preferred that no negotiations begin now say that since the negotiations have been initiated and concluded, that the adverse reaction throughout Latin America and throughout the world in rejecting the treaty would be profound.

I'd like to talk to you for a few minutes about the Panama Canal treaty from the perspective of a President and a political figure. This is one of those items that falls on the shoulders of leaders which is not a popular thing to assume. Because of longstanding misconceptions and because of rapidly changing circumstances that have not yet been explained, I think it is true that many American citizens, well-educated, very patriotic citizens, don't think the treaty at this point is a good idea.

To change their concept based on facts and explanations is my responsibility—not to mislead, not to pressure, not to cajole, but in a way to educate and to lead. And I would like for you to join with me, if you can in good conscience, in that effort.

It requires, as you know, a two-thirds vote in the Senate. There were 40 Senators within the past 12 months or so who signed a resolution deploring the concept of the Panama Canal treaty. I believe I've talked to every one of them, and I can tell you that their response has been very good because they see that their previous concerns have either been corrected or the circumstance are now different. There will obviously be strong opponents to the treaty. I think that our Nation's security interests are adequately protected.

Our original acquisition of the Panama Canal area is one that caused me some concerns, speaking in historical terms. There was not a single Panamanian who ever saw that treaty before it was signed by Panama and the United States, in the middle of the night, when the Panamanian leaders, including their President, were trying to get to Washington before the treaty was signed. Hastily, the treaty was signed, and that began the process of constructing the canal which has been beneficial to our country and to Panama and, I think, to the world.

We have never had sovereignty over the Panama Canal Zone, as you undoubtedly know by now. We had control of that zone, as though we had sovereignty, but we have recognized the sovereignty of Panama down through the years.

I believe that the most important consideration is that the canal be open to the shipping from all countries, that the canal be well operated, that there be harmony between us and the Panamanians, and that we, in case of emergency in this century and in perpetuity, have the right to protect the canal as we see fit and the preferential use of the canal by our own warships and by those cargo ships that have strategic purposes. And all those elements have been written into the treaty.

See "Remarks during a Briefing on the Treaty" (30 Aug. 1977), p. 1526. In *Public Papers of the Presidents of the United States: Jimmy Carter, 1977* (Washington, D.C.: Government Printing Office, 1977).

CARTER'S REMARKS AT THE SIGNING CEREMONY FOR THE PANAMA CANAL TREATIES

September 7, 1977

We are here to participate in the signing of treaties which will assure a peaceful and prosperous and secure future for an international waterway of great importance.

But the treaties do more than that. They mark the commitment of the United States to the belief that fairness, and not force, should lie at the heart of our dealings with the nations of the world.

If any agreement between two nations is to last, it must serve the best interests of both nations. The new treaties do that. And by guaranteeing the neutrality of the Panama Canal, the treaties also serve the best interests of every nation that uses the canal.

This agreement thus forms a new partnership to insure that this vital waterway, so important to all of us, will continue to be well operated, safe, and open to shipping by all nations, now and in the future.

Under these accords, Panama will play an increasingly important role in the operation and defense of the canal during the next 23 years. And after that, the United States will still be able to counter any threat to the canal's neutrality and openness for use.

The members of the Organization of the American States and all the members of the United Nations will have a chance to subscribe to the permanent neutrality of the canal.

The accords also give Panama an important economic stake in the continued, safe, and efficient operation of the canal and make Panama a strong and interested party in the future success of the waterway.

In the spirit of reciprocity suggested by the leaders at the Bogotá summit, the United States and Panama have agreed that any future sea-level canal will be built in Panama and with the cooperation of the United States. In this manner, the best interests of both our nations are linked and preserved into the future.

See "Remarks at the Signing Ceremony at the Pan American Union Building" (7 Sept. 1977), p. 1543. In *Public Papers of the Presidents of the United States: Jimmy Carter, 1977* (Washington, D.C.: Government Printing Office, 1977).

TESTIMONY OF RONALD REAGAN

Hearings Before the Senate Subcommittee on Separation of Powers of the Committee on the Judiciary September 8, 1977

Mr. Chairman and members of the subcommittee, thank you for inviting me to appear before you this morning to testify. You are concerned, as I am, with constitutional and other issues arising out of the proposed Panama Canal treaties, and I appreciated this opportunity to share my views with you. It is necessary first to comment on the constitutional issue. . . . The executive branch argues that the President's treaty-making powers under the Constitution are enough to dispose of U.S. territory and property without any implementing legislation by the Congress, and that transfers of property as specified in a treaty become self-executing once the Senate ratifies the treaty. Historically, Congress has held to a different view, though there have been enough ambiguities over the years to revive the argument with each new case. . . . I believe that careful examination of legal cases as well as historical precedent leads one to the inevitable conclusion that Congress does hold exclusive power and that implementing legislation will be needed in the case of the Panama Canal treaties. . . . The face of all the historical and legal evidence indicating that implementing legislation from the Congress will be necessary in the case of U.S. property in the Canal Zone, it is hard for me to believe that the executive branch would want to circumvent the Congress' rights and responsibilities in this matter. If our foreign policy is to be fully effective, cooperation of the Congress is a vital ingredient.

Briefed by Ambassadors Bunker and Linowitz

The constitutional issue is of great importance, but so is the security of the United States and Western Hemisphere. I have not yet received a copy of the treaty draft to read, but members of my staff and I have been briefed on its contents by Ambassadors Bunker and Linowitz and other members of the U.S. negotiating team. I believe the ambassadors worked earnestly and hard under difficult circumstances and there are some commendable ideas contained in the proposed treaties. But, I also believe they have an overriding—indeed, a fatal—flaw. They proceed from a false premise, that we can expect reliable, impartial, trouble-free, secure operations of the canal in the future by relinquishing the rights we acquired in the 1903 treaty.

In that treaty we acquired the rights of sovereignty over the Canal Zone, to the exclusion of the exercise of such rights by the Republic of Panama. . . .

It seems clear, from the language of the 1903 treaty, that the intention of our Government was to acquire a firm, unshakable legal basis for building, operating and defending the canal. We did not acquire the Canal Zone for the purpose of extracting minerals, tilling the soil or establishing a mercantile colony. It was a single-purpose enterprise, but the important thing to remember is that only one nation can exert sovereign rights over a given piece of land at one time; and the 1903 treaty made it clear that we would do so in the Canal Zone and the Republic of Panama would not.

To this day, it is those rights of sovereignty which undergird our ability to operate and defend the canal. We cannot be kicked out summarily on the whim of some Panamanian government.

Nationalization of Canal Possible

Once those rights are removed—and they will be removed immediately if the new treaties become effective—there is nothing to prevent a Panamanian regime from deciding one day to nationalize the canal and to demand that we leave immediately. That would present us with the very thing the treaty advocates say we want to avoid: confrontation, or its alternative, unceremonious withdrawal in the face of an arbitrary demand.

For more than 60 years we have operated the Panama Canal efficiently, impartially and on a not-for-profit basis. The nations of the Western

Hemisphere have come to rely on our stable presence there to make sure that their commerce would get through unhindered.

We cannot be certain, if these new treaties go into operation, that key personnel now operating the canal will not leave a great deal sooner than expected, thus bringing into question the smooth operation of the canal. We cannot be certain that, as the American presence withdraws from the Canal Zone, new demands for accelerated withdrawal will not be made under threat of violence. We cannot be certain that outside influences hostile to hemispheric security will not make their presence felt much greater that before in Panama. We cannot be certain that Americans operating the canal will not be harassed by an unstable and power-hungry dictator.

Fidel Castro, whose interest in exporting revolution is well known, has made quite a show of his friendship for the current military regime in Panama. And, just this summer, a delegation from the Soviet Union visited Panama to look into trade, investigate possible plan locations and even the possibility of opening a bank in Panama. It should never surprise us that whenever the United States withdraws its presence or its strong interest from any area, the Soviets are ready, willing and often able to exploit the situation. Can we believe that the Panama Canal is any exception?

See U.S. Senate. Committee on the Judiciary. *Panama Canal Treaty.* Hearings, 8 September; 13, 28 October; 3, 15 November 1977, 95th Cong. 1st sess. (Washington, D.C.: Government Printing Office, 1977), pp. 7–8, 10, 11.

ENERGY TAXES

Policies are created in response to a perceived need for change. The country's needs, however, can change dramatically over time, which may simply be the result of subtle shifts in public opinion over the course of years. But changes can also be brought about by dramatic events, both domestically and abroad, that can alter the public's perception literally overnight. This type of event opens a "policy window," in essence creating a new environment that is conducive to the introduction of new policies and their subsequent passage.[1] Individuals or groups can take advantage of this "opening" of the political environment to effect policy changes that would have been difficult to pass in the absence of the event. For instance, a shooting at a school can increase support for gun control, giving gun control proponents a better chance of influencing the passage of new policies limiting the use or accessibility of certain guns. Similarly, a scarcity of imported oil, coupled with the increased costs that come from scarcity, can prompt a call for a government response. The country found itself in precisely this latter situation during President

Carter's administration. As a consequence of events in the Middle East that limited the country's access to foreign oil, President Carter was forced to react to the public's calls to solve the nation's "energy crisis."

The crisis as experienced by the United States was, in some respects, created artificially by an organization representing the oil-producing nations of the Middle East. OPEC (the Organization of Petroleum Exporting Countries) is a cartel, an organization that attempts to monopolize the market for a given product. In the case of OPEC, the product was oil, and with the United States and other countries like Japan relying so heavily on oil from the Middle East, the organization was effectively able to control the supply of oil exported by its member countries, and thus its price. This manipulation of the oil market reached an extreme between October 1973 and March 1974, when OPEC refused to sell oil to countries supporting Israel against Egypt and Syria in what was called the Yom Kippur War. The consequences for Americans were significantly higher gasoline prices and shortages at the gas pump.

Although the OPEC oil embargo was lifted by the time Carter took office, the higher prices set by OPEC underscored U.S. dependence on imported oil and the potential crisis this posed to the nation's economy. The effect of increased gasoline and oil prices rippled throughout the economy: Shipping costs soared as trucking companies and other forms of transportation had to boost rates to cover the costs of transporting goods from the manufacturers to the retailers. Because shipping was more expensive, retailers had to pass on the increased costs to the consumers. The situation made it more difficult to mend an already weak economy plagued by prolonged inflation.

For any problem, there are numerous potential solutions. President Carter opted to take a multifaceted approach to the energy crisis. There were several broad tenets of Carter's plan. First was the conservation of energy, including tax credits for homeowners who installed energy-saving devices or utilized alternative energy sources and mandatory energy-efficiency standards for home appliances. Second was to encourage greater reliance on domestic sources of energy, such as natural gas and coal, by removing federal controls on the pricing of domestic sources of energy and providing tax incentives for utilities and industries to use sources of energy more plentiful in the United States. Third, Carter called for energy taxes, including taxes on domestic crude oil and gas-guzzling cars. Carter discussed his plans at a town meeting in Bangor, Maine.

Given the scope of the proposal, it, is not surprising that his energy plan sparked a great deal of controversy. Members of Congress represent very different constituencies across the country, and a policy that would help one area might harm another. For instance, while representatives of coal-mining areas might support legislation to use more coal, representatives in states with large oil refineries, like Louisiana and Texas, might object. Many industries with economic interests in energy policy weighed in as well, generating both support and opposition among industry interest groups.

One facet of Carter's plan was to remove federal pricing controls on domestic oil, allowing it to be sold at market value. Because the market value of a barrel of oil was largely set by OPEC, it was expected that domestic oil producers would enjoy a tremendous increase in profits compared to what they were permitted by federal regulations. Further, it was hoped that these increased profits would provide an incentive to oil producers to explore new sources of domestic oil. Yet, the profit potential was so large that Carter coupled the decontrol of pricing with a tax on the increase in profits, called a "windfall profits tax." As expected, the domestic oil producers favored the decontrol element of the policy, while opposing the proposed tax. Harold B. Scoggins, Jr., representing the Independent Petroleum Association of America, expressed the industry's opposition to the president's proposal in a Senate subcommittee hearing on the issue.

NOTE

1. John W. Kingdon, *Agendas, Alternatives, and Public Policies* (Boston: Little, Brown and Company, 1984).

CARTER'S REMARKS ABOUT ENERGY AT A TOWN MEETING QUESTION-AND-ANSWER SESSION

February 17, 1978

Last year, New England suffered the worst winter ever recorded, and this winter may be just as harsh. Certainly, the blizzard of 1978, just 10 days ago, will go down in history along with the terrible blizzard of 1888.

You are expert in an average year in contending with freezing weather and winds of gale force and in handling large snowfall. And yet in some ways you are more vulnerable to winter that any other section of the country. You don't have access to cheap supplies of natural gas or oil, and you are heavily dependent on imported energy, primarily oil. It costs you more to heat your homes and your factories here than it does anywhere else in the 48 States in this country—Alaska maybe a little more. But even now Alaska has cheaper supplies of oil. Your jobs are in danger of leaving Maine, some of them because to provide a certain amount of heat, the energy costs you about 45 percent more than the average place in our country.

No part of the Nation has suffered more from a lack of a comprehensive national energy plan than has New England. I've tried my best to close that gap, to correct the unfairness in energy distribution and energy prices. The House and Senate have both passed now a version of our energy proposal, and the conference committees are hard at work.

Let me tell you some of the ways, very briefly, that this energy package would make your own lives more prosperous and your own future more sure.

At present, natural gas produced and sold within a State like Louisiana, Texas, Alabama, Mississippi, Oklahoma brings a higher price than gas exported to another State. The energy bill would create a single price so that producers would no longer be discouraged from marketing their natural gas in other regions like your own State.

The energy bill sets efficiency standards for motor vehicles, for appliances, and for buildings, to save energy. The bill gives tax credits to homeowners and business leaders who insulate their buildings and save energy. For those with incomes so low that they don't pay taxes, the energy bill establishes a program to weatherize the houses of the poor at no cost to them.

Local utilities will be required to work with their customers on energy audits to see where energy is being lost and where economies can be effected. Energy bills can be cut down even more by use of solar energy to meet part of your heating needs. The energy bill also encourages this by offering tax credits to those who install solar energy equipment.

The bill provides research and development funds to study ways in which we can make better use of energy sources that are renewable, the ones that come from the sun. One of these, obviously, is wood, which has traditionally been an important fuel throughout much of New England and also in my own home State of Georgia. But wood can be used in many new and innovative ways, and we aim to explore those ways by research and development.

I don't mean to suggest that any of these things can come about easily or overnight. The problem of energy has been ignored too long for us to expect any quick solution. But we need to start down the road, or we will never bring our demand for energy into balance with our continuing supply. Nor are there any attractive shortcuts. Our progress will be slow and sometimes hard to measure. But we must save oil. We must encourage energy production in our own country, and we must shift to more plentiful supplies of energy.

One immediate step that we can take is to lessen our dependence on foreign oil by conserving energy now. Some people have argued that conservation, the elimination of waste, will slow down our economic growth and cost jobs. But this is the opposite truth. Not only does energy conservation create jobs in the building industry and elsewhere, but conservation also means saving money by the efficient use of energy. It means the return to self-reliance in energy matters. Simply stated: Conservation means thrift. And since when does thrift mean stagnation? Any New Englander knows the answer. We must have a good, sound, comprehensive national energy policy. You know the answer to that. . . .

See "Bangor, Maine: Remarks and a Question and Answer Session at a Town Meeting" (17 Feb. 1978), pp. 345–346. In *Public Papers of the Presidents of the United States: Jimmy Carter, 1978* (Washington, D.C.: Government Printing Office, 1978).

STATEMENT BY HAROLD B. SCOGGINS, JR., GENERAL COUNSEL OF THE INDEPENDENT PETROLEUM ASSOCIATION OF AMERICA

Hearings before the Senate Subcommitee on Energy and Foundations of the Committee on Finance
June 11, 1979

I am Harold B. Scoggins, Jr., general counsel of the Independent Petroleum Association of America, a national organization of independent petroleum explorer-producers having some 5,100 members in every producing area of the Nation.

We are joined in this statement by the 29 unaffiliated oil and natural gas production organizations listed on the cover of our testimony. These organizations have an aggregate membership that includes most if not all of the 10,000 independent producers in the Nation. . . .

In my statement, I will delineate some considerations which—in our view—clearly demonstrate that the so-called "windfall profits" tax, which in no way is related to profits, is an ill-considered policy which ought to be rejected in both the short- and long-term interest of the Nation. In addition, I want to speak generally to the persisting charges that domestic oil producers are profiting inordinately from the Nation's energy problems, and the false contention that petroleum prices are a major factor contributing to the inflation now troubling all Americans. . . .

The tax as proposed, like so much of the legislation of the recent past affecting independent producers, is so highly complex that it would increase the confusion and uncertainty already existing. Producers would continue to sell multiple categories of oil at a multiplicity of prices. But, in addition, all categories would be taxed at different rates. This system would be a trap in which honest mistakes would be unavoidable, and a briar patch in which dishonest opportunists could employ their imaginations.

Structurally, the tax would be a nightmare of complexity to individual producers and their purchasers.

Economically, the tax would be an impediment to the exploration and development now needed to produce the increased energy supplies required by the American people and by our troubled economy.

Strategically, and this is by far the most important consideration, it would increase rather than reduce our already unacceptable dependence on foreign oil. With the present level of dependence, it is clear that even a partial disruption of U.S. imports for any sustained period would cripple the Nation economically. Our country has no greater imperative than effectively meeting the challenge of developing its own abundant energy resources.

Government energy policy controls the economic climate for energy development, and Government policy since the 1973 embargo has been directed unerringly at constraining domestic development and production and encouraging greater import dependence. It should be a surprise to no one, therefore, that import dependence has grown from 30 percent to 50 percent under the prevailing policies in just 5 brief years.

Adoption of the "windfall profits" tax would constitute another action limiting domestic energy resource development. The economic reasons are not so mysterious that they preclude rational analysis and common-sense conclusions. The domestic petroleum industry has a long history of economic experience which has demonstrated conclusively that increased wellhead prices always have resulted in more exploration, more drilling, and more production of oil and natural gas than otherwise would have occurred.

For example, in the period since World War II, every 10-cent change in per barrel price of domestic oil and gas has been accompanied by a change of about $120 million in expenditures for exploration and development. In the past 2 years, these expenditures have increased beyond historical experience by exceeding substantially their relationship to prices that persisted in the pervious quarter century. . . . This proves what most economists would postulate: that producers of a material in short supply have strained their economic and physical resources to increase supply of that material.

Let us look briefly at the supply response which has occurred. In the 5 years since 1973, we have drilled and completed 100,000 new oil wells in the United States. Had we continued to drill at the 1973 level, only 60,000 wells would have been completed. By drilling 40,000 additional wells, the industry will have added almost 1 million barrels daily to 1979 producing capacity above that which otherwise would have been produced. . . . Except for this substantial additional effort, in other words, our imports of oil in 1979 necessarily would be almost 1 million barrels per day higher. Except for additional drilling, primarily by independent producers, Alaskan North Slope production would have had no material effect in offsetting the decline rate of old wells in the lower 48 States.

Despite these efforts, under these circumstances we have not drilled enough. Production continues to decline. Our reserves continue to drop. It is therefore clear that the higher drilling rate of the past 5 years must be greatly expanded.

Against this clear need for a greater drilling effort, the domestic industry is currently experiencing the sharpest drilling slump in 20 years. A number of factors have contributed, a significant one being progressively inadequate wellhead revenues under the Energy Policy and Conservation Act (EPCA). The provisions of that act have been administered so as to limit industry revenues from crude oil sales to $5 billion less than authorized by Congress. Adjusted for inflation, crude oil prices have been controlled by the Department of Energy at progressively declining levels. By contrast, since 1975 when EPCA was adopted, the cost of the drilling and equipping wells in the United States has increased 45 percent. . . .

The recent decline in drilling must be reversed. Total drilling in the United States can and should be doubled in the 1980s. But this can only occur under Government policies which improve the economic climate for high-risk investment. Enactment of the so-called "windfall tax" on domestic crude oil would permanently cloud, rather than improve, this investment climate. . . .

It will not be easy to induce such unprecedented commitment of capital resources even in the most favorable political and economic climates. It will be impossible unless there is soon a clear and positive signal from the Federal Government, including the Congress, that energy investors will be able to make decisions in anticipation of market prices without punitive taxes or arbitrary controls. Congress is overdue in giving market pricing a chance. If the rewards do not outweigh the costs, controls always can be reimposed.

See U.S. Senate. Committee on Finance. *Crude Oil Severance Tax*. Hearing, 7, 11 May; 11, 25 June 1979, 96th Cong. 1st sess. (Washington, D.C.: Government Printing Office, 1979), pp. 366–368.

CAMP DAVID PEACE ACCORDS

In 1948, after World War II, the United Nations established two new countries from the formerly British-occupied Palestine: one for Palestinians and one for Jews. The creation of Israel, a homeland for Jews in a largely Islamic region of the world, was controversial, to say the least. The surrounding Arabic countries were not supportive of the new country and resentments ran high. The bitterness was certainly strong against the Jews who were immigrating into the area, but there was also a great deal of resentment against the United States for its vocal support of Israel. The most significant point of contention was the issue of the Palestinians, who had been living under British control since 1922 and had played little role in the division of their own country. Although the United Nations' plan to create two states was supported by Jews, Arabs vehemently opposed it. One day after Israel declared itself an independent state on May 14, 1948, armies from neighboring Arab countries invaded Israel. Israel effectively defended its independence and enlarged its territory, from what had been proposed in the UN plan, adding more fuel to the hostilities between it and its neighbors.

The tension between Israel and its neighbors manifested itself several times in wars and in the innumerable instances when personal violence erupted between Palestinians and Jews. The conflict between Egypt and Israel was especially strong, pivoting around the issue of territory seized by Israel from Egypt during the Six-Day War in 1967, including the Sinai Peninsula and the Gaza Strip.

President Carter recognized that conflict in the Middle East was ultimately a threat to the interests of the United States. Because the United States had favored the creation of Israel, it had provided a great deal of support to the country, both in terms of financial assistance and sales of military arms. Although the United States did send foreign aid to some of the Arab countries in the region, the level of support was considerably less than what was provided to Israel. Despite firm American support of Israel, Carter didn't want Israel—and American support of Israel—to be a perpetual source of conflict in the region. In 1978, President Carter invited President Anwar al-Sadat of Egypt and Prime Minister Menachim Begin to the United States to negotiate a peace treaty between the two countries. The peace talks were held at the Camp David presidential retreat between September 5 and September 17. Two agreements were signed at the conclusion of the meetings. The first considered the immediate steps necessary to achieve peace between the two countries, foremost of which was Israel's return of the Sinai Peninsula to Egypt. The second outlined the process for future negotiations regarding issues such as the Israeli occupation of the West Bank and Gaza. The first agreement met with some success, but negotiations deteriorated over various interpretations of the second agreement.

While there was opposition to the Camp David Accords, it generally came from outside the boundaries of the United States—from Arab nations and the Palestinians. Countries of the Middle East tended to believe that Sadat had given up too much to Israel and that Israel would not hold up its end of the agreement. Palestinians, in particular were opposed to any agreement that did not address the issue of a Palestinian state. Within the United States as a whole, support for the agreement was strong. One concern was that the meetings at Camp David would not accomplish much at all in the way of peace between Israel and Egypt.

An article in *The Economist* suggests that President Carter was not doing enough to get the two Middle Eastern leaders to compromise and talk to each other. While the rationale behind meeting at Camp David was to provide a more relaxed atmosphere, one that was presumably more conducive to negotiations, the article asserted that Carter was not actively engaged in the process. It concludes by asserting that in hosting the meetings, President Carter would win politically regardless of the outcome of negotiations. Despite the article's criticisms, peace, albeit a cold peace, has persisted between Israel and Egypt.

MEETING ON THE MIDDLE EAST

Joint Remarks by President Jimmy Carter, President Anwar al-Sadat of Egypt, and Prime Minister Menachim Begin of Israel at the Conclusion of the Summit September 17, 1978

When we first arrived at Camp David, the first thing upon which we agreed was to ask the people of the world to pray that our negotiations would be successful. Those prayers have been answered far beyond any expectations. We are privileged to witness tonight a significant achievement in the cause of peace, an achievement none thought possible a year ago, or even a month ago, an achievement that reflects the courage and wisdom of these two leaders.

Through 13 long days at Camp David, we have seen them display determination and vision and flexibility which was needed to make this agreement come to pass. All of us owe them our gratitude and respect. They know that they will always have my personal admiration.

There are still great difficulties that remain and many hard issues to be settled. The questions that have brought warfare and bitterness to the Middle East for the last 30 years will not be settled overnight. But we should all recognize the substantial achievements that have been made. One of the agreements that President Sadat and Prime Minister Begin are signing tonight is entitled, "A Framework for Peace in the Middle East."

This framework concerns the principles and some specifics, in the most substantive way, which will govern a comprehensive peace settlement. It deals specifically with the future of the West Bank and Gaza and the need to resolve the Palestinian problem in all its aspects. The framework document proposes a 5-year transitional period in the West Bank and Gaza during which the Israeli military government will be withdrawn and a self-governing authority will be elected with full autonomy. It also provides for Israeli forces to remain in specified locations during this period to protect Israel's security.

The Palestinians will have the right to participate in the determination of their own future, in negotiations which will resolve the final status of the West Bank and Gaza, and then to produce an Israeli-Jordanian peace treaty.

These negotiations will be based on all the provisions and all the principles of United Nations Security Council Resolution 242 [the resolution establishing the State of Israel in 1948]. And it provides that Israel may live in peace, within secure and recognized borders. And this great aspiration of Israel has been certified without constraint, with the greatest degree of enthusiasm, by President Sadat, the leader of one of the greatest nations on Earth.

The other document is entitled, "Framework for the Conclusion of a Peace Treaty Between Egypt and Israel."

It provides for the full exercise of Egyptian sovereignty over the Sinai. It calls for the full withdrawal of Israeli forces from the Sinai and, after an interim withdrawal which will be accomplished very quickly, the establishment of normal, peaceful relations between the two countries, including diplomatic relations.

Together with accompanying letters, which we will make public tomorrow, these two Camp David agreements provide the basis for progress and peace throughout the Middle East.

There is one issue on which agreement has not been reached. Egypt states that the agreement to remove Israeli settlements from Egyptian territory is a prerequisite to a peace treaty. Israel states that the issue of the Israeli settlements should be resolved during the peace negotiations. That's a substantial difference. Within the next 2 weeks, the Knesset [the Israeli parliament] will decide on the issue of these settlements.

Tomorrow night, I will go before the Congress to explain these agreements more fully and to talk about their implications for the United States and for the world. For the moment, and in closing, I want to speak more personally about my admiration for all of those who have taken part in this process and my hope that the promise of this moment will be fulfilled.

During the last 2 weeks, the members of all three delegations have spent endless hours, day and night, talking, negotiating, grappling with problems that have divided their people for 30 years. Whenever there was a danger that human energy would fail, or patience would be exhausted or good will would run out—and there were many such moments—these two leaders and the able advisers in all delegations found the resources within them to keep the chances for peace alive.

Well, the long days at Camp David are over. But many months of difficult negotiations still lie ahead. I hope that the foresight and the wisdom that have made this session a success will guide these leaders and the leaders of all nations as they continue the progress toward peace.

Thank you very much.

See "Meeting on the Middle East" (17 Sept. 1978), pp. 1519–1520. In *Public Papers of the Presidents of the United States: Jimmy Carter, 1978* (Washington, D.C.: Government Printing Office, 1978).

"CAN THEY SEE THE WOOD FOR THE TREES AT CAMP DAVID?"

**From *The Economist*
September 16, 1978**

Where nicer to walk and talk in pursuit of peace than the secluded woods of Camp David? Yet, one week into this most curious summit meeting of President Carter, President Sadat and Mr. Begin, there had been remarkably little three-way walking or talking.

On the first two days of the conference, September 6th and 7th, Mr. Sadat and Mr. Begin made long speeches at each other while Mr. Carter took notes. From then on, except for a burst of tourism on Sunday, the Egyptian and Israeli leaders kept to their own log cabins; they negotiated through Mr. Carter and consulted their own delegations (more important for the Israelis than for the Egyptians) but at mid-week had still not talked directly to one another. The abstinence, said Mr. Carter's spokesman, was of no particular import. But it was not exactly evidence of an early meeting of minds. What has been happening most of the time at Camp David is not real negotiation; it is a new and extravagant variety of proximity talks.

There has been no question at Camp David of recapturing the high-flying mood of November in Jerusalem. Mr. Sadat's descent on Jerusalem appeared to shrink mountainous obstacles into hillocks, which men of goodwill could easily bound over. Yet even at the time this could seem to be an illusion: the spirit of the two men was fine but the letter of what they said showed the obstacles to be as big as ever. Now even the spirit may be flagging.

The Egyptians have been negotiating on two levels: on their own behalf to get the Israelis out of the rest of Sinai; and on behalf of their not-very-consenting allies to get Israel out of the West Bank, the Gaza strip and the Golan Heights. In return they could offer the peace that they want as much as the Israelis do.

The biggest obstacle was expected to be the West Bank and in the long run it is bound to be. Surprisingly, in the short term, the negotiations at

Camp David first got snarled up over Israel's reluctance to pull out of its airfields and settlements in Sinai. Mr. Sadat has taken this badly; in November he had gathered that Sinai was his for the asking. But the pressure not to wreck the conference over the Sinai was strong: certainly other Arabs would be quick to point out how much readier Mr. Sadat is to compromise over other issues not directly his own.

As ideas were passed forward and back at Camp David, the limits of what the Palestinians can expect from Mr. Sadat as a negotiator on their behalf became apparent. The extent of their promised self-determination is visibly narrowing.

As the Egyptians see it, Jordan would take back the West Bank; and the proposal that these two entities should start out as two separate and independent Arab states and then join in a confederation can be forgotten. Does King Hussein, whom Mr. Sadat has carefully telephoned several times in London this week, agree with this apparently crude approach? The furthest Mr. Sadat originally seemed likely to go for the Palestinians was some form of referendum after five years to determine the West Bank's permanent form of government. Nor does he regard the Palestine Liberation Organisation as a body fit for negotiation or for rule: the PLO may succeed in changing Arab minds about this but at present it is damned by Egyptians only a little less heavily than by Israelis.

Both Egyptians and Israelis, it is said, are showing flexibility. Egyptian flexibility may, it seems, relate to the degree to which Palestinians may one day be allowed to decide their future. Mr. Begin's religious-nationalist arguments for holding on to the West Bank are not susceptible to counter-arguments about security guarantees. But he has already made a distinction between Israel's "right" to the territory and the decision to exercise this right. If he wants it, the loophole is there. But so far the nearest approach to a compromise on the sovereignty issue is President Carter's suggestion that America might commit itself to get Israel to commit itself eventually to a transfer of sovereignty. Pretty tortuous, even for the Middle East.

Short of a miracle, Mr. Sadat will be left at the end with two bad choices: to stumble on with talks that have made precious little progress so far, or to break them off altogether. A break is tempting in that it has the air of decisiveness, but it does not by itself constitute a policy. It would make quite a few Arabs feel good, but what then?

If Mr. Sadat does not opt for yet another display of his explosive unpredictability, he may prefer to settle for a Camp David quarter-agreement—if Mr. Begin lets him have than much—which might be just enough to keep this three-sided summitry hopping on into the indefinite future. Mr. Sadat told his colleagues on the way to Camp David that, providing there is no total breakdown there, he regards it as the beginning of a process of bargaining reality into the Israelis, not the end.

The answer, many Arabs would say, still lies with Mr. Carter. While apparently working very hard indeed at Middle East peace-making, he is not, they would argue, exercising the powers of persuasion at his disposal. If he brings peace to the holy land, Mr. Carter will be crowned with glory. If he fails, he will nonetheless merit top marks for effort. And that, after all, is not to be sneezed at by a man for whom nearly everything else in his first half term has gone wrong.

See "Can They See the Wood for the Trees at Camp David?" *The Economist* v. 268, September 16, 1978, pp. 55–56.

ANTI-INFLATION PROGRAM

Inflation was an ongoing economic problem throughout the 1970s. Presidents Nixon, Ford, and Carter all had to grapple with a stubbornly stagnant economy—rising wages were offset by increased prices—and each president proposed policies to address the inflation that was plaguing the country. Nixon had imposed mandatory wage and price controls, while Ford tried to jump-start the economy with his "Whip Inflation Now" campaign. Neither policy had any long-term effects, and in 1978, the United States was still facing the problem. On October 24, 1978, President Carter discussed this seemingly perpetual problem in an address to the nation, making several general proposals to combat America's inflation.

Presidents can address the public to convey information, to generate support for their policies, and to provide a voice of leadership in troubled times. Particularly when the country is unsettled, say, because of an unfavorable economy or a strained relationship with another country, the public will turn to the president for leadership and assurance that all will be well. As the only elected representative of the entire country, one of his informal roles is to provide the voice of the nation. While a president can characterize a threat as serious, he is not usually overtly negative in his presentation of the country's command of the problem. In the address on inflation by President Carter, however, the tone was discouraging and ominous. Although he outlined his plan to further combat inflation, it was presented as yet another strategy to curb inflation, following up on plans that had failed in the first two years of his term. The potentially upbeat information that unemployment was finally under control was merely offered as a prelude to comments about what the country had to lose if inflation wasn't curbed. Unfortunately for the president, the substance of his plan became mired in the foreboding tone of his address.

The substance of the plan was simple. The government would attempt to get its own house in order, cutting spending, maintaining taxes at their current levels, and keeping government hiring down. He also included the private sector in his plan, eliminating needless government regulation, encouraging competition, and setting standards for wage and price controls. Several of the president's more specific policies, such as airline deregulation and the decontrol of domestic oil pricing, emerged out of these more general proposals.

Unfortunately, the president had supported a very ambitious policy agenda in 1978, including an entire package of energy policies. Adding a series of difficult and unpopular anti-inflationary measures to Congress' agenda gave opponents of the president's plan the opportunity to play Carter's policies against one another, claiming, for instance, that enacting portions of the president's energy policies would undermine his goal of lowering inflation. The depressing tone of the president's message only added fuel to the fire. In an opening statement at a hearing of the Senate Committee on Banking, Housing, and Urban Affairs, Senator Harrison Schmitt (R-N.M.), commenting on the president's efforts to curb inflation, argued that not only were the president's proposals unwise and contradictory, but he was failing to exert moral leadership of the country as well.

CARTER'S ANTI-INFLATION ADDRESS TO THE NATION

October 24, 1978

Good evening.

I want to have a frank talk with you tonight about our most serious domestic problem. That problem is inflation. Inflation can threaten all the economic gains we've made, and it can stand in the way of what we want to achieve in the future.

This has been a long-time threat. For the last 10 years, the annual inflation rate in the United States has averaged 6 ½ percent. And during the 3 years before my inauguration, it had increased to an average of 8 percent.

Inflation has, therefore, been a serious problem for me ever since I became President. We've tried to control it, but we have not been successful. It's time for all of us to make a greater and a more coordinated effort.

If inflation gets worse, several things will happen. Your purchasing power will continue to decline, and most of the burden will fall on those who can least afford it. Our national productivity will suffer. The value of our dollar will continue to fall in world trade.

We've made good progress in putting our people back to work over the past 21 months. We've created more than 6 million new jobs for American workers. We've reduced the unemployment rate by about 25 percent, and we will continue our efforts to reduce unemployment further, especially among our young people and minorities.

But I must tell you tonight that inflation threatens this progress. If we do not get inflation under control, we will not be able to reduce unemployment further, and we may even slide backward.

Inflation is obviously a serious problem. What is the solution? . . .

I want to discuss with you tonight some of the approaches we have been able to develop. They involve action by Government, business, labor, and every other sector of our economy. Some of these factors are under my control as President—especially Government actions—and I will insist that the Government does its part of the job. . . .

I will concentrate my efforts within the Government. We know that Government is not the only cause of inflation. But it is one of the causes, and Government does set an example. Therefore, it must take the lead in fiscal restraint.

We are going to hold down Government spending, reduce the budget deficit, and eliminate Government waste.

We will slash Federal hiring and cut the Federal work force.

We will eliminate needless regulations.

We will bring more competition back to our economy.

And we will oppose any further reduction in Federal income taxes until we have convincing prospects that inflation will be controlled.

Let me explain what each one of these steps means.

The Federal deficit is too high. Our people are simply sick and tired of wasteful Federal spending and the inflation it brings with it. . . .

Reducing the deficit will require difficult and unpleasant decisions. We must face a time of national austerity. Hard choices are necessary if we want to avoid consequences that are even worse.

I intend to make those hard choices. I have already vetoed bills that would undermine our fight against inflation, and the Congress has sustained those vetoes. I know that the Congress will continue to cooperate in the effort to meet our needs in responsible, noninflationary ways. . . .

This approach I've outlined will not end inflation. It simply improves our chances of making it better rather than worse. To summarize the plan I'm announcing tonight:

We will cut the budget deficit.

We will slash Federal hiring and reduce the Federal work force.

We will restrain Federal pay.

We will delay further tax cuts.

We will remove needless regulations.

We will use Federal policy to encourage more competition.

We will set specific standards for both wages and prices throughout the economy.

We will use all the powers at our disposal to make this program work.

And we will submit new anti-inflation proposals to the Congress next January, including the real wage insurance proposal I've discussed tonight.

I've said many times that these steps will be tough—and they are. But I also said they will be fair—and they are. They apply equally to all groups. They give all of us an equal chance to move ahead.

And these proposals, which give us a chance, also deserve a chance. If, tomorrow or next week or next month, you ridicule them, ignore them, pick them apart before they have a chance to work, then you will have reduced their chance of succeeding. . . .

There are those today who say that a free economy cannot cope with inflation and that we've lost our ability to act as a nation rather than as a collection of special interests. And I reply, "What kind of people do they think we are?"

I believe that our people, our economic system, and our Government are equal to this task. I hope that you will prove me right.

Thank you and good night.

See "Anti-Inflation Program" (24 Oct. 1978), pp. 1839, 1840, 1841, 1844, 1845. In *Public Papers of the Presidents of the United States: Jimmy Carter, 1978* (Washington, D.C.: Government Printing Office, 1978).

OPENING STATEMENT BY SENATOR HARRISON SCHMITT (R-N.M.)

Hearing before the Senate Committee on Banking, Housing, and Urban Affairs
May 22, 1978

The Carter administration's activities become more disturbing as time goes on, and there is a continuing impression that the President blames the country rather than Government for our economic problems.

The President's influence on economic monetary policy is through fiscal, and other policy recommendations to Congress, and through moral persuasion. Frankly, in the eyes of this Senator, both the policy recommendations and the moral persuasion are inadequate. One-shot tax cuts without spending cuts and the magnitude of the recently imposed coal settlement are only the most recent examples of this administration's lack of fiscal leadership.

The Carter administration seems to have recognized that inflation must be reduced, but many of the policies supported by the administration will significantly increase the rate of inflation:

One: New social security taxes for 1978 will add $6.8 billion to employers' payroll costs. Over the next decade, the total increase in social security taxes will amount to $113 billion for employers and the same amount for employees, according to the House Ways and Means Committee.

Two: Proposed energy taxes will mean higher fuel costs for utilities, industry, and consumers. According to testimony given by Treasury Secretary Blumenthal before the House Ways and Means Committee, under the Carter energy plan, if enacted as proposed, the American people would have faced almost $177 billion in new taxes by 1985.

Three: For the businessman and the consumer alike, the cost compliance with Federal regulations and their attendant paperwork represent purely inflationary costs. The cost of federally generated regulations and the attendant paperwork add $102.7 billion in inflationary pressure according to a recent study by Murray Weidenbaum, prepared for the Joint Economic Committee.

It is clear that the most critical economic problems facing us domestically and internationally are government-created inflation, declining productivity, unemployment, and overregulation of the economy. Although the symptoms of these problems reinforce each other, there are gradual, common-sense solutions to each problem. If we begin to solve these problems, and show some patience as solutions begin to take effect, the symptoms will begin to recede.

Let me once again suggest the following "common sense" approaches to these four problems. These approaches should be thought of as an interrelated package of scheduling goals rather than absolute goals.

Inflation

Our 5-year fiscal policy should (1) reduce the net Federal deficit by $10 billion per year; (2) permanently reduce taxes on the productive portions of our economy by $10 billion per year, and (3) reduce the rate of growth of the Federal budget by 2 percent per year.

The Federal funds rate should be held below 7 percent so that the credit market can stabilize and related pressures toward a recession can be reduced or eliminated.

Monetary policy should reduce the gap between the quarterly averaged growth of M1 and the quarterly averaged growth rate of real GNP by 0.5 percent per year until rough equality is reached.

Congress should allow for graduated mortgage rates to reduce any short-term adverse effects of possible increased interest rates as a consequence of tighter money growth.

Management and labor policy in the private sector must jointly bear the burdens of reducing demands for price and wage increases as a strong incentive for the Government to also show restraint.

Unemployment

Tax policy should establish annual permanent decreases in personal and business taxes which will (1) encourage small business development and hiring; (2) create increased long-term demand, and (3) create investment in increased labor-intensive productions.

Congress should gradually increase the incentives for able-bodied persons on welfare to seek private sector employment or training for future private sector employment.

Monetary policy should be one of restraint so that business and investment confidence can contribute directly to the creation of private sector jobs.

Federal tax policy should be one of general reduction so that the bottom rungs of the economic ladder to success are restored for unemployed youth and for those with dreams of starting their own business. . . .

Regulation

Federal regulatory policy must be streamlined so that Congress can review major regulatory programs for their economic, judicial, and paperwork impacts on the economy. I have introduced the Regulation Reduction and Congressional Control Act of 1978, S.2011, which would accomplish this aim.

I hope that during these hearings on anti-inflationary proposals, this committee will give its primary attention to the major source of inflationary pressure in our economy: the Federal Government.

It is a simple fact that every first-year student of economics learns, "As the supply of a commodity increases, its price, or value, declines." That is just what the Government has done with the dollar. By putting too many dollars into circulation, the value of each of them has been diminished. It is pointless to call upon the rest of the country to forgo the pay increases that will allow them to keep up with the declining value of the dollar. We must address ourselves to ending inflation through changes in Federal policies instead.

See U.S. Senate. Committee on Banking, Housing, and Urban Affairs. *Anti-Inflation Proposals*. Hearing, 22–23 May 1978, 95th Cong. 2nd sess. (Washington, D.C.: Government Printing Office, 1978), pp. 2–4.

CREATION OF THE DEPARTMENT OF EDUCATION

Although the president is the head of the executive branch, this branch is significantly larger than simply the president and his staff. While the president can certainly play a primary role in the process, the power to execute the laws passed by Congress generally falls to the many organizations in the executive branch, which collectively are referred to as the bureaucracy. The bureaucracy is broken down into many sections, including departments, agencies, and bureaus, each with responsibility for implementing certain types of policies, as determined by the Congress. Ultimately, outside of constitutionally prescribed offices and functions, Congress has the authority to organize the executive branch of the federal government, but it often follows the recommendations of the president in conducting this activity.

The various sections of the bureaucracy are usually established because of some perceived need for federal activity in a policy area, but the process of creating new parts may involve a political component as well. Presidents are aware that some groups in society are more likely to support them than are others. This support typically stems from the record a president or his party has in making policies favorable to that group. Republican and Democratic candidates for elective office usually garner the support of different groups because these two parties, as well as the people who run under the respective party labels, support different policies to address the needs of the country. Once a president is elected to office, he is well aware of the need to maintain the support of the groups that helped elect him to office. Yet, in looking at the decisions of any given president, it's often difficult to say whether he supported certain interests because of what past support groups have offered him, or whether he simply made decisions that reflected his own policy priorities and the country's needs as he perceived them. In all likelihood, presidential decisions are a combination both of political concerns and presidential priorities.

Some of the strongest supporters of Democratic candidates are organizations representing public education. Education policy is the responsibility of the fifty individual states; the federal government typically plays a minor role in this policy area. In most states, public education is funded by local property taxes and state funds, and this can lead to great disparity in the quality of education and educational facilities between the poorest and richest communities. Democrats have often favored equalizing the funds provided to different schools within states, even relying on federal funds to supplement schools' budgets in certain areas, like free and reduced-price lunch programs, or specific programs for low-income areas. Republicans, on the other hand, generally support a reduced role for the national government, preferring in recent years to put funds for education directly in the hands of parents to spend at whichever school they prefer.

These different approaches to education are based on some significant philosophical differences between Democrats and Republicans. Democrats, at least at the national level, tend to see the national government as a means of achieving the greater goals of society. In essence, the government can introduce programs and policies to address inequality and other social ills. Republicans, on the other hand, tend to see too much intervention by the federal government as imposing a burden on society, and as such, conclude that the best thing government can do to achieve the goals of society is to minimize its role. These broad philosophical differences, as well as the parties' specific differences in the area of education policy, help explain the conflict that arose when President Carter announced his intention of adding a Department of Education to the executive bureaucracy.

Creating a new executive department means that the president and Congress consider the policy issues to be addressed by the department central to the goals of the country. Cabinet-level department heads, called secretaries, are appointed by the president to help initiate and direct national policy in their purview, as well as provide insight and information to the president. Thus, for President Carter to propose the creation of the Department of Education, he demonstrated the key position he thought education should play in the policy agenda of the national government. The newly-formed Department of Education would take on functions that had previously been handled by the Department of Health, Education, and Welfare (HEW), including divisions to focus on vocational and adult education, special education and rehabilitative services, and educational research and improvement, in addition to divisions addressing issues relating to more mainstream elementary and secondary education. One other important function of the Department of Education would be to coordinate and provide education for American children whose parents were stationed in foreign countries. In his message to Congress on February 13, 1979, he articulates the need for the new department, both to centralize the federal government's activities in education, as well as to demonstrate symbolically the primacy of education in the United States.

Critics of the proposed new department voiced both specific and more general concerns. First, some feared that the creation of a Department of Education would result in the loss of local control over education. These critics focused on the specific functions of the department and how the education system of the United States would be harmed if the federal government acquired more control over the process. Second, there was the more general concern that the creation of the department represented yet another increase in the size of the federal bureaucracy, resulting in more government intrusion into people's lives. Monsignor Wilfrid H. Paradis, secretary for education of the U.S. Catholic Conference, expressed both of these concerns in his testimony before the Senate Committee on Governmental Affairs. He also incorporates concerns often expressed by religious organizations that parents need to maintain the greatest control over their children's education, and that a more centralized governmental presence in education could be detrimental to parental rights.

CARTER'S MESSAGE TO THE CONGRESS TRANSMITTING PROPOSED LEGISLATION TO ESTABLISH THE DEPARTMENT OF EDUCATION

February 13, 1979

To the Congress of the United States:

I am sending to the Congress today my proposal to establish a Department of Education.

There is a compelling need for the increased national attention a separate Cabinet department will bring to education issues. Our Nation's pluralistic education system, considered the most competent and open in the world, faces many problems and challenges: a decline in public confidence in the quality of education; unacceptably high rates of high school dropouts and of young people who lack basic educational tools and specific skills for productive employment; and increasing demands for retraining and learning opportunities.

The primary responsibility for education in our Nation lies with State and local government. The Federal government has a limited, but critical responsibility to help public and private institutions meet these challenges; to ensure equal educational opportunities; to increase access to postsecondary education by low- and middle-income students; to generate research and provide information to help our educational systems meet special needs; to prepare students for employment; and to encourage improvements in the quality of our education. The achievement of each of these goals will be enhanced by a new Department of Education. . . .

[First,] a Department of Education will bring our Nation's educational challenges and the Federal government's role in meeting them to the forefront of domestic policy discussion. Such discussion is vital to an activity that directly affects 60 million students, teachers and educational employees and constitutes a $120 billion public and private enterprise.

Establishing a separate Department will create, for the first time, a

Cabinet-level advocate for education with direct access to the President, the Congress, and the public.

Second, it will give Federal education programs the full-time, high-level leadership and management that they cannot receive in a structure so large and complex as the Department of Health, Education, and Welfare. This will allow the Federal government to fulfill its responsibilities in education more effectively. It will eliminate duplication in the administrative and staff support activities within the Office of the HEW Secretary and the Education Division. It will allow improved financial management and more efficient administration of education programs. Separation of the education functions of HEW will also promote improved management of its closely related health and welfare responsibilities.

Third, it will provide greater accountability. Submerged beneath HEW's dominant functions of health and welfare, Federal education programs lack full-time accountability at the Cabinet level. With a separate Department of Education, one Cabinet member will report directly to the President and be accountable to the Congress and the American people for the conduct of Federal education policies.

Fourth, the new Department will allow better coordination of education programs with related Federal activities, such as employment programs and research. It will also allow high-level consideration of the impact of other Federal policies, such as tax and energy, on education institutions and students.

Under the proposal I am submitting today, the Department of Education will include more than 150 programs and 16,200 employees. With a budget of more than $13 billion, this Department will be larger than five other Departments including Energy, Commerce, Justice, Interior and State.

In addition to the 140 programs in the Education Division of the Department of Health, Education, and Welfare, the new Department of Education will handle educational activities now carried out by several other departments. These include: the U.S. Department of Agriculture School, certain science education programs of the National Science Foundation, the overseas dependents' schools of the Department of Defense, the college housing loan program of the Department of Housing and Urban Development, the Law Enforcement Internship Program of the Department of Justice, and the Migrant Education programs of the Department of Labor.

The proposed legislation establishes within the Department of Education separate Offices for Civil Rights, Elementary and Secondary Education, Postsecondary Education, and Educational Research and Improvement, each headed by an Assistant Secretary. It establishes an office to administer functions related to the education of overseas dependents of Department of Defense personnel, an Inspector General, and a 20-member Intergovernmental Advisory Council on Education, appointed by the President, to promote better relations with the various levels of government and private institutions.

I urge the Senate and the House of Representatives to act promptly on this important proposal.

See "Message to Congress Transmitting Proposed Legislation" (13 Feb. 1979), pp. 264–265. In *Public Papers of the Presidents of the United States: Jimmy Carter, 1979* (Washington, D.C.: Government Printing Office, 1979).

TESTIMONY OF MONSIGNOR WILFRID H. PARADIS, SECRETARY FOR EDUCATION, U.S. CATHOLIC CONFERENCE

Hearings before the Senate Committee on Governmental Affairs
February 7, 1979

. . . I am testifying in behalf of the U.S. Catholic Conference Committee on Education which has the responsibility for recommending policy positions on educational matters.

The Catholic community in this country consists of approximately 49 million persons and includes 14.8 million children and youth of elementary and high school age; 11.5 million are in public schools, and approximately 3.5 million are enrolled in some 11,000 Catholic elementary and secondary schools. These statistics alone are ample evidence of our serious concern for both public and private education. Consequently, the Catholic community has a vital interest in how Federal elementary and secondary education programs are administered.

I would like to pass over our praise of the work being done by Congress, especially of ESEA [Elementary and Secondary Education Act] and other legislation that you gentlemen have done and just want you to know how much we appreciate these things.

However, the U.S. Catholic Conference Committee on Education which is as I have mentioned, a high-level policy advisory board, has concluded after considerable study, discussion and consultation that there is no clear justification for the creation of a new Cabinet-level Department of Education within the Federal Government.

Consequently, the committee reaffirms a longstanding U.S. Catholic Conference position in opposition to the creation of a Department of Education.

There are a number of reasons for opposing establishment of a separate Cabinet-level Department of Education. I would like to share simply a few of these with this committee. You will note that there is . . . a great deal of similarity in my testimony [to that] of Dr. Bartlett, the president of the Association of American Universities.

We believe first of all that the education of children and youth is primarily a parental responsibility. This responsibility has traditionally been shared between the home and local school authorities who are responsive to the rights and wishes of the parents. This relationship among home, school, and community which has been forged over the years and generally characterized by mutual concern, trust, and collaboration has proven to be an asset of the individual family and the U.S. society at large.

There is good reason to fear from our point of view that a new Department of Education will further increase Federal interference in both public and private education in areas that rightfully belong to parents and to the local community.

We also believe that the decision to establish a Cabinet-level Department of Education in itself is a policy decision which apparently has been made in large part to make good on a political campaign promise and with little or no prior discussion and debate on this important issue.

The consequent result of this hasty decision will be the creation of an executive office where basic responsibility will be to formulate further national policy dealing with education and education-related issues, thus as we see it, gradually eroding the policymaking responsibilities of the State and local communities. We are also disturbed by the continued development of a philosophy of education, which runs counter to the Nation's traditional acceptance of and respect for pluralism in education; that is, that it is wholesome and advantageous for this country to have a diversity of schools in addition to private schools.

This also touches upon the rights of parents to select the type of education they want for their children and youth within a minimum of carefully and sensitively established parameters set by the Government. This trend could well be continued and even accelerated if, as it is feared, the new Department becomes dominated by public school interest groups almost exclusively committed to the public school education and with little understanding for and appreciation of the value and rights of nonpublic education.

Such a result would neither be in the best interests of the country nor would it contribute to the health and vitality of education in our pluralistic society.

The major arguments proffered by the proponents of a Department of Education is that such a department would raise education to the level of prominence it justly merits and that the funding of education by the Federal Government would be increased. We support the proposition that there is a need to strengthen the position of education as a national concern among competing Federal priorities.

However, we do not agree that creating a separate Department of Education is the appropriate means of achieving these goals. We are of the opinion that these objectives could readily be accomplished through a creative reorganization within the Department of Health, Education, and Welfare.

This approach would have the additional merit of insuring the necessary coordination of welfare and health benefits with those of education as they impact upon the local community. We also agree with the proposition that there is a need for increased Federal assistance to elementary and secondary education.

Currently the Federal expenditures for education programs amounts to only 8 percent of the Federal budget. This figure has consistently held at this level over the past several years despite all efforts on the part of the education community to have the administration increase the percentage of the Federal educational assistance. There is no guarantee that the Federal share of the cost of education will be any greater because of a separate department.

In fact, we contend that the creation of a separate Department of Education in order to give education greater prominence and visibility would result in greater Federal expenditures solely to maintain a high-level bureaucracy. . . .

Nothing we have heard so far has convinced us of the advantages of a separate department without such conviction. Therefore, we cannot support the enactment of S.210.

See U.S. Senate. Committee on Governmental Affairs. *Department of Education Organization Act of 1979*. Hearing, 6–8 Feb. 1979, 96th Cong. 1st Sess. (Washington, D.C.: Government Printing Office, 1979), pp. 186–188.

SALT II

When the original SALT treaty was negotiated and signed by Richard Nixon in May 1972, the issue of whether the United States and the Soviet Union would limit their offensive nuclear weapons was essentially delayed. The primary issue on which both parties could agree and was ultimately included in SALT I was the limitation on the scope of each country's antiballistic missile program. Because the issue of limiting offensive nuclear weapons was so contentious, the two countries addressed the question in an interim agreement, rather than including it in the formal treaty. Although the interim agreement did include some guidelines for nuclear weapons systems, it was essentially an agreement between the two countries to begin negotiations on the topic in the future. These negotiations began on the heels of SALT I, in November 1972.

In negotiating treaties, countries have to balance the goals of the treaty with their own national interests. As such, the process can take years to complete. Negotiations for SALT II took 6 ½ years, beginning in President Nixon's first term of office and concluding in June 1979 during President Carter's third year in office. The broad goals of the negotiations were to limit strategic offensive weapons systems. Yet, as with SALT I, the difficulty was in defining which weapon systems actually fell under the scope of the treaty, since both sides wanted to maintain as much of an advantage over the other as possible. One issue that threatened to derail negotiations on several occassions was whether a weapon unique to the Soviet Union, called the Backfire, should fall under the limits set by the treaty. The Americans wanted the treaty to apply to the Backfire; the Soviets wanted their weapon excluded.

When Jimmy Carter took office in 1977, he stressed the importance of successfully negotiating SALT II, and although it took another 2 ½ years of nearly continuous negotiations, he signed the treaty on June 18, 1979. In an attempt to build support for the treaty prior to its completion, President Carter addressed the American Newspaper Publishers' Association in New York in April 1979. He provided information about the treaty and insight into what he believed the treaty would accomplish. In short, he thought that SALT II would bear witness to the U.S. desire for world peace and demonstrate its leadership in accomplishing this goal.

As with all treaties signed by presidents, SALT II had to be ratified by the Senate before it was officially approved by the United States. In July 1979, the Senate Committee on Armed Services held hearings on the treaty, receiving testimony from witnesses from the administration in support of SALT II. Senator Sam Nunn (D-Ga.), a well-respected senator with a great deal of expertise in foreign affairs, was specifially critical of the treaty, but also more generally critical of the president's lax attitude toward defense spending. In a statement before the committee, Senator Nunn explained that it was his understanding that the Soviet Union had surpassed the United States in its military preparedness, and, as a result, approval of the treaty would require a much greater commitment of resources in the area of defense. He criticized the president for allowing SALT II to lull him into a false sense of security, as evidenced by his declining budget requests for defense spending. SALT II faced tremendous opposition in the Senate, but the fact that a senator as highly regarded as Sam Nunn was opposed to it did not bode well for the treaty's success.

The treaty did not ultimately come to a vote in the Senate. When the Soviet Union invaded Afghanistan in December 1979, the prospects for success sank to new lows. Even President Carter considered the invasion cause for stepping back from his support of SALT II, and on January 3, 1980, he requested that the Senate withdraw its consideration of the treaty. Although both the United States and the Soviet Union agreed to comply with its provisions, the treaty was never ratified.

CARTER'S REMARKS ON SALT II BEFORE THE AMERICAN NEWSPAPER PUBLISHERS' ASSOCIATION

April 25, 1979

Each generation of Americans faces a choice that defines our national character, a choice that is also important for what it says about our own Nation's outlook toward the world.

In the coming months, we will almost certainly be faced with such a choice—whether to accept or to reject a new strategic arms limitations treaty. The decision we make will profoundly affect our lives and the lives of people all over the world for years to come. We face this choice from a position of strength, as the strongest nation on Earth economically, militarily, and politically. . . .

Because SALT II will make the world safer and our own Nation more secure, it is in our national interest to control nuclear weapons even as we compete with the Soviets elsewhere in the world. . . .

It's a delusion to believe that rejection of a SALT treaty would somehow induce the Soviet Union to exercise new restraints in troubled areas. The actual effect of rejecting such a treaty might be precisely the opposite. The most intransigent and hostile elements of a Soviet political power structure would certainly be encouraged and strengthened by our rejection of a SALT agreement. The Soviets might very well feel that they then have little to lose by creating new international tensions.

A rejection of SALT II would have significance far beyond the fate of a single treaty. It would mean a radical turning away from America's long-time policy of seeking world peace. We would no longer be identified as the peace-loving nation. It would turn us away from the control of nuclear weapons and from the easing of tensions between Americans and the Soviet people under the system of international law based on mutual interests.

The rejection of SALT II would result in a more perilous world. As I said at Georgia Tech on February 20, each crisis, each confrontation, each point of friction—as serious as it may be in its own right—would take on an added measure of significance and an added dimension of danger, for it would occur in an atmosphere of unbridled strategic competition and deteriorating strategic stability. It is precisely because we have fundamental differences with the Soviet Union that we are determined to bring this most dangerous element of our military competition under control.

For these reasons, we will not try to impose binding linkage between Soviet behavior and SALT, and we will not accept any Soviet attempt to link SALT with aspects of our own foreign policy of which they may disapprove.

Again, SALT II is not a favor we are doing for the Soviet Union; it's an agreement carefully negotiated in the national security interests of the United States of America.

I put these issues to you today, because they need discussion and debate and because the voices of the American people must be heard. . . .

As the national discussion takes place, let us be clear about what the issues are—and are not.

Americans are committed to maintaining a strong defense. That is not the issue.

We will continue to compete—and compete effectively—with the Soviet Union. That is not the issue.

The issue is whether we will move ahead with strategic arms control or resume a relentless nuclear weapons competition. That's the choice we face—between an imperfect world with a SALT agreement, or an imperfect and more dangerous world without a SALT agreement.

With SALT II, we will have significant reductions in Soviet strategic forces; far greater certainty in our defense planning and in the knowledge of the threats that we might face; flexibility to meet our own defense needs; the foundation for further controls on nuclear and conventional arms; and our own self-respect and the earned respect of the world for a United States demonstrably committed to the work of peace.

Without SALT, the Soviets will be unconstrained and capable, and probably committed to an enormous, further buildup.

Without SALT, there would have to be a much sharper rise in our own defense spending, at the expense of other necessary programs for our people.

Without SALT, we would end up with thousands more strategic nuclear warheads on both sides, with far greater costs—and far less security—for our citizens.

Without SALT, we would see improved relations with the Soviet Union replaced by heightened tensions.

Without SALT, the long, slow process of arms control, so central to building a safer world, would be dealt a crippling and, perhaps, a fatal blow.

Without SALT, the world would be forced to conclude that America had chosen confrontation rather than cooperation and peace.

This in an inescapable choice we face, for the fact is that the alternative to this treaty is not some perfect agreement drafted unilaterally by the United States in which we gain everything and the Soviets gain nothing; the alternative now, and in the foreseeable future, is no agreement at all.

I am convinced that the United States has a moral and a political will to control the relentless technology which could constantly devise new and more destructive weapons to kill human beings. We need not drift into a dark nightmare of unrestrained arms competition. We Americans have the wisdom to know that our security depends on more than just maintaining our unsurpassed defense forces. Our security and that of our allies also depends on the strength of ideas and ideals and on arms control measures that can stabilize and finally reverse a dangerous and a wasteful arms race which neither side can win. This is a path of wisdom. This is a path of peace.

See "Remarks at the Annual Convention of the American Newspaper Publishers Association" (25 Apr. 1979), pp. 693, 694, 698, 699. In *Public Papers of the Presidents of the United States: Jimmy Carter, 1979* (Washington, D.C.: Government Printing Office, 1979).

STATEMENT BY SENATOR SAM NUNN (D-GA.)

Hearings before the Senate Committee on Armed Services
July 25, 1979

We have heard from the Secretary of Defense, we have heard from the Assistant Secretary for Research and Development. Now we have heard form the Joint Chiefs. I believe, Mr. Chairman, that the Joint Chiefs have been candid and honest in their assessment of not only the SALT II Treaty but our overall balance of power. They have testified that, at least as I understand it, No. 1, there has been a progressive and unfavorable shift in the military balance between the United States and the Soviet Union over the past 15 years and that this shift will continue well into the 1980s.

No. 2, SALT II Treaty will not arrest this dangerous shift.

No. 3, the treaty limitations on strategic arms are sufficiently permissive to allow the momentum of present and projected Soviet strategic nuclear programs to drive the strategic balance further against us in the early 1980s.

No. 4, the United States will lose essential equivalence in the early 1980s with or without SALT despite Secretary Brown's testimony that the maintenance of essential equivalence is critical to America's security.

No. 5, "Our ability to take the necessary programmatic actions to assure the maintenance of essential equivalence is the ultimate test for SALT II" and that No. 5 is a direct quote, and that the treaty doesn't prevent us from doing so.

No. 6, we cannot afford again to rob Peter to pay Paul by financing the necessary increase in investment in strategic forces through cuts in general purpose force funding.

No. 7, SALT II is a modest but useful step if it is accompanied by the resolve to provide adequate commitment to regain essential equivalence after the early 1980s.

And finally, and I think one of the most important points that I understand the Joint Chiefs to have advised us, the Senate and the country, SALT II must not be allowed to become a tranquilizer of national resolve to compete effectively with the Soviet Union in the military arena.

In summary, Mr. Chairman, as I understand the advice of the Joint Chiefs to the Senate, and this is not in their words but in my understanding of what they have testified to, if you believe that the United States will undertake and vigorously pursue the military programs necessary to reverse the current shift in the balance of power, you should ratify SALT II.

If however you believe SALT II will serve as a tranquilizer which will prevent our Nation from taking the necessary steps to reverse these trends, it should be rejected. . . .

In summary, the Secretary of Defense endorses SALT II but also makes it clear that the balance of power is shifting and that the trends are adverse to the United States.

The Joint Chiefs have made a case that SALT II should be accepted provided the corresponding programmatic and budgetary commitments in the arena of national security are undertaken and maintained.

In the same testimony, however, in answer to questions, the Chiefs have made it abundantly clear that this parallel commitment by the Carter administration has not been fully undertaken and it is not now being maintained. That is my understanding of the testimony. In my view the administration already appears to have succumbed to what the Joint Chiefs have called the tranquilizer effect.

I will reserve final judgment on my vote on this treaty until the committee has heard from other key witnesses. I must, however, observe at this juncture that:

No. 1, the erosion in the military balance during the past decade is indisputable and has been documented by the administration's witnesses.

No. 2, the administration's budget for the past 2 years and the President's defense budget projection through fiscal year 1984 together with the Secretary of Defense's own testimony make it abundantly clear that the Carter administration is not yet prepared to compete effectively with the Soviet Union in the military arena.

No. 3, the Joint Chiefs have said clearly that effective competition is necessary if SALT is to have any meaning for our Nation.

I am hopeful that the Senate will be able to examine the fiscal year

1981 military budget and the new 5-year defense projections prior to our final vote on SALT II. Perhaps the administration will significantly change its course. At this juncture, however, the burden of proof is clearly on the Carter administration. In the absence of such a commitment, the SALT II Treaty will become nothing more than an instrument for registering Soviet military superiority.

In the absence of such a commitment and of a demonstrated willingness of this administration to make the hard political and economic choices necessary to undertake and also to sustain that commitment, based on what I have heard so far and based on the budget trends, I could not at this stage in good conscience support ratification of the SALT II Treaty.

U.S. Senate. Committee on Armed Services. *Military Implications of the Treaty on the Limitation of Strategic Offensive Arms and Protocol thereto (SALT II Treaty)*. Hearing, 23–26 July 1979, 96th Cong. 1st sess. (Washington, D.C.: Government Printing Office, 1979), pp. 286–287.

THE CARTER DOCTRINE

Although presidents generally run their election campaigns on domestic issues such as the economy and education, once elected they tend to turn their attention more to foreign policy matters. This is due to several factors. First, the president faces greater competition in setting the domestic policy agenda than in dealing with foreign policy matters. Other parts of government such as the Congress and the state governments have a greater interest in domestic policies, largely because voters are more interested in issues that affect them personally. Since members of Congress represent fewer people than does the president, they tend to be more in line with their voters' interests. Thus, while the president certainly does involve himself in domestic policy matters, he is only one person out of many who are attempting to shape these policies. Second, and related to the first, members of Congress tend not to be as interested in foreign policy matters, choosing instead to let the president take the lead in this area. From a practical standpoint, it's easier to allow one person to speak for the United States than it is for a large and disparate group like the Congress to do so. In addition, most people look to the president to provide leadership in this area.

Yet the president faces a serious quandary: Foreign policy is often made in reaction to situations that are not of one's own making. When the Soviets invaded Afghanistan in December 1979, the United States in general—and President Carter in particular—was put in the position of developing policies in response to this action. Although President Carter did take specific action against the Soviets in retaliation for their invasion, such as the suspension of grain sales and, later, the boycott of the 1980 Summer Olympics in Moscow, the president also developed a more comprehensive policy against threats toward the Middle East in general. This policy became known as the "Carter Doctrine" and it became the justification for the actions taken against the Soviet Union.

The Carter Doctrine stated that the United States had a vested interest in the stability of Middle Eastern countries, primarily because of our country's reliance on oil from the region. It was the president's assertion in his State of the Union Address of January 1980 that the United States would view any attempt to hamper the flow of oil from the Middle East, and particularly through the Persian Gulf, as an attack on its national interests. While President Carter did employ the Carter Doctrine to justify his actions against the Soviet Union, its influences were seen as late as the administration of George Bush, in his decision to retaliate against Iraq for its invasion of Kuwait during the Gulf War. While Bush explained his decision to retaliate militarily in humanitarian terms, certainly much of his concern was with the effect the invasion would have on the oil supply out of the region.

In a prescient statement before the Subcommittee on Europe and the Middle East of the House Committee on Foreign Affairs, Marvin Zonis, professor at the University of Chicago, concluded that the Carter Doctrine was not relevant given the actual threats facing the Middle East. He argued that the Carter Doctrine was based on the premise that intervention by countries outside the Middle East would pose the biggest risk to U.S. interests in the region. Yet, it was Zonis's contention that the most likely threat, and one which was not addressed by the Carter Doctrine, was an internal threat, emerging out of the religious and political turmoil within Middle Eastern countries. Thus, his criticism of the Carter Doctrine was based on his belief that it did not match the reality of circumstances in the Middle East.

CARTER'S STATE OF THE UNION ADDRESS

January 23, 1980

The region which is now threatened by Soviet troops in Afghanistan is of great strategic importance: It contains more than two-thirds of the world's exportable oil. The Soviet effort to dominate Afghanistan has brought Soviet military forces to within 300 miles of the Indian Ocean and close to the Straits of Hormuz, a waterway through which most of the world's oil must flow. The Soviet Union is now attempting to consolidate a strategic position, therefore, that poses a grave threat to the free movement of Middle East oil.

This situation demands careful thought, steady nerves, and resolute action, not only for this year but for many years to come. It demands collective efforts to meet this new threat to security in the Persian Gulf and in Southwest Asia. It demands the participation of all those who rely on oil from the Middle East and who are concerned with global peace and stability. And it demands consultation and close cooperation with countries in the area which might be threatened.

Meeting this challenge will take national will, diplomatic and political wisdom, economic sacrifice, and, of course, military capability. We must call on the best that is in us to preserve the security of this crucial region.

Let our position be absolutely clear: An attempt by any outside force to gain control of the Persian Gulf region will be regarded as an assault on the vital interests of the United States of America, and such an assault will be repelled by any means necessary, including military force.

During the past 3 years, you have joined with me to improve our own security and the prospects for peace, not only in the vital oil-producing area of the Persian Gulf region but around the world. We've increased annually our real commitment for defense, and we will sustain this increase of effort throughout the Five-Year Defense Program. It's imperative that Congress approve this strong defense budget for 1981, encompassing a 5 percent real growth in authorizations, without any reduction.

We are also improving our capability to deploy U.S. military forces rapidly to distant areas. We've helped to strengthen NATO and our other alliances, and recently we and other NATO members have decided to develop and to deploy modernized, intermediate-range nuclear forces to meet an unwarranted and increased threat from the nuclear weapons of the Soviet Union.

We are working with our allies to prevent conflict in the Middle East. The peace treaty between Egypt and Israel is a notable achievement which represents a strategic asset for America and which also enhances prospects for regional and world peace. We are now engaged in further negotiations to provide full autonomy for the people of the West Bank and Gaza, to resolve the Palestinian issue in all its aspects, and to preserve the peace and security of Israel. Let no one doubt our commitment to the security of Israel. In a few days we will observe an historic event when Israel makes another major withdrawal from the Sinai and when Ambassadors will be exchanged between Israel and Egypt. . . .

We've reconfirmed our 1959 agreement to help Pakistan preserve its independence and its integrity. The United States will take action consistent with our own laws to assist Pakistan in resisting any outside aggression. And I'm asking the Congress specifically to reaffirm this agreement. I'm also working, along with the leaders of other nations, to provide additional military and economic aid for Pakistan. That request will come to you in just a few days.

Finally, we are prepared to work with other countries in the region to share a cooperative security framework that respects differing values and political beliefs, yet which enhances the independence, security, and prosperity of all.

All these efforts combined emphasize our dedication to defend and preserve the vital interests of the region and of the nation which we represent and those of our allies—in Europe and the Pacific, and also in the parts of the world which have such great strategic importance to us, stretching especially through the Middle East and Southwest Asia. With your help, I will pursue these efforts with vigor and with determination. You and I will act as necessary to protect and to preserve our Nation's security.

See "State of the Union Address" (23 Jan. 1980), pp. 197, 198. In *Public Papers of the Presidents of the United States: Jimmy Carter, 1980* (Washington, D.C.: Government Printing Office, 1980).

COMMENTS BY MARVIN ZONIS, PROFESSOR, UNIVERSITY OF CHICAGO

Hearings before the House Subcommittee on Europe and the Middle East of the Committee on Foreign Affairs
May 5, 1980

I have a great deal of trouble understanding what the Carter doctrine would mean in practice. As I can understand it from the State of the Union message and from subsequent glosses, the Carter doctrine seems to be something which I consider dangerous in the sense that its fulfillment requires a military capability that we are not now able to deliver and suggests military processes which we will not be able to control.

Clearly, the United States would have to meet an effort by an outside power to control to our detriment the export of Persian Gulf oil. This would be a major threat to the United States, one which would undoubtedly require a military response.

There is no question in my mind that such a response would be to the point and appropriate. The problem is that the most likely threat, and here, perhaps, I share the perception of Saudi leaders, is not going to be in the form of massive military intervention by an outside power. That type of threat demands a military response and would undoubtedly receive one, although not necessarily in the region of the Persian Gulf itself. Insofar as this represents the principal thrust of the Carter doctrine it is relatively unexceptionable. But, the major security problems of the gulf will not stem from such interventions, but from political turmoil internal to this region which will accelerate toward the end of this decade. That kind of turmoil cannot be responded to by American military power. . . .

Among the issues I see becoming of increasing political importance are issues which will accompany the transformations of these societies. For example, the issue of income inequality will become highly politicized, especially in the event that there is an economic downturn. That is what happened in Iran during the summer of 1977. People who felt that the extent of income inequality in Iran was insignificant because they eventually would earn riches, suddenly saw the likelihood of their succeeding collapse, with the credit constriction meant to reduce inflation. It is inevitable that income inequality will become a politicized issue.

Second, people inevitably demand the right to participate in their own political system in some sense which they define as meaningful. One key problem is to sustain already extant identifications with the regimes while facilitating new forms of participation for newly mobilized segments of the population, if traditional identifications prove insufficient. The danger, of course, is that a regime may alienate its traditional supporters while failing to win [over] the new groups. Saudi Arabia has already begun to struggle with this problem through the creation of some form of Parliament and elections. . . .

I think there is a transformation going on that's fueled by very powerful and very deep-rooted passions. It would be a misunderstanding to equate those passions with Islam. They have nothing inherently to do with the religion. Rather, the religion is being used as a language with which to express these passions, a counterrevolution against westernization and the loss of indigenous culture.

One thing we can do is to understand what the Middle Easterners are feeling in the processes through which they are passing. . . .

What we have to do is recognize and confirm the passions which are at work in the region. I personally feel that there is not any one particular set of Western or American actions which will convince Middle Easterners that we are their partisans, nor should that be surprising. For they are looking for rationalizations to justify these processes through which they are passing. This is a period of enragement against the West which is then cloaked in Islamic garb. It has very little to do with Islam. But it is also not something which the United States can alter by its contemporary policies.

If we act as a coherent, unified, powerful nation through an understanding of the process besetting the region and the nature of our interests there, it will be entirely feasible for us to live with the revolution.

See U.S. House. Committee on Foreign Affairs. *U.S. Interests in, and Policies Toward, the Persian Gulf, 1980.* Hearing, 24 March; 2 April; 5 May; 1, 28 July; 3 September 1980, 96th Cong. 2nd sess. (Washington, D.C.: Government Printing Office, 1980), pp. 147, 148, 151.

SOVIET GRAIN EMBARGO

One of the functions the president of the United States fulfills is to represent the United States to the world's many countries. He is the one elected official who represents the entire country, and, as such, is often called on to "speak" for the United States as a whole. This may be as simple as offering condolences to a country facing tragedy or the loss of a leader, or it may be as complex as representing the nation's interests in negotiating a treaty with other countries. There are times, however, when presidents must express U.S. disapproval or outrage at the actions of another country. The most extreme method of expressing disagreement over the actions of another country is to use military force, but presidents are, of course, reluctant to proceed with military force unless the action has a direct bearing on our nation's or our allies' security or economic interests. Most often, the president will employ other expressions of disapproval, such as economic sanctions, a reduction in aid, or a cooling of relations between the United States and the offending country.

President Carter was put in the difficult position of responding to the military actions of another country in December 1979, when the Soviet Union invaded neighboring Afghanistan. At the time of the invasion, Afghanistan had been struggling to establish a stable government for years. In the 1970s alone, the country witnessed two military coups, the first in 1973, when a pro-Soviet government was established by Mohammed Daoud, and the second in 1978, when a communist regime was established after Daoud had forged closer ties to the West.

After the People's Democratic Government of Afghanistan was established by the 1978 coup, Islamic groups opposed to the communist regime and its ties to the Soviet Union began rebelling. By March 1979, these groups, called the Mujahadeen, or "warriors," had instigated a civil war that posed a serious threat to the communist regime. The Soviet invasion, begun on December 24, 1979, was initiated to support the faltering pro-Soviet government against the threat posed by the Mujahadeen. The ensuing ten-year Soviet occupation of Afghanistan was largely an extension and broadening of the civil war that had developed between the Muslim groups in Afghanistan, which wanted the country's government to reflect the principles of Islam, and the communist government supported by the Soviets. Ultimately, the rebel groups, supported in part with arms and funds provided by the United States, prevailed and in 1989, then Soviet Premier Mikhail Gorbachev ordered the withdrawal of Soviet troops from Afghanistan. In 1996, some of the more extremist rebel groups eventually took control of Afghanistan's government, establishing the Taliban government. It is interesting to note that Ronald Reagan continued to provide financial support and armaments to the rebel groups during his administration. By the 1990s, these very groups were providing a safe haven to terrorist leader Osama bin Laden and to groups allegedly responsible for flying commercial jets into the Twin Towers of the World Trade Center in New York City and the Pentagon on September 11, 2001.

One of the first steps President Carter took in response to the invasion was to suspend the sale of grain to the Soviet Union. In 1975, the United States and the Soviet Union approved a trade agreement, in which the United States would sell grain, such as wheat, soybeans, and corn, to the Soviet Union. Farmers in the United States had been producing a surplus of grain and the agreement allowed American farmers to effectively expand their market. In 1979, the Soviet Union experienced a particularly bad year for grain production; as a result, the Soviets had reached an agreement with the United States to buy 17 million tons of grain in excess of the 8 million tons they had already planned to purchase in accordance with the 1975 agreement. It was this 17 million tons of grain that the president refused to sell to the Soviets in protest against their military invasion.

Through the suspension of grain sales, Carter hoped to pressure Soviet leaders into reconsidering their invasion of Afghanistan, as well as to concretely communicate the disapproval of the United States toward their actions. In his State of the Union Address in January 1980, President Carter explained his decision to suspend sales as well as his plans to protect the interests of farmers who would be left with the excess grain. In responding to an event such as the invasion of Afghanistan, presidents have to weigh their options carefully. In no way did the United States support the actions of the Soviets, but were the interests of the United States threatened enough to justify military action? In this particular case, President Carter opted to use economic sanctions to convey the sentiments of the country, rather than resorting to military means.

Oftentimes, the sentiments of the country as expressed by the president are not always the sentiments of every sector of the country. In the case of the grain embargo, American farmers did not echo the president's call for the suspension of sales. They contended that it was U.S. farmers, not the Soviets, who would ultimately be harmed by Carter's decision. Without the expected sale of the 17 million tons, that grain would be put on the market for sale, effectively flooding the market with grain and driving down prices. An editorial in the periodical *Farmer's Digest* explained the perspective of farmers, who were less than sanguine about the president's proposals to protect American farmers. *Farmer's Digest's* predictions were dire: Not only would the Soviet Union hesitate to buy American grain in the future, the publication editorialized, but other countries, too, would be wary of buying food from the United States.

CARTER'S STATE OF THE UNION ADDRESS

January 21, 1980

Soviet Grain Embargo

In response to the Soviet armed invasion of Afghanistan on Christmas Eve, I took several actions to demonstrate our Nation's resolve to resist such hostile acts of aggression against a sovereign, independent nation. One of the most important of these actions was the suspension of grain sales to the Soviet Union beyond the 8 million tons provided under our 1975 grain agreement. The Soviet Union had intended to purchase an estimated 25 million tons of U.S. wheat and feed grains. Thus, the suspension of sales above the 8 million ton agreement level is expected to result in the freeing of about 17 million tons.

My decision to suspend these sales was a difficult one, but a necessary one. We could not continue to do business as usual with the Soviet Union while it is invading an independent, sovereign nation in an area of the world of strategic importance to the United States. I am fully committed to a policy of promoting international trade, and particularly the expanded export of U.S. agricultural products. I am proud of my Administration's record in this regard. Because of the aggressive efforts of American farmers and businessmen, working in cooperation with Federal representatives, and the provision of new authorities by Congress, we have set new export records in each of the past 3 years. Even with the Soviet suspension, we intend to set still another record in the coming year. In making my decisions on the suspension, I believed it would be unfair to ask the American farmer to bear a greater share of the burden and sacrifice than their fellow Americans were asked to bear. Farmers should not be penalized simply because they are part of an agricultural machine that is of growing strategic importance in the world.

To protect American farmers from the price-depressing effects of the grain suspension, I directed the Secretary of Agriculture to take several actions:

The Commodity Credit Corporation will assume the contractual obligations for grain previously committed for shipment to the Soviet Union.

The Department of Agriculture, acting through the Commodity Credit

Corporation, will purchase wheat contracted for export to the Soviet Union for the purpose of forming an emergency international wheat reserve. In this connection, I will propose legislation authorizing release of this wheat for international aid purposes.

To encourage farmers to place additional grain in the farmer-held grain reserve, the Secretary of Agriculture has made several modifications in that important program.

The Commodity Credit Corporation will purchase corn at the local level to alleviate the congestion within the transportation system caused by the refusal of the International Longshoremen's Association to load grain up to the 8 million metric ton level.

In combination, these actions are expected to isolate from the market an amount of grain equivalent to that not shipped to the Soviet Union, thereby avoiding a decline in grain prices. I am pleased to report that these actions are having the desired results and that American farmers are being protected from the effects of the suspension.

If further actions are necessary to insure that American agriculture does not bear a disproportionately large share of the burden associated with this action, I will not hesitate to take them.

See "State of the Union Address" (21 Jan. 1980), pp. 160–161. In *Public Papers of the Presidents of the United States: Jimmy Carter, 1980* (Washington, D.C.: Government Printing Office, 1980).

"SUDDENLY, THE MARKETPLACE HAS CHANGED"

Editorial in *Farmer's Digest*
February 1980

President Carter's embargo on grain to the Soviet Union has brought a fundamental change in price expectations.

A Farmer's Digest Report

Corn prices in 1980 are more likely to be set in the White House than in the marketplace. When President Carter cut off shipments of grain to the USSR last month, he completely changed the fundamentals of the market for all grains.

We have been producing record yields of grain on the assumption that the world urgently needed them. But when the president cut off the Russians, he left 17 million metric tons of grain on the beach. This is roughly equivalent to 10 percent of last year's corn harvest. The price tag is about $2 billion. The eventual cost to the government (taxpayers) may be $3 billion or more. And farmers will feel the effect for years to come.

We may sell some of this corn to other customers, particularly if prices remain low. However, this doesn't seem very likely. The extra corn is going on welfare.

Washington had informally told Moscow it would have another 17 million metric tons, to help make up for a bad 1979 Soviet crop, and this is the grain, mostly wheat and corn, which won't be delivered. So far, about five million metric tons has been exported to the Soviet Union this marketing year.

To keep this extra grain from flooding U.S. markets and depressing prices, the administration has asked Congress for authority to purchase four million metric tons of wheat for eventual distribution among poor countries.

The Agriculture Department also announced steps to nearly double the nation's 17.5 million metric ton reserve of corn and other feed grains and to boost the existing six-million-ton wheat reserves. The administration said it also will encourage other countries by guaranteeing $2 billion of export loans in the fiscal year ending Sept. 30, 1981; for 1980, guarantees of $1 billion plus direct loans of $800 million already were planned.

This is a heavy dose of bad news for corn growers. There may be a little good news in the future but it is hard to find. First the bad news:

Placing grain in a reserve doesn't remove it from the marketplace. That grain will hang heavily on the market and will take the bounce out of prices.

We have lost a good customer. The Soviet Union won't count on U.S. grain again—and you can't blame them. If they don't get the grain, they will have to slaughter livestock and that will cut the market permanently.

Embargoes don't sit will with any customer, even if they strike another country. It will make others nervous about depending on the U.S. for food.

Farmers are caught with the huge 1979 crop in the bin. Their inventory suddenly dropped in value. It has hurt liquidity. Country elevators that had not hedged grain are in trouble, too. This could hurt farm customer and co-op owners. . . .

The embargo may be lifted within this crop year—which also happens to be an election year. The administration will have to write off the farm states if it sticks with the embargo. The pressure will be enormous.

President Carter will eagerly seek a compromise, as he has in the past. Maybe the Russians can convince him there only are a few "training battalions" in Afghanistan.

While Carter's embargo may bring a sharp slump in grain prices for a while, don't expect the 1980s to revert back to the kind of agriculture we had in the 1960s. And neither will the 1980s be anything like the 1970s. Instead, you can look forward to an entirely new kind of power balance in the world.

We have been selling two-thirds of our wheat, half of our soybeans and a third of our corn around the world. Now, demand will be reduced substantially. Farm prices can no longer be made in Washington. Instead, the events in Moscow, Peking and even Tehran will have to be considered as you make your plans for 1980 and the years ahead.

See "Suddenly, the Marketplace Has Changed." *Farmer's Digest* v. 43, n. 8. February 1980, pp. 1–3.

OLYMPIC BOYCOTT

All presidents have to make difficult decisions. Often, decisions are difficult because the "right" course of action is simply difficult to ascertain. Yet at other times, the difficulty lies in the fact that the course of action a president may think is the best for the interests of the country may not be what is popular with the American public, or at least with vocal sectors of the American public. It was the latter type of choice that faced President Carter in the months following the Soviet invasion of Afghanistan. The president's immediate response to the invasion had been the grain embargo, and although farmers were dissatisfied with the decision, public sentiments were generally supportive. Yet, the Soviets persisted in their military advances into Afghanistan, forcing Carter to address the situation yet again.

Several factors contributed to the difficulty in making any decision in this regard. First, the American hostages in Iran continued to be held as prisoners, and the American public was growing weary of Carter's inability to secure their release. He was perceived as being weak in dealing with the Iranians, and a poor decision regarding the Soviet invasion might solidify that impression. Second, 1980 was a presidential election year, and Carter was seeking reelection. Like other elected officials, presidents are concerned with their ability to be reelected, and making unpopular decisions, especially in an election year, can come back to haunt a president as he seeks reelection. Thus, Carter was faced with a difficult foreign policy situation, a situation that was not of his making, a situation that he adamantly opposed, yet any decision in this regard could have very real political consequences for the 1980 presidential election. The situation was made even more difficult since Carter's likely Republican opponent was the popular governor of California, Ronald Reagan.

In March 1980, Carter decided to take a symbolic stance against the Soviets by prohibiting American athletes from participating in the 1980 Olympic games, which were to be held in Moscow, if the Soviet Union did not withdraw from Afghanistan by February 20. While the grain embargo had been a more direct and concrete reprimand of the Soviets, the move to withdraw American athletes was designed more to embarrass the Soviet Union, which had always taken pride in the successes of its athletes. To keep the Americans from participating in the Olympics would presumably diminish the value of any gold medals the Soviet athletes would win, because their favorite rivals would be absent. The Soviet Union had also spent a great deal of money on securing and preparing for the games, and its leaders had hoped that holding the Olympics in their country would cast the U.S.S.R. in a more positive light around the world. A boycotted Olympics would certainly tarnish the image of the games and the locale where they were held.

While public support was relatively high for the president's decision, certain groups were highly critical of the decision. The majority of the athletes who had planned on competing were very disappointed that they would not be permitted to attend the games. In a meeting held with representatives of the Olympic athletes, President Carter explained his decision and asked for their support, but many criticized the president for inappropriately linking sports and politics. And because the policy was ineffective—the Soviets maintained their presence in Afghanistan past the February 20 deadline—criticism ran high among the media. George Plimpton, a magazine editor, author, and actor, contributed to *Newsweek* magazine a parody of an interview regarding the boycott. As has become common on late-night talk shows and sketch-comedy shows like *Saturday Night Live*, presidents often serve as the butt of jokes. In a similar vein, Plimpton's mock interview with President Carter used humor to criticize Carter's decision. He compares the Soviets' invasion of Afghanistan with the U.S. interference in Vietnam, identifies other groups that have politicized the Olympics, such as the Nazis, and uses irony to demonstrate the ineffectiveness of this purely symbolic act.

CARTER'S WHITE HOUSE BRIEFING ON THE 1980 SUMMER OLYMPICS

Remarks to Representatives of the U.S. Teams
March 21, 1980

The highest commitment that I have in my official capacity as President is to preserve the security of the United States of America and to keep the peace. Every decision that I make, every action that I take, has to be compatible with that commitment. . . .

I'm determined to keep our national interest paramount, even if people that I love and admire, like you, are required to share in disappointment and in personal sacrifice. I don't say that lightly, because my admiration of you and my appreciation of you is very deep and very sincere.

But it is absolutely imperative that we and other nations who believe in freedom and who believe in human rights and who believe in peace let our voices be heard in an absolutely clear way, and not add the imprimatur of approval to the Soviet Union and its government while they have 105,000 heavily armed invading forces in the freedom-loving and innocent and deeply religious country of Afghanistan. Thousands of people's lives have already been lost. Entire villages have been wiped out deliberately by the Soviet invading forces. And as you well know, the people in the Soviet Union don't even know it. They do not even realize that 104 nations in the United Nations condemned the Soviet Union for their invasion and called for their immediate withdrawal from Afghanistan. The people of the Soviet Union don't even know it.

The Olympics are important to the Soviet Union. They have made massive investments in buildings, equipment, propaganda. As has probably already been pointed out to you, they have passed out hundreds of thousands of copies of an official Soviet document saying that the decision of the world community to hold the Olympics in Moscow is an acknowledgment of approval of the foreign policy of the Soviet Union, and proof to the world that the Soviets' policy results in international peace.

I can't say at this moment what other nations will not go to the Summer Olympics in Moscow. Ours will not go. I say that not with any equivocation; the decision has been made. The American people are convinced that we should not go to the Summer Olympics. The Congress has voted overwhelmingly, almost unanimously, which is a very rare thing, that we will not go. And I can tell you that many of our major allies, particularly those democratic countries who believe in freedom, will not go.

I understand how you feel, and I thought about it a lot as we approached this moment, when I would have to stand here in front of fine young Americans and dedicated coaches, who have labored sometimes for more than 10 years, in every instance for years, to become among the finest athletes in the world, knowing what the Olympics mean to you, to know that you would be disappointed. It's not a pleasant time for me.

You occupy a special place in American life, not because of your talent or your dedication or your training or your commitment or your ability as an athlete, but because for American people, Olympic athletes represent something else. You represent the personification of the highest ideals of our country. You represent a special commitment to the value of a human life, and to the achievement of excellence within an environment of freedom, and a belief in truth and friendship and respect for others, and the elimination of discrimination, and the honoring of human rights, and peace. . . .

That's why it's particularly important that you join in with us, not in condemnation, even of the Soviet Union, not in a negative sense at all, but in a positive sense of what's best for our country and best for world peace. There must be a firm, clear voice of caution given to the Soviet Union, not just in admonition and criticism of what they have already done to despoil a small and relatively weak country but to make sure that they don't look upon this as an achievement without serious adverse consequences which can then be followed up with additional aggression along the same lines. . . .

And I'd like to remind you that everything we have done has been not only for the ultimate purpose of peace but has been done with peace. I've got powerful forces available to carry out my command, military forces, the most powerful on Earth, and I did not exercise any military option. We exercised political options by asking the other nations to join in with us at the U.N. to condemn the Soviet Union, and 103 others did it. . . .

I'm very grateful that you came, and I hope that you will help me, and I hope that you will agree, if possible. But this is a free country, and your voice is yours, and what you do and say is a decision for you to make. But whatever you decide, as far as your attitude is concerned, I will respect it. And I appreciate this opportunity for me as President to meet with you to discuss a very serious matter as equals, as Americans who love our country, who recognize that sometimes we have to make sacrifices and that for the common good, for peace and for freedom, those sacrifices are warranted.

Thank you very much.

See "White House Briefing on the 1980 Summer Olympics" (21 Mar. 1980), pp. 518–521. In *Public Papers of the Presidents of the United States: Jimmy Carter, 1980* (Washington, D.C.: Government Printing Office, 1980).

"I'D DIE FOR THE DEAR OLD BOYCOTT"

***Newsweek*, by George Plimpton**
May 12, 1980

Q. I wonder, sir, as we wait here waiting for the rain to stop, and the tarpaulins to be removed and the teams to take to the field, if I may ask you a few questions about the U.S. boycott of the Moscow Olympics?

A. You may presume.

Q. First of all, do you approve of the boycott?

A. To me, it is the grandest expression of the national endeavor and unity since the U.S. Olympic hockey team won the gold medal at Lake Placid.

Q. But, sir, isn't that a rather awkward analogy—considering you approve doing away with our involvement this summer?

A. There is a considerable difference between Lake Placid and Moscow. In Lake Placid no one was allowed in without proper credentials. In Moscow, as I understand, a great number of people without proper credentials are being moved out.

Q. Do you think the boycott will have any effect?

A. Oh, my, yes. It's one of the cleverest things we've done—right up there with the CIA's notion of putting depilatory powder in Castro's bedroom slippers so his beard would fall out. I don't know why we ever dropped *that* idea.

Q. What will be the result of the boycott?

A. Everyone in Russia will sulk. Objects will be thrown at Brezhnev when he reviews the May Day parade, and he will be told to get the Russian boys out of Afghanistan by June 20, or they will start looking for someone to take over from the House of Romanov. It may be the beginning of the end for Communism as we know it.

Q. What is your own evaluation of the Afghanistan crisis?

A. It is the most serious threat to our national security since the War of 1812, when the British burned the White House.

Q. On television the other day, an Olympic swimmer said she couldn't understand, if national security was so threatened, why the draft wasn't in effect, or that some sort of mobilization wasn't going on.

A. I saw that girl. She was wearing braces on her teeth. You can't expect questions of substance from people that immature.

Q. What are the Russians doing in Afghanistan?

A. They're looking for oil and a warm-water port. Everyone knows that the Russians have warm-water ports on the brain.

Q. But Afghanistan doesn't have oil or a seacoast?

A. When the Russians find that out, they'll look elsewhere. Mark my words, the next place they'll try will be Iowa.

Q. Why do you think sports journalists have been so universally supportive of the boycott?

A. Because they know that the place to be in mid-July is not eating second-rate borscht in Moscow but a hot dog in the press box in St. Louis while the Cards play the Pirates. That's the American way, and thank goodness sportswriters know it.

Q. What about the politicians? Why are they so solidly behind the President's actions?

A. They all think very highly of the group that wants to take over in Kabul after the Russians are out.

Q. Who are these people?

A. Sgt. Samuel K. Doe. He's probably one. But you'd better ask Dan Rather. He was with them for "60 Minutes" up on top of a mountain, panting in the dawn. They all looked like chaps who could run a country.

Q. What is the difference between the Kabul regime asking for the Soviet Union's help in overcoming an anarchic situation in their country and the Diem regime in the 1960s asking us to intervene in Vietnam?

A. Distance. We had to send our troops 6,000 miles. Also defoliants. Fortunately, we were able to use them in Vietnam, but Afghanistan has no trees.

Q. But then, doesn't it seem somewhat hypocritical—if not sanctimonious—to criticize the Soviets? After all, they turned up at the Games in Montreal and Munich while we had our forces in Southeast Asia.

A. Very grave error. The Russians should never have shown up. Neither should the Japanese have come to the Olympics after President Ford insulted them by wearing the pants of his cutaway above his ankles in the photo with the Emperor. Nor should the Mexicans wish to compete after President Carter's gibe about Montezuma's revenge. Why should our country wish to walk on the Olympic fields with the Pakistanis after those ingrates referred to our $400 million loan offer as "peanuts?" And the French—why should the French want to compete with us after a U.S. fashion expert referred to the new dress designs as "Coptic oddities," or we with them after Michel Poniatowski characterized President Carter as an "imbecile?" Why would the Saudis want to play field hockey against the British after the scandal of the Princess Misha film?

Q. So you strongly believe the Olympics should be politicized?

A. Absolutely. Adolf Hitler did it in 1936. The PLO did their best in Munich. The Third World withdrew its teams four years ago because New Zealand had played rugby in South Africa. So if everyone else does it, why shouldn't we leap on the bandwagon?

Q. And must we learn to think of athletes as political pawns?

A. Yes. Athletes should be our first line of defense in any moral equivalent of war. Think of the impact of sending Reggie Jackson up to
   the plate without a bat.

Q. What good would that do?

A. Who knows? But it's a hell of a symbolic gesture, don't you think?

See George Plimpton. "I'd Die for the Dear Old Boycott," *Newsweek* v. 95, n. 15,
12 May 1980, p. 15.

ATTEMPTED RESCUE OF AMERICAN HOSTAGES IN IRAN

With a few exceptions, most of the countries in the Middle East region
of the world are arid or semiarid. On the surface, it is a harsh terrain,
ranging from the rolling sand dunes of Saudi Arabia to the rugged,
craggy mountains of Iran and Afghanistan. This terrain, however, belies
the great value of the area, in that nearly two-thirds of the world's oil
reserves are located in the Middle East, and nearly a quarter of the
world's oil is exported from the Persian Gulf countries alone. Because
the oil that we use today was created over millions of years, oil is considered a nonrenewable resource; as reserves are depleted, they cannot
be replaced. The West's dependence on Middle Eastern oil prompts
countries like the United States to claim that political or military distur-
bances in the region affect their own national interests, often justifying
intervention into the affairs of these countries. Unfortunately, this intervention usually breeds resentment and even contempt among the people
of the Middle Eastern countries against the intervening nations.

The United States experienced this hostility in Iran during 1979. In
January, Iranian rebels ousted the pro-American government and established a government more in line with their Muslim beliefs. The ruling
Shah, who had been widely supported by the United States, left the
country and was, within a few months, replaced by the Islamic religious
leader Ayatollah Ruhollah Khomeini, who called the United States the
"Great Satan." When the exiled Shah was admitted to the United States
on October 22, 1979 for medical treatment, many Iranians demonstrated
against the United States, demanding the extradition of the Shah to Iran.
Matters became more serious on November 4, 1979, when a mob of Iranian students stormed the American embassy, ultimately taking fifty-two
Americans hostage, and holding them for 444 days.

This event dramatically affected the collective psyche of the American
public. Yellow ribbons were displayed around the country, outside both
businesses and homes, to demonstrate support for the hostages. Network
news programs began each edition with the number of days the hostages

had been held, a daily reminder of the crisis. President Carter, wanting to avoid a military altercation, attempted to negotiate with the Iranian government but was not able to secure the release of the hostages. He resorted to economic sanctions against Iran, freezing Iranian government assets in the United States and ceasing the importation of Iranian oil. Carter's national security advisor, Zbigniew Brzezinski, urged the president to attempt a rescue of the hostages, although Secretary of State Cyrus Vance was opposed to the idea, preferring to rely on negotiations as the new government in Iran became more stable. Choosing to follow the suggestions of Brzezinski, Carter approved a plan to send a rescue team to Tehran, Iran, where the hostages were being held. Although any military rescue plan would be risky, this one was especially so because of the isolation of Tehran. Not only did troops have to infiltrate enemy territory, but they also had to refuel their aircraft in the process. Tehran was simply too far from any base the Americans were able to use.

Unfortunately for the Americans, the harsh terrain of Iran played a pivotal, tragic role in the rescue operation. To have even a chance of success, the operation needed a minimum of helicopters to get the required troops into Tehran to free the hostages and still have enough room for the fifty-two hostages. To help guarantee that this minimum number would be available, the Americans sent numerous helicopters into the mission. The one thing the planners didn't count on was the abrupt change in the weather. Because the helicopters were flying at low altitudes in order to elude enemy radar, they were particularly susceptible to sandstorms that developed in the area of their refueling rendezvous point. On April 24, 1980 several helicopters had to turn back because of low visibility, and in the course of landing for refueling, two of the remaining helicopters crashed into each other, damaging the aircraft beyond use and killing eight members of the mission team. With the number of working helicopters below the required number for the mission, the remaining team evacuated the area, and in their haste, failed to destroy the damaged aircraft. As a consequence, the Iranians were able to get hold of the top-secret plans of the mission and subsequently scattered the hostages to various places in Tehran, effectively ending any possibility of rescue.

On April 25, 1980, President Carter announced to the country that a rescue had been attempted, but had failed. In many ways, this failure presaged Carter's defeat in the 1980 election. The nation's collective worry about the hostages turned to collective disappointment, with President Carter as the perceived source of that disappointment. Carter made a point of explaining that the rescue attempt had not been a military operation directed against Iran. It was, instead, a "humanitarian" operation. The distinction was important, given that the War Powers Act of 1973 requires the president to consult with the Congress before undertaking a military operation. President Carter had not informed the Congress prior to the rescue attempt. Opponents criticized the president for failing to inform the Congress before the mission and questioned his motivations for not including the Congress, or at least the leadership, in the decision. Senator Richard G. Lugar (R-Ind.) expressed his opinion on the matter in a statement before the Senate Committee on Foreign Relations, stating explicitly that the president didn't inform the Congress simply because he didn't want opposition, opposition which was certain to have been articulated. In fact, Carter faced criticism by members of his own administration regarding the decision to rescue the hostages, Secretary of State Cyrus Vance resigned over his opposition to the decision.

CARTER'S ADDRESS TO THE NATION ABOUT THE HOSTAGE RESCUE ATTEMPT

April 25, 1980

Late yesterday, I canceled a carefully planned operation which was underway in Iran to position our rescue team for later withdrawal of American hostages, who have been held captive there since November 4. Equipment failure in the rescue helicopters made it necessary to end the mission.

As our team was withdrawing, after my order to do so, two of our American aircraft collided on the ground following a refueling operation in a remote desert location in Iran. Other information about this rescue mission will be made available to the American people when it is appropriate to do so.

There was no fighting; there was no combat. But to my deep regret, eight of the crewmen of the two aircraft which collided were killed, and several other Americans were hurt in the accident. Our people were immediately airlifted from Iran. Those who were injured have gotten medical treatment, and all of them are expected to recover.

No knowledge of this operation by any Iranian officials or authorities was evident to us until several hours after all Americans were withdrawn from Iran.

Our rescue team knew and I knew that the operation was certain to be difficult and it was certain to be dangerous. We were all convinced that if and when the rescue operation had been commenced that it had an excellent chance of success. They were all volunteers; they were all highly trained. I met with their leaders before they went on this operation. They knew then what hopes of mine and of all Americans they carried with them. . . .

The mission on which they were embarked was a humanitarian mission. It was not directed against Iran; it was not directed against the people of Iran. It was not undertaken with any feeling of hostility toward Iran or its people. It has caused no Iranian casualties.

Planning for this rescue effort began shortly after our Embassy was seized, but for a number of reasons, I waited until now to put those rescue plans into effect. To be feasible, this complex operation had to be the product of intensive planning and intensive training and repeated rehearsal. However, a resolution of this crisis through negotiations and with voluntary action on the part of the Iranian officials was obviously then, has been, and will be preferable.

This rescue attempt had to await my judgment that the Iranian authorities could not or would not resolve this crisis on their own initiative. With the steady unraveling of authority in Iran and the mounting dangers that were posed to the safety of the hostages themselves and the growing realization that their early release was highly unlikely, I made a decision to commence the rescue operation plans.

This attempt became a necessity and a duty. The readiness of our team to undertake the rescue make it completely practicable. Accordingly, I made the decision to set our long-developed plans into operation. I ordered this rescue mission prepared in order to safeguard American lives, to protect America's national interests, and to reduce the tensions in the world that have been caused among many nations as this crisis has continued.

It was my decision to attempt the rescue operation. It was my decision to cancel it when problems developed in the placement of our rescue team for a future rescue operation. The responsibility is fully my own.

In the aftermath of the attempt, we continue to hold the Government of Iran responsible for the safety and for the early release of the American hostages, who have been held so long. The United States remains determined to bring about their safe release at the earliest date possible.

As President, I know that our entire Nation feels the deep gratitude I feel for the brave men who were prepared to rescue their fellow Americans from captivity. And as President, I also know that the Nation shares not only my disappointment that the rescue effort could not be mounted, because of mechanical difficulties, but also my determination to persevere and to bring all of our hostages home to freedom.

We have been disappointed before. We will not give up in our efforts. Throughout this extraordinarily difficult period, we have pursued and will continue to pursue every possible avenue to secure the release of the hostages. In these efforts, the support of the American people and of our friends throughout the world has been a most crucial element. That support of other nations is even more important now.

We will seek to continue, along with other nations and with the officials of Iran, a prompt resolution of the crisis without any loss of life and through peaceful and diplomatic means.

Thank you very much.

See "Address to the Nation" (25 Apr. 1980), pp. 772–773. In *Public Papers of the Presidents of the United States: Jimmy Carter, 1980* (Washington, D.C.: Government Printing Office, 1980).

STATEMENT OF SENATOR RICHARD G. LUGAR (R-IND.)

Hearing before the Senate Committee on Foreign Relations
May 8, 1980

At the beginning of the difficulty on November 4, it appeared to be our official position that our Embassy was invaded by militants or militant students, that is, people other than officials of the Government of Iran. It was a private action of those citizens.

In due course, however, the President indicated that our responses to that situation could be many, and in early November he indicated that he had not ruled out the use of military force. Many observers said that this was a turn in events. It came almost at the same time, as I recall, as an aircraft carrier came from the Pacific.

From that point or thereabouts, it now appears in retrospect that the rescue mission was conceived. At least some reconstructions have led us to believe this.

The reason I raise this question with regard to the War Powers Act is this. At the point the President indicated that military action might be involved, he could have asked the Congress to declare a status of hostilities, or at least to take some formal action that might have given some latitude for further activity. He did not do so, and, as I recall, for some time the interpretations of those of us who asked about this is that we were not at war with Iran because the Government of Iran had not, in fact, occupied our Embassy or taken our hostages. Rather it was still private persons who were involved. The degree of Government sponsorship became more important as time went on.

Now I suppose that is still the case. We are not at war with Iran. We have not taken formal action. One way in which the President gets off the hook altogether, I suppose, is to ask for the Congress to declare war. In that way the full Congress is involved. And, in the event that a declaration has occurred, it seems to me that the President is free as Commander-in-Chief to conduct any number of actions.

The dilemma is that he has not asked for this and, as a matter of policy, has not decided that we are at war or in a state of hostilities. But at the same time we prepared for this action.

So, we come now to this crucial point in which the President decided to implement it.

Senator [Frank] Church, I think, has made an important point this morning and it is on that I share. It is this.

I suspect that one reason the President did not want to invite some people to the White House for consultation is that he sensed that they might be in disagreement with the use of military force or military action in this situation. Indeed, that has been a general debate in our country for some time. Although the President had indicated he had not ruled it out, there were a good number of people in the State Department, and even among the staff members in the White House, apparently 2 or 3 days before the action who indicated that they thought we were sliding into hostilities. . . .

I would suggest that this is likely to be repeated because, until there is some consensus within the administration and clearly within the Congress with regard to military action, a President who feels it is absolutely vital will look for ways to find that the War Powers Act is not quite operative in that instance.

To take any other course, it seems to me, would court some very real problems.

I simply want your comment, without having any idea what your viewpoint was all the way through this argument. Secretary Vance indicated in a way what his viewpoint was. Would it not have been better much earlier on for the President or you who are advising the President, knowing that you are rehearsing a military rescue operation, to have asked Congress for some formal action that would give the administration the latitude to employ military activity or, more limited than that, a rescue mission, and have at least that degree of consensus so that we would not come to a constitutional struggle over the War Powers Act which, I think is in this instance, is acute? . . .

In short, I do not see how we can move regarding Iran without the Congress having a debate of sorts as to whether it is going to support military action if that is required. I do not think the President is in a position to use military action if it is required without coming into constitutional difficulty over the War Powers Act.

As I understand the Act, as Senator [Jacob] Javits and certain others have explained it, it is to cover precisely this hiatus where there has not been a mandate from the Congress to do anything at all, where there has been no debate by the public. It is to prevent a President literally from waging war and telling the Congress about it later on.

This is the dilemma. This is my own judgment and I appreciate that it is not shared by many people. The clean-cut way to handle the situation is to declare a status of hostilities. It does not mean that we send bombers over Iran or that we take some provocative action. It simply indicates after a Congressional debate and an up or down vote in this body that we are in that sort of situation. The President, as our Commander-in-Chief, is the Executor of that policy.

See U.S. Senate. Committee on Foreign Relations. *The Situation in Iran*. Hearing, 8 May 1980, 96th Cong. 2nd Sess. (Washington, D.C.: Government Printing Office, 1980), pp. 37–39, 40.

SUPERFUND

Although the public's concern for environmental issues appeared to peak in 1970 with Earth Day and the creation of the Environmental Protection Agency, public calls for environmental policy continued well into President Carter's administration. Unfortunately, much of the continued concern for the environment was precipitated by several catastrophic events, including the discovery in 1976 that a chemical waste dump, previously abandoned by the Hooker Chemical Company, was leaking hazardous chemicals into the soil and groundwater in Niagara Falls, New York. In 1978, hundreds of families were evacuated from the Love Canal area of Niagara Falls when it was discovered that the leaking chemicals were extremely toxic and could cause numerous health problems for those exposed to them.

The public was outraged that chemical companies had done so little to protect the health and well-being of citizens in areas adjacent to their waste sites. Groups such as the Love Canal Homeowners' Association turned to the federal government to solve the problem of abandoned, hazardous waste sites and to address as well their consequent environmental and health damage. The tremendous media coverage of the Love Canal incident also helped trigger increased national awareness of the dangers and prevalence of hazardous waste sites around the United States. Yet in developing a policy to address a problem as pervasive as abandoned waste sites, the federal government faced the very real problem of financing such extensive cleanup efforts.

In response, Congress introduced the Comprehensive Environmental Response, Compensation, and Liability Act, commonly known as "Superfund." The bill included a "polluter pays" provision, in which those who were deemed responsible for a particular site would be obligated to finance the cleanup efforts. It was the responsibility of the Environmental Protection Agency to identify hazardous sites as well as to identify those responsible for each site's recovery. However, because not all sites would have an evident "culprit," either because there were no records regarding an abandoned site or because the offending company no longer existed, the Act also imposed taxes on the violating industries to help finance the restoration of these sites. The chemical manufacturers were particularly singled out to help finance these anonymous efforts.

In July 1980, President Carter expressed his support for the legislation during comments made in Jacksonville, Florida. During his campaign for president, Carter had articulated his commitment to environmental protection, and the Superfund policy was defined in his comments as a significant step toward addressing the problem of hazardous waste sites. While increased taxes are not generally welcome, he claimed that the policy targeted only a very few industries and would not create an undue burden on the chemical industry or the consumers of these chemicals. Not surprisingly, the chemical manufacturers were not as sanguine about the legislation as was the president. Robert A. Roland, president of the Chemical Manufacturers' Association, testified at one of the many hearings held by congressional committees on Superfund. At the hearing held by the House Committee on Interstate and Foreign Commerce, Roland was in agreement that those responsible for a hazardous dump should be required to rectify the situation. However, he disagreed ardently with the proposal to establish a superfund through the taxation of the industry as a whole in order to pay for "orphaned" sites. He proposed instead a system in which abandoned sites would be cleaned up at taxpayers' expense, since the problem was ultimately generated by all sectors of society, not just the chemical industry.

Despite considerable controversy over the policy, the legislation was passed into law on December 11, 1980. Interestingly, the bill was passed in a flurry of activity after the presidential election of 1980, in which Ronald Reagan, an outspoken critic of environmental policy, was elected president. Reagan did not take office until January 1981, and proponents of the Superfund knew the bill would stand no chance of passage if it weren't signed into law before President Carter left office. This was incentive enough for even weaker supporters of the bill to solidly get behind the president and vote for Superfund's passage. Since the inception of Superfund, the policy has been amended several times and is routinely criticized by environmental groups and industry groups alike, albeit for different reasons. It has, however, prompted the EPA to identify and address some of the more egregious hazardous waste sites around the country.

CARTER SPEAKING ON SUPERFUND LEGISLATION

July 17, 1980

When I was Governor and when I served on local governments as well and when I campaigned around this Nation, it became increasingly evident to me that because Americans had not faced up to this problem in past years, that it had reached almost crisis size.

The Love Canal incident in New York State has been highly publicized because there was, in effect, a garbage dump for chemical wastes for generations. And now, all of a sudden, people started dying; they have something wrong in their blood. The reports are that some of them might be seriously injured in the future. We don't know for sure yet about the permanent consequences. But we've had to move 700 families out of that region, because they had built their homes in a place they thought was safe.

We have about 50,000 places potentially like that in this country, where hazardous chemical wastes have in the past been dumped, and the people who lived there didn't really know it. As a matter of fact, the people who dumped the waste didn't know about the long-term effects of some of those chemicals. It would cost the Federal Government an unbelievable amount of money if the taxpayers of the Nation had to pay all of the damages that have been caused and to clean up those dump sites and to determine who is legally responsible.

So, what we thought we would do, after literally almost 2 years of hard work, was to set up a kind of insurance fund; we call it the superfund. It doesn't involve very much public money—a little bit of taxpayers' money to administer the program. But what it will do is this—to oversimplify a complicated thing. It will require chemical manufacturers to add a very tiny percent to the cost of their product, and the people who buy those chemicals will pay a little bit more, not enough to really hurt. Out of that small amount that's withheld, we will create, in effect, an insurance fund to help over a long period to clean up those dump sites and also help to pay for damages once those damages are revealed.

The Congress has responded well to this proposal, and it's making good progress in the House and has strong support in the Senate. It's one of the five or six top-priority bills of my administration. I think that I can predict to you that because of widespread support by the League of Women Voters and many others—and not opposed, by the way, by the chemical industry or others—that this is the proper way to go about correcting this longstanding problem. I believe we will be successful. And when we are successful, it'll help every community in the Nation.

See "Jacksonville, Florida" (17 July 1980), pp. 346–349. In *Public Papers of the Presidents of the United States: Jimmy Carter, 1980* (Washington, D.C.: Government Printing Office, 1980).

TESTIMONY ON SUPERFUND LEGISLATION BY
ROBERT A. ROLAND, PRESIDENT, CHEMICAL
MANUFACTURERS ASSOCIATION

Hearing before the House Committee on Interstate and Foreign Commerce
October 10, 1979

I am Robert Roland, president of the Chemical Manufacturers Association. I am speaking on behalf of CMA representing almost 200 company members producing more than 90 percent of the basic industrial chemicals in this country.

We appreciate the opportunity to present our views on the superfund concept as it relates to the cleanup and containment of uncontrolled abandoned or inactive hazardous waste disposal sites.

The members of our association are acutely aware of the problems caused by some of these sites and the need to deal with them in a prompt and effective manner.

At the outset I would like to express our very strong support for legislation that will address the problem of abandoned and uncontrolled sites. We believe existing law is not adequate in this area and that new legislation on old sites is needed. At the same time we do not believe that the sweeping superfund or ultrafund approach is an appropriate way of resolving the uncontrolled site problem.

The following is an effort to represent a summary of the legislative position of the Chemical Manufacturers Association with respect to the superfund concept.

We believe that the concept of combining oil spills, hazardous substances spills and abandoned and inactive hazardous waste disposal sites all into one liability and compensation fund is inappropriate.

These subjects are different in nature and are addressed in differing degrees by societal and legal mechanisms already in place and should receive separate and distinct consideration. . . .

We are addressing today the specific problem of abandoned or as we express them orphan dump sites and Congress should establish a Federal fund to provide for emergency assistance and containment of orphan dump sites where there is an imminent threat to public health and where no other party is taking responsible action.

The fund should be financed by Federal appropriations, recoveries from wrongful dumpers and matching moneys from State governments.

The new Federal program should focus on orphan sites which are dangerous and where no action is being taken to eliminate that danger.

An orphan site in our definition is one which first does not achieve interim RCRA [Resource Conservation and Recovery Act] standards; second it is a failing site; third, the failure is causing a health danger; and fourth, no action is being taken to arrest the danger because of the inability to locate a liable party or where a legal dispute would lead to an inordinate delay.

We believe the fund should be derived from regular Federal appropriations, from which matching funds are contributed by the States and as I said, from wrongful dumpers.

General revenue funding is appropriate for reasons of equity and sound public policy. It is unfair to place the burden on today's companies, shareholders, or customers for practices, failures, or shortcomings of yesterday's industrial producers.

Furthermore hazardous wastes are not the product of chemical manufacturing activities alone. Rather they are an integral byproduct of our industrial society and byproducts of the daily life of every citizen.

The problems associated with abandoned hazardous waste disposal sites reflect more than 100 years of industrial development in the Nation. Hazardous wastes have been and will continue to be generated by a wide range of industries, business concerns, Government agencies and defense installations, municipalities and scientific facilities. The problem is societal in scope and the mechanisms for coping with this segment of the problem should reflect its societal nature just as the benefits of resolving the problem will inure to all elements of the country.

Only through the use of appropriated funds, both State and Federal, can this general responsibility be fairly discharged.

It is unfair to single out the chemical industry for punishment in a fee system. EPA has itself identified 17 industries whose operations result in generation of hazardous wastes.

Wrongful dumpers—whether from the chemical industry or some other—should be required to pay for cleanup to the extent that they contributed to the problem. Recovery should be based on the comparative contribution of the party who generated the problem.

No contribution for abandoned or inactive sites should be required where the disposal or participation in disposal was in accord with applicable rules and regulations and state-of-the-art at the time of disposal. . . .

One of the most confusing things to me in the testimony and the various proposals which have been put forward is the inadequacy of the data base we are dealing with here. We hope this will be rectified in the near term. To me it seems imperative that we get a handle on this. To say that sites range from 1,500 to 35,000 and have the EPA produce a document as recently as July of this year indicating there are 151 sites that they have identified that may produce hazardous wastes leads to a terrible confusion not just in my mind but certainly in the public's mind.

What is the scope of this problem? I think we ought to know that.

An EPA contractor, F. Hart and Associates, developed a preliminary assessment of the number of abandoned hazardous waste disposal sites. Although we do not agree with the format and the way the data base was developed, some interesting conclusions were made by the developer of the document.

There are almost as many Government-owned disposal facilities and four times as many hospital disposal sites as there are chemical manufacturing sites. In addition hospitals accounted for more than two-thirds of the abandoned disposal sites and the residuals from hospitals are predominantly biological in composition.

With five-sixths of the abandoned sites alluded to in the Hart study being other than the chemical manufacturer and with over 90 percent of the disposal sites utilized by our industry being onsite and identifiable, it is inappropriate to place, in our opinion, the emphasis of control and cost on chemical manufacturers alone.

See U.S. House. Committee on Interstate and Foreign Commerce. *Superfund.* Hearing, 19 June; 17 August; 10, 11 October 1979, 96th Cong. 1st sess. (Washington, D.C.: Government Printing Office, 1979), pp. 346–349.

RECOMMENDED READINGS

Abernathy, M. Glenn, Dilys M. Hill, and Phil Williams, eds. *The Carter Years: The President and Policy Making.* New York: St. Martin's Press, 1984.

Campagna, Anthony S. *Economic Policy in the Carter Administration.* Westport, Conn.: Greenwood Press, 1995.

Fink, Gary M., and Hugh Davis Graham, eds. *The Carter Presidency: Policy Choices in the Post–New Deal Era.* Lawrence: University Press of Kansas, 1998.

Jordan, Hamilton. *Crisis: The Last Year of the Carter Presidency.* New York: Putnam, 1982.

Kerr, Malcolm H. *America's Middle East Policy: Kissinger, Carter, and the Future.* Beirut: Institute for Palestine Studies, 1980.

Maga, Timothy P. *The World of Jimmy Carter: U.S. Foreign Policy, 1977–1981.* West Haven, Conn.: University of New Haven Press, 1994.

Neuringer, Sheldon Morris. *The Carter Administration, Human Rights, and the Agony of Cambodia.* Lewiston, N.Y.: E. Meelen Press, 1993.

Rosenbaum, Herbert D., and Alexij Ugrinsky, eds. *The Presidency and Domestic Policies of Jimmy Carter.* Westport, Conn.: Greenwood Press, 1994.

Skidmore, David. *Reversing Course: Carter's Foreign Policy, Domestic Politics, and the Failure of Reform.* Nashville: Vanderbilt University Press, 1996.

Strong, Robert A. *Working in the World: Jimmy Carter and the Making of American Foreign Policy.* Baton Rouge: Louisiana State University Press, 2000.

BIBLIOGRAPHY

Barron, Rachel. *Richard Nixon: American Politician.* Greensboro, N.C.: Morgan Reynolds, 1999.

Blue, Rose, and Corinne J. Naden. *The Modern Years, 1969–2001.* Austin, Tex.: Raintree Steck-Vaughn, 1998.

Brzezinski, Zbigniew K. *Power and Principle: Memoirs of the National Security Advisor, 1977–1981.* New York: Farrar, Straus and Giroux, 1985.

Cannon, James M. *Time and Chance: Gerald Ford's Appointment with History.* New York: HarperCollins, 1994.

Carter, Jimmy. *Keeping Faith: Memoirs of a President.* Fayetteville: University of Arkansas Press, 1995.

Cohen, Daniel. *Watergate: Deception in the White House.* Brookfield, Conn.: Millbrook Press, 1998.

Dudley, Mark E. *United States v. Nixon: Presidential Powers.* New York: Twenty-First Century Books, 1994.

Feinstein, Stephen. *The 1970s from Watergate to Disco.* Berkeley Heights, N.J.: Enslow Publishers, 2000.

Ford, Gerald R. *A Time to Heal: The Autobiography of Gerald R. Ford.* Norwalk, Conn.: Easton Press, 1987.

Fremon, David K. *The Watergate Scandal in American History.* Springfield, N.J.: Enslow Publishers, 1998.

Garrison, Jean A. *Games Advisors Play: Foreign Policy in the Nixon and Carter Administrations.* College Station: Texas A&M University Press, 1999.

Greene, John Robert. *The Limits of Power: The Nixon and Ford Administrations.* Bloomington: Indiana University Press, 1992.

———. *The Presidency of Gerald R. Ford.* Lawrence: University Press of Kansas, 1995.

Haas, Garland A. *Jimmy Carter and the Politics of Frustration*. Jefferson, N.C.: McFarland and Company, 1992.

Hargrove, Erwin C. *Jimmy Carter as President: Leadership and the Politics of the Public Good*. Baton Rouge: Louisiana State University Press, 1988.

Hurst, Steve. *The Carter Administration and Vietnam*. New York: St. Martin's Press, 1996.

Jones, Charles O. *The Trusteeship Presidency: Jimmy Carter and the United States Congress*. Baton Rouge: Louisiana State University Press, 1988.

Kaufman, Burton Ira. *The Presidency of James Earl Carter, Jr*. Lawrence: University Press of Kansas, 1993.

Kirchberg, Connie, and Marc Hendricks. *Elvis Presley, Richard Nixon, and the American Dream*. Jefferson, N.C.: McFarland, 1999.

Lazo, Caroline Evensen. *Jimmy Carter: On the Road to Peace*. Parsippany, N.J.: Dillon Press, 1996.

Lynn, Laurence, E. *The President as Policymaker: Jimmy Carter and Welfare Reform*. Philadelphia: Temple University Press, 1981.

Maroon, Fred, J. *The Nixon Years, 1969–1974: White House to Watergate*. New York: Abbeville Press, 1999.

Melanson, Richard A. *American Foreign Policy Since the Vietnam War: The Search for Consensus from Nixon to Clinton*. Armonk, N.Y.: M.E. Sharpe, 1996.

Morin, Isobel V. *Impeaching the President*. Brookfield, Conn.: Millbrook Press, 1996.

Morris, Kenneth Earl. *Jimmy Carter, American Moralist*. Athens: University of Georgia Press, 1996.

Moss, Ambler H. *Reflectons on U.S. Policy Toward Central America: The Transition from Carter to Reagan*. Coral Gables, Fla.: Institute of Interamerican Studies, University of Miami, 1983.

Muravchik, Joshua. *The Uncertain Crusade: Jimmy Carter and the Dilemmas of Human Rights Policy*. Lanham, Md.: Hamilton Press, 1986.

Reichley, James. *Conservatives in an Age of Change: The Nixon and Ford Administrations*. Washington: Brookings Institution, 1981.

Robertson, David Brian, ed. *Loss of Confidence: Politics and Policy in the 1970s*. University Park: Pennsylvania State University Press, 1998.

Robinson, Jerry, ed. *The 1970s, Best Political Cartoons of the Decade*. New York: McGraw-Hill, 1980.

Sarkesian, Sam C., ed. *Defense Policy and the Presidency: Carter's First Years*. Boulder, Colo.: Westview Press, 1979.

Smith, Gaddis. *Morality, Reason, and Power: American Diplomacy in the Carter Years*. New York: Hill and Wang, 1986.

Spencer, Donald S. *The Carter Implosion: Jimmy Carter and the Amateur Style of Diplomacy*. New York: Praeger, 1988.

Thornton, Richard C. *The Carter Years: Toward a New Global Order*. New York: Paragon House, 1991.

United States. *Public Papers of the Presidents of the United States*, Washington, D.C.: U.S. Government Printing Office.

Wandersee, Winifred D. *On the Move: American Women in the 1970s*. Boston: Twayne Publishers, 1988.

Wilson, Robert A., ed. *Character Above All: Ten Presidents from FDR to George Bush.* New York: Touchstone, 1997.

———. *Power and the Presidency.* New York: Public Affairs, 1999.

Woodward, Bob. *Shadow: Five Presidents and the Legacy of Watergate.* New York: Simon & Schuster, 2000.

INDEX